BAD TIDINGS:

Communication and Catastrophe

COMMUNICATION

A series of volumes edited by:
Dolf Zillmann and **Jennings Bryant**

Zillmann/Bryant: Selective Exposure to Communication

Beville: Audience Ratings: Radio, Television, Cable, Revised Edition

Bryant/Zillmann: Perspectives on Media Effects

Goldstein: Reporting Science: The Case of Aggression

Ellis/Donohue: Contemporary Issues in Language and Discourse Processes

Winett: Information and Behavior: Systems of Influence

Huesmann/Eron: Television and the Aggressive Child: A Cross-National Comparison

Gunter: Poor Reception: Misunderstanding and Forgetting Broadcast News

Olasky: Corporate Public Relations: A New Historical Perspective

Donohew/Sypher/Higgins: Communication, Social Cognition, and Affect

Van Dijk: News Analysis: Case Studies of International and National News in the Press

Van Dijk: News as Discourse

Wober: The Use and Abuse of Television: A Social Psychological Analysis of the Changing Screen

Kraus: Televised Presidential Debates and Public Policy

Masel Walters/Wilkins/Walters: Bad Tidings: Communication and Catastrophe

Salvaggio/Bryant: Media Use in the Information Age: Emerging Patterns of Adoption and Consumer Use

Salvaggio: The Information Society: Economic, Social, and Structural Issues

Olasky: The Press and Abortion, 1838–1988

BAD TIDINGS:

Communication and Catastrophe

Edited by

Lynne Masel Walters
Houston Area Research Center

Lee Wilkins
University of Colorado-Boulder

Tim Walters
University of Texas at Austin

LAWRENCE ERLBAUM ASSOCIATES, PUBLISHERS
1989   Hillsdale, New Jersey   Hove and London

Copyright © by Lawrence Erlbaum Associates, Inc

All rights reserved. No part of the book may be reproduced in any form, by photostat, microform, retrieval system, or any other means, without the prior written permission of the publisher.

Lawrence Erlbaum Associates, Inc., Publishers
365 Broadway
Hillsdale, New Jersey 07642

Library of Congress Cataloging-in-Publication Data

Bad tidings: communication and catastrophe/edited by
Lynne Masel Walters, Lee Wilkins, Tim Walters.

   p. cm.
   Bibliography: p.
   Includes index.
   ISBN 0-89859-951-2
   1. Disasters in the press—United States—Case studies. 2. Mass media—United States—Psychological aspects—Case studies.
3. Television broadcasting of news—Social aspects—United States—Case studies. 4. Broadcast journalism—United States—Case studies.
I. Masel Walters, Lynne. II. Wilkins, Lee. III. Walters, Tim.
PN4888. D57B3 1988
303.4'85—dc19

                                                              88-7186
                                                                CIP

Printed in the United States of America
10 9 8 7 6 5 4 3 2 1

Contents

PREFACE xi

1
THE SOCIAL SCIENCE STUDY OF DISASTERS AND MASS COMMUNICATION
E. L. Quarantelli   1

The Development of Research *3*
General Observations
   and Findings *5*
Specific Studies *7*
Some Significant Research
   Themes *12*
Future Research Agenda *16*

2
BHOPAL: THE POLITICS OF MEDIATED RISK
Lee Wilkins   21

Chemical Spills as Political
   Accidents *21*
The Mediated Story
   of Bhopal *22*

The Public Memory
  of Bhopal *27*
Elites as Adaptation *29*
The Cutural Myth
  of Bhopal *31*
The Politics of Risk *32*

3
THE SOUND AND THE FURY: MASS MEDIA AND HURRICANES
John A. Ledingham and Lynne Masel Walters   **35**

4
COMMUNICATING THREAT INFORMATION FOR VOLCANO HAZARDS
Ronald W. Perry and Michael K. Lindell   **47**

Current Volcanic Dangers *49*
Volcano Information
  Dissemination *51*
Channels for Information
  Receipt *54*
Assessments of Source
  Credibility *57*

5
TMI: THE MEDIA STORY THAT WILL NOT DIE
Sharon M. Friedman   **63**

Pre-Accident Information
  Efforts *64*
Pre-Accident Media
  Coverage *65*
The Accident Itself *67*
Lessons Learned From
  the Accident *71*

Media Coverage From
   1983–1987 *74*
Commentary on Later TMI
   Media Coverage *76*
Conclusions *81*

6
PREVENTIVE JOURNALISM AND AIDS EDITORIALS: DILEMMAS FOR PRIVATE AND PUBLIC HEALTH
Gene Burd   **85**

News Coverage of the Causes
   of AIDS *86*
Editorials on Preventing
   AIDS *88*
An Update: Coverage Between
   February 1985 and February 1987 *109*

7
THE HOSTAGE TAKER, THE TERRORIST, THE MEDIA: PARTNERS IN PUBLIC CRIME
Joseph Scanlon   **115**

Incidents Reported Differently *116*
Criminal or Terrorist? *118*
Not Ordinary Crimes *118*
The Hostage Taking *119*
Effects of Reports
   are Critical *119*
Why the Fascination? *122*
Those Involved Know This
   and Use It *122*
Copy-Cat Hijackings *124*
Other Problems *125*
The Media Often
   Cooperate *127*
Extraordinary Measures Needed *128*

8
REPORTING CHERNOBYL: CUTTING THE GOVERNMENT FOG TO COVER THE NUCLEAR CLOUD
Philip Patterson   **131**

Introduction *131*
The Theoretical Frame *132*
The Qualitative Study
 of Television News *134*
Technological Disasters
 and the Media *135*
The Influence of Stereotype
 on Television Content *136*
The Atomic Context *140*
The Sourcing Problem *143*
Conclusion *144*

9
IT'S THE NUCLEAR, NOT THE POWER AND IT'S IN THE CULTURE, NOT JUST THE NEWS
Russell E. Shain   **149**

10
TALES FROM THE DARKSIDE: ETHICAL IMPLICATIONS OF DISASTER COVERAGE
Deni Elliott   **161**

Functional Obligations *162*
Tensions of Interdependence *163*
The Role of Media
 in Disaster Preparation *165*
The Media Myth
 of Helpless Victims *166*
Deaths in Living Color *167*
How Media Ought
 to Cover Disasters *169*

11
CONCLUSION: ACCIDENTS WILL HAPPEN
Lee Wilkins   **171**

Media Performance *172*
The Culture of Disaster *173*
The Role of Further
 Research *175*

REFERENCES 179

AUTHOR INDEX 191

SUBJECT INDEX 195

Preface

In the 1970s, a book collecting research about the mass media and their role in disasters would have been unimaginable. Five years ago it would have been almost impossible to compile. With just a few noteworthy exceptions, including work by Henry Quarantelli and Joseph Scanlon, both of whom are contributors to this volume, the entire field of disaster- media research has developed in just the past few years.

Indeed, this mushrooming research development is one of the reasons for this book. Although much of the work in "disaster studies" was begun by sociologists and geographers, psychologists and communications scholars in recent years have assumed a more dominant role. The result is a variety of research informed by different disciplines with different theoretical frames. The debates in disaster research now range not only between those who study "natural" as opposed to "technological" hazards, but between different epistemological approaches, some of which treat the mass media as tangentially important, whereas others view the media as a major player in the hazard mitigation game.

This book, then, is an attempt to compile a somewhat ecclectic view of research on mass communication and catastrophe. The editors have attempted to provide a sampling of the most recent empirical work on the mass media and disasters, including everything from content analysis of media reports to studies of audience response to those events. Imbedded in this research, most of it informed by the various social science disciplines, is an attempt at theory building, at least as theory may be used to link empirical observations with a more predictive view. In this sense, this volume is of interest to students of mass communication, sociology, geography, and political science who seek to link the mass media with broader questions of human behavior.

However, mass communications scholarship has another side—one that owes an epistemological debt to the humanities. This branch of mass communications research focuses on issues of textual interpretation, popular culture, and ethical questions surrounding the issues of human life that disasters and their aftermath throw into sharp relief. Essays representing this branch of disaster studies also are incorporated in this reader. They reflect the editors' beliefs that it is not only social science that is capable of providing insight into human and institutional behavior.

The goal of the book, then, is to allow readers to begin the work of developing an integrated understanding of communication and catastrophe. The chapters in this volume were selected, in part, because they speak to each other. And, although the editors have begun the work of integration in a concluding note, it is their belief that the central work remains one of integration, a task for readers as well as researchers.

Sociologist E.L. Quarantelli (chapter 1), one of the pioneers in the field of disaster research, opens the volume with an insightful review of the current standing of the field. Quarantelli provides a history of early research on the role of the mass media in disasters, emphasizing not only media performance but also the institutional constraints under which the media function. He outlines several significant trends that have emerged from research in the field, including the media's tendency to mythologize certain aspects of disasters and the curtailment of gatekeeping functions within news organizations in times of disaster. Quarantelli fits existing research into a matrix that he then uses to suggest future research directions.

Although Quarantelli's contribution provides a scholarly overview, Lee Wilkins' work (chapter 2) places disasters—and media reports of them—in a political context. Based on a concept of politics developed by Harold Lasswell, Wilkins' chapter describes how media coverage of the Bhopal tragedy emphasized an institutional view of political power while omitting other, equally important facets of politics. Her essay, which is based on research into media coverage and public response to the 1984 Bhopal chemical leak, also outlines the emergence of a new disaster mythology, one that is profoundly undemocratic and that does not encourage society-wide efforts at mitigation and the assumption of collective risk.

Two studies of natural disaster follow.

John Ledingham and Lynne Masel Walters (chapter 3), in a longitudinal study of Texas residents' response to warnings about Hurricane Alicia (1983) and Danny (1985), note that the mass media provide an important form of environmental surveillance for natural hazards. The scholars document that mediated evacuation warnings, particularly those broadcast on television, are an important component of individual decisions to evacuate in the face of certain types of threat. However, the media operate within what Ledingham and Walters characterize as a "disaster environment," including past experiences with other storms and discussions with friends and family. Taken in this context, the study suggests the media set an evacuation agenda for readers and viewers, one that is influenced by individual needs and that interacts with a variety of other environmental factors.

One of those additional "factors"—the local emergency management official—is the subject of research conducted by Ron Perry and Michael Lindell (chapter 4). In an analysis of local response to a variety of messages about the 1980 Mt. St. Helens eruption, Perry and Lindell found that local emergency managers need to incorporate the mass media more directly in their plans for warning information and subsequent information about personal protection and mitigation. Washington residents in the midst of a series of volcanic eruptions said they preferred television, radio, and newspapers as a way of conveying warning information. They added mitigation information also could be mediated. Perry and Lindell suggest the mass media have an important role to play in the development of hazard knowledge as well as individual coping skills, at least when volcanoes are the issue.

The next three chapters shift the volume's focus from natural to human-created hazards—and from public response to mediated messages to the messages themselves.

Sharon Friedman (chapter 5), a counsultant to the President's Commission on Three Mile Island, updates her 1979 work on media coverage of the U.S. nuclear accident in "TMI: The Story That Will Not Die." After a review of the initial problems with TMI coverage, including ill-prepared reporters, utility officials, and Nuclear Regulatory Commission staff, Friedman notes that coverage of post-accident events has improved— marginally. Her content analysis of local coverage of the accident found that, although the media provided broader coverage of the questions surrounding the accident, local newspapers have done a better job with the story in the years after the accident. However, Friedman found that coverage of Three Mile Island still represents a clash between the world of the reporter and that of the scientist and engineer. One result of that clash is that events continue to dominate.

The role of journalists in preventing disasters—at least on newspaper editorial pages—is the subject of Gene Burd's (chapter 6) essay on editorial treatment of AIDS. In a detailed examination of editorials on the subject since the disease became news at the beginning of the 1980s, Burd notes that editorial writers generally failed to be specific about how the disease itself is transmitted and to link other events to the spread of the disease. Editorial writers were more concerned about preventing public panic about AIDS, and its possible link to civil rights violations, than about the transmission of the disease itself. Editorials written later in the 1980s supported technical solutions to the problem—such as use of condoms—and occasionally linked the transmission of the virus with television programming. Burd concludes that although editorials might have helped readers deal with the bad news about AIDS, they endorsed old solutions and technology rather than behavior change as a method of mitigating this biological disaster.

Terrorism, and media coverage of it, is the focus of Joe Scanlon's contribution (chapter 7). The Canadian scholar, using a broad definition of terrorism, shows how a predictable pattern of media performance can make journalists unwitting accomplices to terrorist acts. Scanlon's chapter highlights the need for increased advance planning by the mass media for coverage of such events, one that brings readers and viewers the news of the actions without contributing to an escalation of the violence itself.

Three, more humanistic essays conclude the volume.

The Chernobyl nuclear accident—and the social construction of that reality as viewed on American television—provides the core of a chapter that bridges media content and cultural construct. Philip Patterson (chapter 8), based on a content analysis of American network television coverage of the Chernobyl disaster, asserts that news was replaced by propaganda when television reported the Chernobyl story. Stereotypes of the Soviet government and Russian people and an underlying tone of fear of anything nuclear allowed the networks to accept as fact gross inaccuracies and to perpetuate stereotypes in news coverage. The author suggests that such reporting inhibits a realistic discussion of disasters and crises—particularly those that have transnational implications.

In his companion (chapter 9) contribution, Russell Shain concentrates on the cultural construct—particularly as viewed on film. Noting that much of what individuals "know" about disasters emerges not from events themselves but from fictional—as well as factual—portrayals, Shain links "nuclear" films of the 1950s and 1960s such as the government- sponsored *Duck and Cover* or Hollywood's *Attack of the 50-Foot Crab Woman* with a larger popular culture surrounding nuclear technology. Shain answers scientists who assert that the media "aren't doing their job" covering nuclear issues by outlining a popular conception of nuclear power linked to nuclear nightmare, one that is not scientifically accurate but maintains a firm hold on the popular imagination. Efforts to dilute documented pervasive skepticism of "anything nuclear" must thus deal not only with the facts of the nuclear debate but with popular, and often fictional, constructions of it.

In chapter 10, Deni Elliott, currently a Rockefeller Fellow at Dartmouth College, outlines the ethical implications of disaster coverage. Her pioneering effort, one that blends a humanistic tradition with a large body of social science work, establishes an ethical hierarchy of disaster reporting—one that working journalists as well as scholars can use to evaluate media performance. Elliot's essay also suggests areas for improved performance, a common theme throughout many of the selections.

ACKNOWLEDGMENTS

This volume would not have been possible without a wide variety of friendships and support networks.

The editors would first like to thank their contributors for their patience and hard work.

Lynne and Tim Walters thank their family—Amanda and Casey—for their support during the 2 years it took to collect and edit the book chapters. Tim also acknowledges the support of his parents, Dr. and Mrs. Charles E. Walters, and Professor Robert Ferrell, Indiana University, who taught him how to write. Lynne's brothers, Randy Masel and Dr. Brent Masel, provided encouragement when it was most needed, as did Lynne's co-workers at the Institute for Immunological Disorders in Houston, who supported this disaster reader in the midst of their own crisis.

Much of the work outlined in the volume has been encouraged by Dr. Bill Riebsame and Susan Tubbessing at the Natural Hazards Center, University of Colorado, Boulder.

Lee Wilkins also thanks her colleagues at the University of Colorado's Environment and Behavior Program and the School of Journalism and Mass Communication for their support, as well as her husband, David, who was willing to read first drafts, and daughter Miranda, who did not color rainbows on all of them.

Finally Jennings Bryant and Jack Burton, both with Lawrence Erlbaum Associates, provided needed encouragement when the draft was nearing completion. Without these unique contributions, this effort would not have been possible.

1
The Social Science Study of Disasters and Mass Communication

E. L. Quarantelli
University of Delaware

There are five general topics in this chapter. First, there is a brief history of the early social and behavioral science disaster studies both in the United States and elsewhere. One major point is, although the work has come far in the last 35 years, the initial research was rather uneven and many areas remained little examined or almost unexplored, including the operations of the mass communication system in disasters. A few reasons for this selective inattention are suggested.

Second, there is a highlight and summary of some of the more important general themes that have emerged from the numerous studies on all kinds of disaster phenomena. Much of that research has uncovered a great number of myths about individual and organizational behavior at the emergency time period of disasters. Of note is the existence of a disaster mythology that has been partly attributed to what is assumed and reported about such situations by mass media organizations.

Third, a substantive listing of the specific studies undertaken indicates something of the quantity and topical focus of the past and current work on mass communications in disasters. Research on the subject matter has accelerated as have the efforts at theoretical formulations.

The fourth section of the chapter focuses on major themes in the research findings and observations up to this time about mass communication behavior in disasters. In the process, some attention is given to important unknown matters as well as to known themes. A graphic matrix is used to try to depict the present state of knowledge.

Finally, the chapter concludes with a partial agenda for future research on mass communication activities in disasters. Certain innovations in the mass media area, particularly the development of new electronic technology, as well as qualitative changes in the nature of disastrous events, are creating different sets of research questions and issues. What has been learned from the past may not be equally as applicable to the disaster situations of the future.

The chapter's prime interest is in the human, social, group, and organization aspects of mass communication mediated through mass media at times of disasters. More specifically, the major focus is on emergency time-period activities (that is, on preparedness and response). However, such an emphasis does reflect the bulk of the existing literature, because there are very few mass communication studies related to the mitigation and recovery phases of disasters. Similarly, there are only passing allusions to the isolated pieces of research on fictional depictions of disasters (but this topic is partly covered in chapter 9 by Shain, this volume; see also Quarantelli, 1985c).

This overview mostly discusses mass communication in actual or threatened natural and technological disasters. Thus, collective stress or mass emergency situations such as wartime activities, civil disturbances, and riots, terrorist attacks, and other conflict events are outside its scope. Although there are some similarities, there are also some basic differences between mass communication in consensus type (that is, natural and technological disasters) and conflict type (e.g., wars) situations (cf. Kueneman & Wright, 1976; Quarantelli, 1970). However, future research should give high priority to systematic studies of the similarities and differences of mass communication in these two kinds of "collective stress situations" as Barton (1970) called them.

Given a choice, for scholarly purposes it is preferable to distinguish the concept of mass communication from that of mass media, with the former having references to the social processes and groups involved and the latter to the technologies or mechanical means involved. Such an approach would allow an analysis of two related, but, nonetheless, independent phenomena, that is, the technological base and the organizational superstructure. However, rather than attempting to make a case in this chapter for the theoretical and practical usefulness of this distinction, the two terms—*mass media* and *mass communication*—are used interchangeably, as unfortunately, is the tradition in the literature of the area. Included under either one of the terms is the full range of what is usually intended, that is, newspapers and other print outlets, radio and television stations, wire services, cable systems, and the more recently developed, so-called high-tech electronic services (for the last, see Rice et al., 1984).

THE DEVELOPMENT OF RESEARCH

The first systematic social science disaster study ever undertaken was by S. Prince (1920), who, as a part of his PhD dissertation in sociology looked at the social change consequences of an ammunition ship explosion in Halifax, Canada, which killed about 2,000 in 1917. Although an occasional study was done in the years that followed, social and behavioral research of disastrous events did not have any continuity until the end of World War II. Then a body of data began to be produced, especially on the behavior in the emergency time periods of disasters. Particularly important in these early days was the research done at the National Opinion Research Center (NORC) at the University of Chicago (1950-1954), studies by the Committee on Disaster Studies and the Disaster Research Group (DRG) at the National Academy of Sciences (1951-1962), and work by the Disaster Research Center (DRC), established at the Ohio State University in 1963 and relocated to the University of Delaware in 1985. These pioneering efforts, linked together by key NORC personnel who played major roles at DRG and DRC, created, systematized, and institutionalized the field of disaster studies in the United States (see Quarantelli, 1986).

Although most researchers were sociologists, each of the three groups made its own contribution. The NORC work was primarily social psychology in orientation and was concerned mostly with victim reaction to disaster impact. DRG research began to move toward a focus on group behavior in disasters. The DRC studies explicitly concentrated on the preparations and responses of social organizations and communities to quick onset disasters. All three studied both natural and technological disasters and assumed that the distinction was not especially useful for research purposes.

Without making any detailed examination, some of the earlier researchers did note the important role of radio, in particular, in transmitting warnings about potential disasters. Anderson (1970) reported on mass media involvement in the transmission of warnings to the general populace about tsunamies in Crescent City, California, and Hilo, Hawaii, after 1964 and 1965 earthquakes. DRC obtained information from several radio stations regarding their role in warnings about the 1965 Palm Sunday tornadoes in Northern Indiana (Brouillette, 1966). In describing warnings issued in the 1966 Topeka tornado, Stallings (1967) noted how stations passed on messages from the U.S. Weather Bureau.

This pattern of observing that radio and television stations have some part in warning about impending disasters has continued to the present day (e.g., see Ledingham & Masel-Walters, 1985). With some recent exceptions, the research focus is on the warning process rather than on the operation of mass communication. From a theoretical viewpoint, the mass communication system, as such, was more generally ignored, even when the processes of communications in disasters generally was a central focus, as in the doctoral dissertation of Harry Williams (1956).

The pioneering studies paid almost no attention to mass media organizations, as such, or to nonwarning mass communication news or stories at times of disasters. Although it was a research organization attuned to mass media operations, NORC all but totally ignored the area of mass communication (although Bucher peripherally treated the topic in her 1957 independent work on scapegoating). The DRG, either in its own field studies or in research it supported, was almost as disinterested, except for noting the use of radio in warning messages. About the only exception was a 1964 DRC in-depth study of the changes in structure and functioning of a radio station during a major forest fire near Santa Barbara, California. Made public in 1974, the report of this study (written by Adams) is, according to the *Inventory of Disaster Field Studies in the Social and Behavioral Sciences 1919-1979* (Quarantelli, 1984), the first clear-cut piece of research on a mass media organization. The only earlier piece directly focused on some mass communications aspects was in a 1956 Master's thesis by Ewell R. Williams who did a content analysis of letters to the editor published in a newspaper after the 1953 Waco, Texas, tornado. Harry Moore (1958) incorporated the Williams material and presented a more extensive content analysis of that same newspaper's treatment of disaster-related news stories, photographs, and advertisements. For all practical purposes, these three studies constituted the corpus of direct work on mass communication in disasters until the late 1960s.

Few other institutional areas were given so little direct attention. Just a few years ago, in singling out the mass media of communication area, Verta Taylor (1978) said that, "At present, the very few studies which exist in the literature are confined almost exclusively to descriptions and analyses of the news reporting of local radio and televisions in the United States. Much more needs to be done" (p. 274).

To some extent, this omission was the product of 1960s social science research that did little on mass communications, except for certain kinds of market and survey studies. McQuail (1969) described the body of early work in this area as bearing

> the marks of an entirely practical concern with two objectives: the counting and description of audiences and the measurement of direct effects on those exposed to communication. Between them, these two enterprises account for most of the research effort over a period of twenty or thirty years covering the 1930's, 1940's and much of the 1950's. (p. 36)

So the early social science disaster researchers had little to guide them in designing studies of the operation of mass communications systems in disasters. There were other factors involved. One was that the methodology required for similar kinds of quantitative "audience" research would have been extremely difficult to implement in the disaster field. Given enough resources it was not impossible. Witness the NORC classic, and still unmatched, in-depth survey of victims in an Arkansas tornado (see Marks, 1954).

More importantly, the early researchers failed to recognize the dual role of mass communicators in disasters: first, as reporters of events and second, as major organizational actors in preparing for, and responding to, disasters. There was a strong tendency to see the mass media outlets as primarily reporting about events and as poor reporters of disaster happenings. These pioneers found considerable mythology about the supposed behavior of individuals and groups in disaster situations. Lewis Killian (1986), one such pioneer said, "My early field experiences quickly led me to doubt the validity of most press accounts of disasters. They could not be depended upon."

Given a widespread skepticism about mass communication disaster accounts and a failure to appreciate fully mass media organizational operations in disasters, researchers tended to treat the mass media as at best a secondary, and none too reliable, source of information about a disaster event. Some early work even decided that press accounts of "panic" could safely be ignored as valid data (Quarantelli, 1954).

No doubt, the little governmental funding available to study the topic abetted the general neglect of the mass communication area. Perhaps there was a reluctance, as on some other research topics, to fund research that might be politically sensitive. More likely, funding agencies remained passive, given their view of mass communicators as reporters rather than as participants in disaster responses, a perception that remains widespread.

Outside of the United States, pioneering disaster research has been criticized as being somewhat parochial and reflective only of the American scene (e.g., Dombrowsky, 1981). Although social science disaster studies were initiated in Canada in the mid 1950s and in Japan and France in the early 1960s, the status of research on mass communication was not that different elsewhere. Eventually the operations of mass communications in disasters became a central focus of attention in Japan, but disaster researchers outside the United States also generally neglected the topic in the early years of study.

GENERAL OBSERVATIONS AND FINDINGS

Since the 1960s, disaster research has increased tremendously, with probably more studies being undertaken in a single year of the 1980s than were conducted in the first 10 years of pioneering work combined. There is no question that the later research is not only quantitatively, but qualitatively far superior to the early studies. This acceleration can be seen by contrasting the first research codification effort that was made by NORC (see Fritz & Marks, 1954), and the massive inventory of just sociological findings recently produced by Drabek (1986). The former, a 15-page article, stands in marked contrast to the latter, a 509-page book that draws 1,232 empirically supported conclusions on 146 subtopics derived from nearly 1,000 published reports.

Although these and all other literature reviews and codifications say little about the topic of mass communications in disasters, some major themes in the research findings and observations do emerge. These bear indirectly on a suggested relationship between what mass media outlets and communicators report about individual and group emergency-time behavior and what social science researchers have found out about such behavior. Even keeping in mind the different objectives of workers in the two areas, as Weller (1979) has pointed out, the differences are marked.

One theme in the research literature is that human beings respond remarkably well to extreme stress. Those threatened by disasters do not break into panic flight. Likewise, they seldom engage in antisocial or criminal behavior such as looting. Similarly, on the whole victims neither go "crazy" or psychologically break down, nor do they manifest severe mental health problems as a result of disasters. Those officials and others with community responsibilities do not abandon their work roles to favor their family roles. In the aftermath of a disaster impact, survivors do not passively wait for outside assistance, but actively initiate the first search-and-rescue efforts, taking the injured to medical care and doing whatever can be done in the crisis. Mass shelters are avoided. Those forced out of their homes go overwhelmingly to places offered by relatives and friends.

Although other characteristic behavior in disasters could be cited, a central theme in the research literature (see Barton, 1970; Drabek, 1986; Dynes, Quarantelli, & Kreps, 1981; Fritz, 1961) is that victims cope well with the extreme stress they are exposed to in major community emergencies generated by either natural or technological agents.

This general conclusion of how humans respond in such situations varies from what is generally believed both by the public at large and even community officials (cf. Wenger, Dykes, Sebok, & Neff, 1975). Based on research findings, such beliefs have been characterized as the myths of disasters (Quarantelli & Dynes, 1972). Researchers explain the discrepancy between what is commonly believed and the actual behavior in several ways. One is attributed to journalistic reporting. Researchers see disaster mythology as partly rooted in mass communication system expectations and accounts of how people supposedly behave in such situations. As Kreps (1980) wrote:

> There appears to be a long-standing assumption among disaster researchers that the media are deficient in disaster reporting. The media have been accused of inaccurately reporting disaster impacts, of giving undue emphasis to the sudden and dramatic, and of conveying false images about disaster behavior. (pp. 40-41)

It has been argued that mass media accounts are also deficient in reporting organizational behavior in disasters as well as misrepresenting individual behavior. Although the research literature emphasizes the coping and adaptive behavior of human beings in disasters, a second theme is that, in contrast, much organizational behavior is inefficient and ineffective, if not actually dysfunctional. In fact, one point more often stressed in the literature is that the organizations that converge to help in the emergency situation are frequently not only the locus, but also the source of the problem (cf. Quarantelli, 1985b).

Thus, the research literature suggests that, if there are negative mental health, or at least psychological, problems, they are seldom the direct consequence of the disaster. More likely, they are the result of inept management and poor decisions by public and private bureaucracies trying to help in the emergency or immediate postimpact period (cf. Quarantelli, 1985a). Similarly, research studies have consistently documented serious organizational problems in mobilization of relevant resources, in intra- and and interorganizational communication and coordination, and in appropriate management of disaster problems and difficulties (Drabek, 1986).

Although the point is sometimes only implicit, researchers often seem to be saying that mass media accounts of most disasters simply fail to depict the actual behavior of organizations in such situations. Whereas journalistic accounts seem to stress the negative about individual behavior, there is a tendency to focus on the positive about organizational behavior. Although some stories about emergency time and postrecovery activities of helping groups may point out difficulties, most accounts of responding organizations during these times stress what they have done and accomplished.

In fact, some researchers have stated that mass media personnel tend to take a "command-post" view of disasters. This view sees disasters primarily as events that are defined and explained by key emergency organizations involved, such as police or high local government officials who are unlikely to have other than a formal bureaucratic view of the situation (cf. Quarantelli, 1981). Mass media organizations seldom report the problematic picture of organizational preparedness and response to disasters uncovered by the systematic social science work.

SPECIFIC STUDIES

It is difficult to advance a definite figure either on the number of studies and/or the number of publications that have focused on mass communication in disasters. Although much depends on the definition of a study, a publication, and/or mass communications in disasters, some rough estimates can be made if certain criteria are used.

If a study is defined as "a data-gathering effort undertaken by some kind of a social scientist in a systematic manner," then there are probably less than several dozen pieces of research at most. A recent DRC compilation used to develop an annotated bibliography on the mass media and disasters (Friedman, Lockwood, Snowden, & Zeidler, 1986) supports this estimate. Found were 26 different studies of 49 different disasters or situations (but several events such as Three Mile Island were studied by different researchers) and 29 different publications are mentioned. The DRC compilation, although acknowledged to be incomplete, does include research that produced only limited circulation working papers or reports. To put the results in a larger context, the *DRC Inventory of Field Studies* found studies of 353 different disasters up to 1979 that had resulted in more than 1,080 publications (Quarantelli, 1984).

These compilations and bibliographies deal primarily with English language literature sources. One consequence is a slight underestimate of the total. Consider the work of the Japanese, where mass communications specialists at the Institute of Journalism and Communications Research at the University of Tokyo have conducted a core of social and behavioral disaster research. (For an English language summary and annotation of Japanese studies done up to 1981, see Yamamoto & Quarantelli, 1984; for later work see Hirose, 1986). Not always noted have been Swedish, Italian, and French researchers who have done occasional studies of mass communication in crisis situations (e.g., Lagadec, 1985; Rosengren, Arvidson, & Sturesson, 1975; Santoianni, 1983). Nor has all the work by Scanlon and his colleagues at the School of Journalism at Carleton University in Canada been captured in summaries and reviews of mass media literature. This may be because that research focuses as much on interpersonal communication flow as on mass communication and looks at both consensus and conflict-type collective stress situations (e.g., Scanlon, 1978; Scanlon & Alldred, 1982; Scanlon, Dixon, & McClennan, 1982; Scanlon & Frizzell, 1979).

Nonetheless, even when all these, and other more fugitive references, are included, the total body of work on mass communications in disaster seems to number less than 50. If the term *research* is used more narrowly, the number shrinks to not more than 36. If reference is made to a systematic, empirical study of some kind, this total is also too high.

Even the research that exists has problems. It is uneven in focus and leaves major areas and questions unexplored. Although studies like Wilkins (1986) of the Bhopal chemical disaster and Morentz (1980) of the Sahel drought looked at wire service reports, the international media of the wire services have been mostly ignored. Similarly, the operation of national systems in disasters has been generally unexamined, although Nimmo (1985) did study CBS, NBC, and ABC telecasting about the Three Mile Island nuclear plant accident, and Rogers and Sood (1980) examined NRC reporting about the Andhra Pradesh cyclone. The functioning of cable systems in disasters had been almost totally unexamined. Only a few studies of disaster-relevant aspects of magazine productions have been undertaken. Alexander (1980) studied two Italian magazines' coverage of the Florence flood, whereas Wenger and Friedman (1985) conducted a content analysis of reports on Hurricane Alicia in *Time* and *Newsweek*.

As might be anticipated, print media studies have been more common than studies on electronic media. On the other hand, there has been more research on individual radio and television stations than on individual newspapers. Figures from the DRC bibliography, which should be treated with considerable caution, show that although there were 17 major studies of 42 newspapers and at least 4 magazines, there had been 4 studies of 67 radio stations and 5 studies of 52 television stations.

Substantively, what has been studied? Besides the earlier mentioned research by Adams (1974), E. Williams (1956), and Moore (1958), Alexander did a content analysis of British and Italian print media coverage of the 1966 floods in northern Italy. Brooks (1970), as part of his PhD dissertation, looked at the emergency and disaster planning of 20 radio and 13 television stations in the United States. Sharon Friedman (1981) did interviews and content analyses of eight newspapers in the Three Mile Island area. Goltz (1984) did a content analysis of the reporting of two California papers of the Alaskan, Imperial Valley, Algerian, and 1980 Italian earthquakes. In DRC studies, Green (1983) looked at how local newspapers helped generate emergent citizens groups around disaster issues, and Hannigan (1976) did a content analysis of a newspaper in flooded Wilkes Barre.

Harless and Rarick (1974) interviewed radio personnel in six cities that had natural disasters. Jensen (1972) did a content analysis of three newspapers in his study of a Southern California fire. From DRC, Kueneman and Wright (1976) reported on the disaster news policies of 72 radio and television stations in a dozen cities in the United States. Mazur (1984) has looked at the reporting about the Love Canal chemical disaster and the Three Mile Island nuclear plant accident. Morentz (1980) did a content analysis of 750 wire service reports, special and mass media articles, and press releases about the Sahel drought in 1974-1975. Nimmo's (1985) comparative study of how the three American television networks reported the Three Mile Island nuclear plant accident will be repeated by a DRC study of how those networks initially reported the Chernobyl disaster. Rogers and Sood (1980) have done content analyses of coverage by the *New York Times, Le Monde, Time,* NBC, and several others of the Andhra Pradesh cyclone and the Sahel drought. Rogers and Sood (1981) have also looked at local and American media reporting of Hurricane David's landfall on the island of Dominica. Scanlon (1979) tested hypotheses about the adequacy and completeness of media coverage of the 1978 Canadian Terrace floods. He also looked at Darwin, Australia, after Cyclone Tracy to analyze a situation in which a community's local mass media outlets were initially all made nonfunctional (Scanlon, 1978). Sood (1981) analyzed interview and content data in a study of news gatekeeping in Hurricane David in Dominica, a blizzard in Seattle, and a mudslide in Los Angeles.

Turner (1980) and his colleagues (Nigg, 1982) looked at how six major newspapers and selected radio and television broadcasts in Southern California reported earthquake news. In a partial parallel study, Hirose (1986) examined mass media coverage in Japan of earthquake prediction. McKay (1984) has provided information about the reporting of three newspapers of a bushfire in Australia. As part of DRC research, Waxman (1973) examined the gatekeeping process of local radio stations in four flood-sticken communities, and Weller (1979) performed a content analysis of a local paper in the Alaskan earthquake, in a major snowstorm in Chicago, and in a tornado in Topeka. A test of the perpetuation of "disaster myths" was done by Wenger and Friedman (1985) in their content analysis of Hurricane Alicia coverage by *The Houston Post*, theI Washington Post, The New York Times, USA Today, Newsweek, and *Time*. Wilkins (1986) conducted a content analysis of Bhopal coverage by commercial news network broadcasts, the wire services, the East Coast "prestige press," and national news magazines. Beady and Bolin (1986) have reported on pioneering research on the role of the Black media in disasters by looking at the contents and uses of newspapers, radio and television stations in Mobile, Alabama, during Hurricane Frederic. Finally, DRC and collaborating Japanese colleagues are getting ready to publish the results of a study of the processing of news by the local mass media in two major disasters in both societies. (The Japanese results have been partly set forth in Hiroi, Mikami, & Miyata, 1985.)

There has clearly been an acceleration of empirical research on mass communications in disasters in recent years. There was an upsurge as a result of the Three Mile Island nuclear plant accident (e.g., Krieghbaum, 1979; Stephens & Edison, 1980, 1982), and multiple studies are ongoing in Sweden, Italy, India, France, and the United States as a result of the Bhopal and Chernobyl disasters. (See, for example, the analysis made of Soviet mass media reporting of the nuclear disasters in Sanders, 1986, and in Shabad, 1986.)

In addition to this empirical work, theoretical formulations about mass media operations are appearing, although there is nothing that could remotely be called a middle-range theory of mass communications in disasters. Earlier codifiers of the disaster literature said almost nothing about this. In his comprehensive codification of research results, Dynes (1974) did not allude to mass communications organizations during disasters, except for an introductory vignette of radio station operations primarily during the Warner Robbins tornado. Fritz (1961), in the area's earliest codification effort, paid even less attention to media operations, and Barton (cf. 1970), in the most systematic theoretical overview of collective stress situations, almost exclusively refers to how a few characteristics of disasters will affect news media coverage. In contrast, Drabek (1986), in the latest major codification attempt, included discussions about mass communications and mass media operations in each of the eight substantive chapters of his book. A few years earlier, the Committee on Disasters and the Mass Media (1980) produced for a National Academy of Sciences study a volume dealing solely with the general role of the mass media in disaster reporting. More limited efforts at theoretical generalizations can be found in the treatment of the command-post perspective of mass communicators in Quarantelli (1981), in the examination of news media responsibility for disaster myths perpetuation as as described in Goltz (1984), and in the assessment of factual accuracy of the media's coverage of community crises as analyzed in Scanlon, Tuukko, and Morton (1978).

The increase in empirical research and theoretical formulations can be attributed to several factors. As a matter of organization research policy, DRC has deliberately chosen to open continually new questions and issues in the disaster area. The bulk of the Japanese disaster researchers, given their institutional base and journalism and mass media studies and working in collaboration with DRC personnel, were strongly inclined to look at mass communications in disasters. Also, disaster researchers who had undertaken studies of American urban and ghetto civil disturbances in the late 1960s and early 1970s had been impressed by the role of mass media in the generation, development, and continuation of such collective behavior (e.g., Dynes & Quarantelli, 1973, as well as specific studies of mass media organizations and activities as reported by Quarantelli, 1971, and Kueneman & Wright, 1975). This latter work led directly to the DRC-Japanese collaborative research on local mass media operations in disasters and to the current DRC study on the processing of news on community disasters by media organizations.

Although DRC policy had a role in increasing empirical research and theoretical formulations, the National Academy of Sciences 1978 appointment of a committee to look at the role of the mass media in disasters was probably the most important factor in accelerated social sciences work. No particular event sparked the committee's establishment. But Charles Fritz, a pioneer disaster researcher who was an executive secretary of different disaster-related committees at the Academy in the 1970s, had long been interested in systematically examining mass communications in disasters. He saw the time as opportune to approach the National Science Foundation for a grant to make a state-of-the-art assessment of the topic.

Despite two major rewritings, the committee's final report was never publically issued because it failed to meet the quality standards of the Academy's own reviewers. Intellectual differences between the researchers and the journalists on the committee may have contributed to the problem. What many outsiders have taken as the committee's report, *Disasters and the Mass Media* (1980), is actually only the set of the proceedings of an early workshop that the committee had held. It is not a committee report as such and does not reflect later deliberations that took place over more than a year. Nonetheless, that volume has become known as a milestone in the development of mass communications in disaster studies and is almost certainly the most cited reference in the literature on the topic.

Finally, greater sophistication of recent disaster and mass communications research probably has influenced the increased efforts at theoretical formulations about mass media in disasters. Drawing both from mass communication and the disaster research areas, Wenger (1985) sets forth a number of problematical aspects about mass media operations in disasters, noting both functional and dysfunctional features, as well as within and outside the mass media, perceptual evaluations of performance in disasters.

SOME SIGNIFICANT RESEARCH THEMES

In his recent massive effort to codify the results of sociological disaster research, Drabek set forth a number of specific propositions and hypotheses about mass communications in disasters (1986; see, e.g., pp. 41-42, 122-123, 165-169, 222-223, 336-338). In the following discussion, rather than repeating those specifics, the most significant themes, either from a theoretical or practical point of view, have been isolated. No effort is made to depict systematically all the discernible themes in the literature.

To see what has been (and what has not been) found, some kind of framework must be used (Quarantelli, 1980). Different frameworks could be used for this purpose, including the following matrix. Along one side, media systems and outlets can be distinguished. Along the other, distinctions can be made between communicators, contents, audiences, and consequences of mass communications. This can be seen in graphic terms in the chart appearing on the next page.

Using this matrix to examine the research findings and observations about mass communications in disasters, the general conclusion would have to be that the knowledge base is rather limited. Many of the cells are all but empty or would have only one or very few empirically based statements (e.g., cells 1-4, 21-32). In rising from the level of empirical generalizations to basic themes, only a cell here and there exists about which general statements could be made (among the strongest candidates would be cells 9-11, 13-15, 17-19). With respect to level A, there are practically no studies about international media systems, such as the major wire services or videotape distributors. This is not surprising, because they have been little described or analyzed even outside the disaster area.

One discernible theme in the disaster literature is that general knowledge and perception of most disasters anywhere, but especially in developing countries, is almost exclusively dependent on reporting by the Western World mass media. Slow moving disasters such as the Sahel drought and the Ethiopian famine were well

		Communicators	Contents	Audiences	Consequences
A.	International Systems (e.g., wire service)	1	2	3	4
B.	National Systems (e.g., BBC, NHK)	5	6	7	8
C.	Local Community Systems				
	Print outlets	9	10	11	12
	Radio outlets	13	14	15	16
	Television outlets	17	18	19	20
	Cable outlets	21	22	23	24
	Film outlets	25	26	27	28
	Other electronic outlets	29	30	31	32

developed before they were suddenly and dramatically announced to the rest of the world. Not only are there such selective delays in reporting, but there are many severely damaging natural disasters in Latin American, Asia, and Africa that never circulate in world press accounts. On the other hand, the Bhopal, India, chemical poisoning; the Amareo, Columbia, volcanic eruption; and the Mexico City earthquake did get considerable exposure in the international mass media. Also, disasters that cut across national boundaries, such as fallout from the Chernobyl nuclear plant accident in the Soviet Union and the partial toxic chemical pollution of the Rhine River as the result of a Swiss fire incident, appear to have been over-reported. But this and other thematic notions would have to be almost all speculation because there are practically no empirically based studies at the international level (cells 1-4).

The situation is only slightly better at level B, that of national mass media systems. There are a handful of studies, especially of the contents of national communication systems (cell 6). Dominating any thematic observation is the fact that domestic disasters are major news stories in almost all communications systems, a not self-explanatory point given that only in the last few years have such events been reported in the Soviet Union and that a few developing countries continue to underplay or ignore such happenings. Another theme that emerges from both Japanese and American studies is that different national television networks have different styles of reporting news about disaster emergencies. Also clear is that the content of national and local media coverage is rather different. A weaker theme is that audiences do not necessarily receive what they want. Still, there are huge gaps in our knowledge. For example, there are no disaster area studies parallel to those in organizational research done on the factors and decisions made in the U.S. national television network news coverage of President John Kennedy's assassination (Love, 1969).

Such knowledge as exists about mass communication in disasters is mostly about aspects of level C, local community systems. These are primarily concerned with American, Canadian, and Japanese situations with a few Australian, Swedish, Italian, and French insights. Among the more significant themes in the research literature is that different news media differentially deviate from normal processing of news stores at times of disasters. Radio stations change the most, newspapers the least, and television stations fall in the middle (provided the media facilities are undamaged in the disaster).

Another theme is that there is no across-the-board response in the different American and Canadian media outlets of a local mass communication system. A few go to all-disaster news focus, and some devote much attention to the community emergency. Many either cease operation for the emergency's duration or continue more-or-less normal programming. So the local system, especially the larger it is, responds selectively and not as a holistic entity. The very largest and the very smallest local media outlets change the least at disaster times.

There also seems to be a consensus that the everyday gatekeeping process of mass communication systems is considerably altered, if not truncated, during the emergency time periods of disasters. The generally negative view of mass communication personnel held by emergency organization officials also comes through strongly. Most, but not all, of the research indicates that the criteria used to identify a "news" story at times of disaster do not differ that much from what is used on an everyday basis.

A strong theme regarding story content is that media reports of disaster do not reflect reality, but are a matter of social construction in the sense that Tuchman (1978) and Altheide (1976) argue is true of most news. In fact, many researchers working in the area appear to believe that the definitional process of mass media considerably determines what comes to be or not to be defined as a potential or actual disaster. Another strong suggestion is that what is reported by the mass media perpetuates the "myths" of disaster behavior. A developing theme, perhaps not totally consistent with the perpetuation concept, is that disaster stories are not as factually inaccurate as once believed. A concurrent and widespread theme is that news coverage of disaster events and/or victims tends to focus on the more extreme cases. Some, but not all, researchers believe that news reporting of technological disasters is less well handled than that about natural disaster agents.

On the other hand, there are no clear themes about the visual imagery used by television disaster reporting, as have been developed about depictions as events such as violence, war scenes, pornography and sexual behavior, as well as general news reporting. Not only do we not know if disasters, for instance, are depicted from a bird's eye or worm's eye point of view (Tuchman, 1978), but there does not appear to be even one empirical study of the full content of a local radio station reporting of a major disaster. The use of mass media to deliver personal messages at emergency times, while observed both in Japan and the United States, has not been examined either in terms of functions or content.

Most themes about audiences at times of disaster rest on relatively weak empirical studies. A prevalent idea is that no matter how extensive the mass media system, its disaster-relevant information will not reach some segments of the population. Paralleling what has been found out about normal daily operations, distrust of disaster reports by the media seems to exist among minority groups. Similarly, mass communication content at times of disasters is processed by existing interpersonal communication links.

Not surprisingly, the cells in our matrix covering "consequences" are devoid of much empirical data and do not allow for generalizations, given that scholars know very little about who listens or watches what, with whom, where, and for what purposes during the emergency time periods of disasters. Although many think otherwise, researchers really have little hard data that audiences have greater exposure to, and use mass communications more, during disasters than normal times. Developing audience profiles during major community crises would aid the research effort.

Although there are some studies about the consequences of mass media reporting or information, the work is less than might be expected. And, apart from some having to do with the warning process, it is difficult to discern empirically well grounded general themes. Thus, Hartsough and Mileti (1985) commented:

> There is a great deal of opinion, usually in the form of "conventional wisdom" about the topic of psychological disaster impacts and the mass media, but very little systematic data are actually available.... In fact, there seems to be a paucity of scientific studies on the effects of mass media...on behavior in general.... To our knowledge, the only study of the topic of postdisaster mass media psychological effects is reported by Murphy. (pp. 282-283)

In line with this, frequent assertions are made that the well-known convergence phenomena in disasters can partly be attributed to mass communication reports. This may be true, but apart from the fact that convergence itself has not been very well documented in systematic empirical studies, there does not appear to be any piece of research directly demonstrating a link between mass communication and convergence behavior. There are also a few theoretical formulations that hypothesize that the bigger and more sudden a disaster, the greater the media coverage that, in turn, leads to more attention and conversations about the disaster among the victims (Barton, 1970, p. 222). This also may be true, but it would be difficult to find any systematic research that has actually gathered data on such linkages. Apart from a general statement that some media communicators provide some media content with some media effects, there are no specific themes about the consequences of mass communications in disasters (but see the educated speculations in Kreps, 1980; Larson, 1980).

FUTURE RESEARCH AGENDA

There are three clearly indicated future research paths. The first, although really a more minor one, is to build on what scholars now think they know, or at least strongly suspect, about mass communications in disasters. Among others, studies should attempt to confirm (a) the truncated gatekeeping that seems to occur at emergency times, (b) the differential media deviation from normal everyday operations, (c) the influence of organizational size in mass media changes at times of disaster, and (d) the differences in local community and national level reporting.

Some observations of these issues have been inconsistent with one another. Gans (1979) advanced several plausible, but not altogether consistent, impressions about the number of people who might be affected by a disaster and the probability of that event being reported by the mass media he studied. Research needs to establish the universalities and limitations about what has already been found. Scholars also need to examine the complex intermixture of mass media communications and interpersonal communications in the receiving and using of warning messages (cf. Scanlon, 1976).

A more important path for study would be research on the many questions and issues that have been barely addressed. With respect to the matrix, these would include almost everything except cells 6, 9-10, 13-14, and 17-18. In many instances, there are not even descriptive accounts or case studies of those aspects of mass communication in disasters. In particular, there may be some comparative studies at the national level (cells 5-8) that would lend themselves well to a cross-societal approach. Unless there are several studies using a sophisticated approach (e.g., Hannigan & Wigert, 1973) from which themes can be derived for every matrix cell, researchers cannot even pretend to claim an understanding of mass media operations in disasters.

Unfortunately, even if such knowledge were not available, there would still be a rather large research agenda. Both the nature of disasters and the nature of mass communications are rapidly changing so what current studies suggest now will not possibly provide a good picture of both the near and distant future. Researchers should recognize that: (a) not only will there be quantitatively more disasters, but also the quality of disasters is changing in some respect, and (b) the rapid changes and development of new electronic technologies in mass media are basically altering the whole phenomena of mass communication in disasters.

Because of factors like the continuing population growth, greater population density in high risk areas, more property to be impacted, and greater interdependence of social operations, there is an increased disaster potential. Just look at the New Madrid, Missouri, earthquakes of 1811-1812. At the time, there were few social consequences, but today there could be thousands of casualties, immense economic damage in Memphis and St. Louis, as well as at least a temporary disruption of the larger American society. So even with the best mitigation measures, there will be more and worse disasters in the future, even if assessed only in quantitative terms.

Yet, the qualitative changes and consequences are even more important. Technological accidents of a chemical, biological, or nuclear nature were all but nonexistent a few decades ago. Now possible, these create hazards that can have major consequences distant in time and place from the source. The potential of the Three Mile Island and the reality of the Chernobyl nuclear plant accidents was that populations remote in time and place could be endangered. The Rhine River toxic spill affected several nations. And it is possible to visualize a biogenetic engineering mistake threatening the ecological life cycle of whole regions of the world. The extreme dependence of highly developed societies on the continual functioning of interrelated computers linking vital sectors of the social system also suggest new qualitative threats. But because the threats often are not easily seen, the danger can become very diffuse in many of these newer, technologically rooted disasters.

To be realistic, research on mass communication will have to assume that disasters that will occur will be generally both quantitatively and qualitatively different from those of the present (e.g., the analysis of newspaper stories on major oil spills in the oceans and hazardous materials as examined by Lagadec, 1985; Molotch & Lester, 1974, 1975).

Although disasters themselves are changing, so is mass communication. What are the implications for disaster preparations and responses of the reception of distant stations via cable? There are now cases of audiences in one section of the United States receiving tornado or flood warnings meant for the area around the original transmitting station in another section of the country. Some anecdotal examples raise even more interesting questions. In one case studied in the field by DRC, an incident fire commander used the on-the-scene reporting of a hazardous toxic spill by the local television station to make field decisions. Simultaneously, that official was being interviewed by a reporter on what was happening. In another instance, guests trapped in their rooms in a high-rise were informed of the fire's progress and given instructions on what to do by on-the-scene reporting by mobile vans from local television stations. Many new technologies, from cellular telephones to direct broadcast satellites to videocassette recorders, intervene in new ways between the initial communicator and information recipient. These phenomena are rather different from the traditional view of mass media use in disasters.

According to Rice et al. (1984), the new media mean:

> new ways of encoding, transmitting, distributing, and displaying information most overtly in the form of new communication technologies. For example, digital, as compared to analog, encoding dramatically increases the speed, accuracy, and volume of information that can be exchanged. It efficiently integrates voice, data, and video. It facilitates signal processing and coding techniques. It offers greater privacy and security. But more important, humans are beginning to communicate in new ways as well. New media—from videotext to personal computer networks, from communication satellites to fiber optics—are blurring distinctions that seemed so clear and useful a generation ago. (p. 34)

The importance of such developments is that, of course, they add an interactive and feedback element absent from the one-way media of the past. What will the increasing addition of computers and interactive media technologies do to the operation of local emergency management agencies as they attempt to mobilize resources, exchange information, and coordinate activities in disasters? Certainly the new technologies will make a difference, but scholars have few notions of how they will do so and in what ways. Future research needs to be done on such matters, research that avoids simple-minded treatment of mass communication in disasters as primarily a matter of studying what warning messages reach potential audiences. There is a tendency for both disaster planners and disaster researchers to look at past disasters. If they are to improve their performances, they would be better off projecting likely scenarios of the future, in which both the nature of disasters and of the mass communications involved will be generally different from the past and present.

Although this chapter has focused on communications in consensus-type community emergencies, it would be worthwhile to examine the similarities and differences between mass media reportage of the full range of crises affecting public life, including wars, civil disturbances, and terrorist attacks. There has been a slight start in this direction by those, for example, who argue a command-post perspective is likely to dominate all local reporting of any emergency (e.g., Quarantelli, 1981), and by those who note a differential and selective reporting of riots in American society as compared to news coverage of disasters (Kueneman & Wright, 1975).

Whatever the direction, the fields of disaster research and study and of mass communication can be mutually beneficial. Instead of approaching the problem as if there were not a very extensive body of general mass communication literature providing theoretical notions, conceptions distinctions, and empirical generalizations (an odd position taken in e.g., Lindy & Lindy, 1985), those in the disaster area can use what already exists to guide their work. In turn, students of mass communication can learn from disaster research some of the limits and qualifications of their view (e.g., Wenger, 1985).

ACKNOWLEDGMENT

While some of this work was undertaken under National Science Foundation grant ECE-8504423, the views and opinions expressed are those of the author.

2
Bhopal: *The Politics of Mediated Risk*

Lee Wilkins
University of Colorado-Boulder

> Politics is the study of the changing value hierarchy, the pyramids of safety, income, and deference. Some symbols embody definite demands or expectations or identifications and may be called political symbols in the narrower sense of the word, without losing sight of the larger problem of discovering the actual significance which can be attached to them in redefining the value pyramid.
> —Harold Lasswell (1965, *World Politics and Personal Insecurity*)

CHEMICAL SPILLS AS POLITICAL ACCIDENTS

About 10 months after the December 3, 1984, Bhopal, India, disaster, a private consultant to the federal government reported there had been at least 6,928 chemical accidents in the United States since 1980. In those accidents, the bulk of which occurred during the manufacturing process, 1,500 persons were injured and 135 killed.

The consultant's report itself was one element in the Congressional debates created by the Bhopal disaster—a chemical accident in Central India in which the gas methyl isocyanate, used as the base of a series of environmentally safe pesticides, leaked from a Union Carbide plant. Ultimately killing from 2,700 to 8,000 people, depending on the source, and injuring an additional 200,000, the Bhopal disaster was the worst industrial accident in human history.

The tragedy also became a world-wide political symbol rooted in the cross currents of Third World development, political independence, and capitalist economics. As such, Bhopal was a highly visible marker in a shifting value hierarchy that sometimes pits national welfare, founded on economic and political independence, against low probability but potentially devastating threats to individual safety. Bhopal represents a uniquely tangled 20th-century political dilemma. How do societies, particularly democratic societies, balance the costs of national development—the income portion of the political pyramid—and those of individual security, a unit of analysis that revolves around safety and the individual deference that underlies it?

Just as the December 3, 1984, accident represented a normal part of the work of a highly industrialized society that results from collective choice, it also represented another form of doing business, that highly visual story with human impact and drama that is a staple of modern news reporting.

Although journalists might report any such disaster as an unfolding story, such accidents are not free-standing events (Perrow, 1984). They arise from the synergy created by highly complex, technological systems in which scientific knowledge and technological expertise is tightly coupled with economic and political demands in national and international settings.

Despite this complex infrastructure, recent studies (Graber, 1980; Nimmo, 1985; Wilkins, 1987) suggest that such events are reported as melodrama rather than as news that is both analytic and predictive. In this sense, journalistic accounts of the disaster hue to what Harold Lasswell (1965) called the traditional vocabulary of American public life, "...legal, ethical, and theological rather than analytical; and, where it is analytical, it is personal and partisan rather than impersonal" (p. 164). It is a journalistic world of "real fictions" (Fisher, 1970) where a certain form of environmental surveillance, one that emphasizes the "body count" aspect of a disaster, is substituted for a more thorough analysis.

Thus, media coverage of the Bhopal tragedy foreshadows another sort of tragedy, one in which the politics of the short term almost certainly supercedes any agenda for long-term collective decision making.

THE MEDIATED STORY OF BHOPAL

Any mass-mediated reality (McQuail, 1983; Tuchman, 1978) is a composite comprised of what the media said as reflected and enhanced by individual perceptions (Lippmann, 1949). Yet, a mediated reality is not neutral. Scholars have noted that media reports emphasize the dramatic and the unique rather than the patterns of events and decision making underlying the apparent aberrations usually reported as "news." In this sense, news accounts are the reworking of stylized information, information couched in the form of symbolic strategy (Carey, 1969, p. 36).

Whether in print or on television, modern disaster reportage conforms to a symbolic strategy that is perhaps unique to the genre. As many have noted, disaster reports emphasize a form of environmental awareness designed to alert society either to impending problems or to the actual onset of an event. This "command-post" viewpoint (Quarantelli, 1981) emphasizes the media's surveillance function, enabling community members to extend their knowledge of events beyond experience (Lasswell, 1965).

If acted upon, surveillance enables society to exert some control over those forces, enhancing individual and collective safety. For surveillance to produce this effect, it must place events in a context that allows both decision makers and voters to understand the new configurations of the political value pyramid.

Media coverage of the Bhopal disaster provided only a truncated notion of surveillance.[1] News reports provided Americans with news stripped of cultural and historic context (Altheide, 1976), providing surveillance of an immediate event rather than the conditions giving rise to it. In addition, the demands of individual media outlets influenced the news reports as much as did the event itself.

The Overall Portrait

Media reports of the Bhopal disaster were almost exclusively event centered. About 85% of all stories focused on discrete events in the crisis. This failure to generalize was noteworthy because of the obvious American tie with events in Bhopal, the sister chemical plant located in Institute, West Virginia. Although 21.6% of what was printed or broadcast mentioned that relationship, only 10.5% generalized from the American link to the larger issue of the impact of technological hazards on modern society.

The absence of discussion of the leak's environmental and health consequences strikingly demonstrates the media's concentration on a specific event, rather than on long-term impact. About 62% of the stories did not contain any reference to questions of long-term health, environmental, social, and legal impacts of the leak. Of those that did mention long-term consequences, 25% focused strictly on what has become a standard of the American political vocabulary—the issue of immediate legal culpability.

Only 5.6% of what was written and broadcast fell into the warning and preparedness phase of the disaster. Although 48% of the stories fit into the rehabilitation and reconstructive phase, the vast majority of these also centered on discrete events such as Operation Faith in Bhopal or plant inspections and Congressional hearings in the United States. Longer term issues of rehabilitation and planning were seldom mentioned.

Analysis of more profound issues, tied to problems of technological hazards that are shared by all nations, received even less attention. Just two stories, one carried by Reuters and the other by UPI, mentioned the Green Revolution and India's stated political goal of feeding herself. Only 2.6% of the stories discussed the economic and political reasons the plant was built in India; none of them included any form of institutional analysis.

What these figures demonstrate is that the generalized surveillance provided by media had a distinct focus emphasizing events rather than underlying structural causes. It was an emphasis on immediate individual safety, buttressed by some generalized view of income as defined by capitalistic economics. Concepts of individual safety interwoven with societal well being, the relationship between societal goals and the assumption of collective risks, and the potential political and economic shifts that debate in these areas might create, were absent from almost all media reports. Of course, different outlets, provided slightly different emphases, and certain important variations did emerge.

The Wire Service View

Wire services, which collectively are the primary data-gathering agency for almost all American news organizations, remained most firmly in the surveillance-of-visible-events mold. In almost 75% of what the American wire services produced (74% for AP and 73% for UPI), the tangible connections between the Institute, West Virginia, and Bhopal, India, plants were never mentioned. Reuters' focus was more Indian-event oriented.

The same pattern was evident in wire coverage of long-term issues. Except for repeated body counts and enumerations of the various injuries, relatively little space was devoted to discussion of long-term consequences to human health. AP discussed health problems in only 16% of its stories and environmental questions in only 10% of the stories that moved across the wire.

UPI and Reuters had a similar emphasis. Reports on cultural background of the disaster fared even worse; only 14 individual stories (2.7%) included such information. Economic background was scarce; only 13% of the wire stories mentioned economics and even these focused on the impact the leak would have on Union Carbide's corporate health instead of on structural questions.

Taken as a whole, wire service accounts concentrated on a specific event and its aftermath, not on the conditions giving rise to it. Such reportage was skewed to the anecdotal and atheoretical, a pattern, with some shifts, that was repeated in the prestige press.

The Prestige Press Provides Some Context

Although prestige publications repeated the event oriention of the wires, the *New York Times* and the *Washington Post* did not, in fact, report and write the same story. The *Times*, with its reputation as the national paper of record and its emphasis on international coverage, provided the most complete record of the Bhopal tragedy of any medium studied.

Although the *Times* sustained an event-oriented focus, it was also the only media outlet studied to conduct any independent investigation of the leak. As a result, news of the social, historic, and cultural conditions contributing to the infrastructure of the disaster also appeared significantly more frequently in *Times* reports than in those of the *Washington Post*.

On the other hand, the *Post* reported the politics of Bhopal. The *Post* did not separate Bhopal from the political reaction to it, and hence to some potential alterations in the value pyramid. For example, the *Post* linked the story more closely to Institute, West Virginia, that did the *Times*, and almost one-fifth of the *Post*'s reports used conceptual issues surrounding technological hazards as a primary focus.

Although the *Post* reported the generalized issue of which Bhopal was merely a symbol, it did so in a way that left some doubt about human consequences. Only 13.5% of the *Post*'s reports carried information about the long-term health and environmental consequences of the leak. Of the *Times*' stories, 30% did so.

Blame was framed differently in the two publications. Most stories did not discuss the issue. When the *Times* did, the question was generally contextual, multifaceted, and systemic. The *Post* repeated the pattern established by the wires. When blame was mentioned, it was almost always through quotations by attorneys involved in litigation.

As a result, readers of the two prestige publications received a slightly more contextual view of the disaster. Although the event emphasis remained, *New York Times* readers were made aware of the tragedy's cultural, historic, and social underpinnings. Those who read the *Washington Post* were treated to renditions filled with political connections and some coverage of the accident's underlying conceptual issues. Yet, both newspapers framed these issues in largely traditional ways, reports of what happened and, within certain circumscribed views, what could be done to clean up the mess.

News Magazines Respond to Audiences

Readership demographics, more than the traditional wisdom that "magazines provide more depth," characterized portraits of the leak by three national news magazines. With its more conservative audience, *U.S. News and World Report* covered Bhopal as the story of Union Carbide's survival. *Time* and *Newsweek* shifted to a more event-centered perspective. Both magazines published vivid descriptions of activity in Bhopal and spent a significant amount of space discussing medical and environmental problems. And, although both outlined the economic impact on Union Carbide and the looming legal battles, they were less prominently reported.

Not only did magazine reports place little emphasis on the Institute connection but contributory cultural and social conditions rarely were discussed. When Union Carbide's survival was excluded from the analysis, the various long-term questions received merely sporadic attention. Only 47% of the magazine articles focused on long-term rehabilitation and reconstruction efforts, and much of that was a review of Operation Faith. All other reports were devoted to coverage of the leak itself and to its immediate aftermath.

Despite the shortcomings, the tone of magazine reports varied from that of other print outlets. Through individual words and pictures, as much as through any set of facts, the magazines connected Bhopal more directly to some of the larger issues. *U.S. News* reports relied on smokestacks as an extended metaphor. Witnesses were quoted as saying that the leak had made Bhopal "like a big gas chamber," an image reinforced by discussion of the chemical "fallout" in the Kenaway Valley and the higher than normal regional cancer rates. *Time* quoted witnesses saying that the leak had been like an atomic bomb. In a story focusing entirely on technological hazards, the magazine linked Bhopal to hazardous nuclear waste dumping, environmental poisoning, and Love Canal. In a similar portrayal, *Newsweek* published some of the most graphic pictures that appeared in any media outlet.

Such tones were subtleties, not the major thrust of magazine coverage. Although magazines attempted to make some links between events in Bhopal and larger issues like corporate stability or technological hazards, these connections were far from systematic.

Televison and the Drama of Bhopal

Television repeated the pattern of imagery used in the magazines, and it was videotape, rather than words, that made the Bhopal story such ideal television material. The unfolding drama of Bhopal was a top television news story, one of the top three in network newscasts 71% of the time it appeared.

Although the story gathered more than 2 hours of airtime during the study period, almost all of the television coverage appeared within 2 weeks of the event, an indication that television's view was strictly event centered. Despite Bhopal's obvious connections to the United States and the time devoted to the story itself, television portrayed the leak as primarily an Indian tragedy. More than half of the stories did not mention the Institute connection, 70% included no reference to health and environmental consequences, and 90% of the stories did not mention the larger issue of technological hazards or who or what was to blame for the disaster.

Of course, television does not function by words alone. Modern network news coverage is based on a visual imperative. Those visuals provided some unsystematic clues as to changes in the underlying political value structure that gave rise to the tragedy.

Multiple images of the dead and injured were common, and the injured often were portrayed through the suffering of women and children. In more than 33% of the stories, television broadcasts identified individual victims in the script as well as on videotape. This televised body count was human drama at its most poignant.

Television added one additional image to its Bhopal video vocabulary. Bhopal footage became synonymous with gas. Smokestacks, graphics containing animated clouds of gas, and, in one case, old newsreel footage of World War I trench warfare, complete with troops wearing gas masks, all became part of television's coverage of Bhopal. In all, 68% of the televised reports included a gas image. Those 28 stories contained 115 separate images of gas, or of objects that were capable of producing emissions.

Taken in its entirety, media coverage provided some environmental surveillance, regardless of specific media outlet. Readers and viewers were alerted to the event itself, and to subsequent recovery and rehabilitation efforts in India. Television coverage, focusing as it did on victims, also alerted viewers to some of the human costs of the leak, an important inclusion if environmental surveillance is to be made salient to individual media consumers.

Yet, what the media provided was far from complete, even if surveillance is assumed to be the media's primary function in the coverage of disasters. Bhopal reports consistently decontextualized the event. The reports also fragmented the event in a more profound way, for linkages between what was happening in India and what could—and eventually did—happen in Institute did not permeate media coverage of Bhopal. What readers and viewers were alerted to was an event that happened far away, not one that reflected, in a most concrete way, some fundamental political questions facing a technological society.

THE PUBLIC MEMORY OF BHOPAL

Public opinion polls taken in Charleston, West Virginia, the metropolitan home of the Bhopal sister plant, and Eugene, Oregon, a community that considers itself "environmentally aware" but nestled in a benign environment, show that disaster news coverage was memorable 7 months after the leak. Residents of both communities learned something from the news reports, but the differences in "memory" between the two communities indicate that the media do play a surveillance role for those in the more risky environment. Personal memory and media reports also were linked in subtle ways, correlating with personal feelings of helplessness about technological hazards. Such a linkage indicates that surveillance is not the only role media coverage of disaster plays, because individuals are likely to retain images that may reinforce existing beliefs in certain critical ways.

Factual retention of some aspects of the Bhopal story was widespread. Although 32% of those surveyed could not supply a correct association with the world "Bhopal," 68% provided a number of correct associations—chemicals, death, and India being the most common. Almost 33% of the sample knew that Institute was the site of the sister plant, whereas an equal number knew the plant was located somewhere in the United States. Considering the rather secondary connections the media made between Bhopal and Institute, readers and viewers apparently connected some of the tragedy's relationships without a great deal of media prompting. Only 25% of those sampled could not provide an estimate of the number of people who died, and more than 33% were able to give the precise estimates prominent in media coverage. Recall of the number of injured was much less vivid; more than half (54%) could not supply any injury estimate.

The long-term health impact also was vividly etched in the minds of those who responded. The vast majority said they believed the accident would cause permanent lung damage (90%) and eye problems (86%). Almost 75% said they believed the leak would cause cancer, an anomaly considering the issue is still open to scientific debate and received relatively little media coverage.

Survey respondents also provided some indication of their own views of their ability to mitigate the impact of a local chemical spill. Of those surveyed, 75% agreed that "we should be able to prevent accidents like the one in Bhopal," whereas 56% believed that "increased government regulation" would decrease the number of such accidents. People were less certain about their abilities to protect themselves; 48% said they would be able to "do some things to protect" themselves and their families. They also believed accidents such as the one in Bhopal would harm future generations, a finding that matches some of Robert Lifton's (1967) work on the psychological impact of the atomic blast at Hiroshima on the Japanese.

For all those surveyed, the most memorable medium was television. Less than 33% said they had not retained some specific televised image of the tragedy. And there were relationships between what people remembered and feelings of individual helplessness concerning technological hazards. Those who said they believed Bhopal-type accidents were inevitable were significantly more likely to recall images of death on television. They were less likely to recall images of medical problems, cooperation, or stories directed to local aspects of the event. Images of death also dominated the memories of those who said such accidents would harm future generations, whereas those who did not subscribe to that belief were more likely to recall other sorts of stories.

Although drawing any firm conclusions from such correlations is another form of risk, hazards scholars have found that a major component of individual response to hazards is a sense of efficacy, that is the individual's recognition of a capacity to act during and after a hazard coupled with an individual willingness to do so (Burton, Kates, & White, 1978). Such a sense of efficacy, which political scientists have documented as a component of voting behavior (Campbell, Converse, Miller, & Stokes, 1960), underlies individual willingness to undertake societal changes. As such, this efficacy forms a base, or perhaps a predisposition, to engage in many kinds of political activity, including those involved with hazard mitigation.

How that sense of powerfulness interacts with retention of certain mediated images and the apparent exclusion of others is a central question facing hazards research in the future.

Considering the mediated portrait of power in news reports, it is unlikely that close attention to news coverage of a disaster like the one in Bhopal would enhance an individual's sense of power and efficacy. Michael J. Robinson (1976), who coined the term videomalaise, provides insight into this question. Robinson found that those who viewed public affairs documentaries were "at least as willing to doubt their own capability to comprehend politics as they were to question the legitimacy of the institutions involved. In fact, it appears as if they were actually more likely to deprecate themselves" (p. 413). Such an apparent abridgement of individual effectiveness should provoke concern about media coverage of events founded in democratic decision making.

ELITES AS ADAPTATION

In this information age, information is power. And, whether it was the sources cited, those people portrayed as powerful actors, or the overall impression of "helplessness" that reports conveyed, institutions were the mediated entities capable of altering the value hierarchy.[2]

Certainly, reliance on elites to make key political and economic decisions is a tested adaptation strategy. However, political science literature indicates that potential elite policy alternatives become relatively restricted in time of extreme social stress or when competing powerful interests take vigorously opposing stances on particular issues. In severe cases, such as during a political revolution, elites can be so constrained as to be rendered impotent, forcing the hands of those of those who would lead mass movements (Davies, 1971).

Modern democratic theory, particularly as it has developed in the United States, also has vested significant political control in the corporate-driven economic system (Mills, 1956; Dye & Ziegler, 1971). In this view, there is a clash between economic power and individual political and social welfare, two fundamental forces in a democratic society. The existing political bias means that the forces of corporate lobbying are opposed by relatively powerless and underfunded groups and individuals representing the constituency for political and social welfare. Such an imbalance has been widely credited with the relatively weak stance the federal government has taken with regulation of the chemical industry, including "right-to-know" laws.

Sometimes critical events can alter this existing power constellation (Kraus, Davis, Lang, & Lang, 1975). The accident at Three Mile Island so aroused citizen groups and potent legal forces that further development of the U.S. nuclear industry stalled. Although such a development reflected a change in Lasswell's political value hierarchy, it was one that was truly accidental rather than the product of a deliberate working of a political process.

Bhopal could have functioned as such a critical event. But media portraits consistently placed both the knowledge and power for change in the hands of bureaucries and corporations. Such an adaptation strategy has its drawbacks, particularly when the problem is pervasive and unlikely to resolve itself if market forces alone are viewed as the solution.

This mediated reliance on elites was evident in several ways. In general, the number and types of sources cited in news reports of this highly complex and technical story were similar to sources for more traditional sorts of news. Regardless of media outlet, government and corporate spokespersons, and, sometimes, records, were the most frequently cited sources almost 33% of the time.

Some media outlets exceeded even this percentage. The *Washington Post*, because of the particular version of the story it reported, relied on government officials as the first, second, and third most frequently cited source more than 33% of the time. Television news generally relied on government or Union Carbide officials as the chief news sources. Government officials were the most frequently cited source in 40% of all television stories, whereas Union Carbide officials were the most frequently cited sources in an additional 33% of those reports. The two groups merely traded places when the second most frequently cited source in television news was the issue. The wire services, the prestige press, and the news magazines repeated the pattern, and only the mass media themselves, primarily the Indian news media, emerged as significant third-level sources in these print reports.

Citizens, doctors, and scientists, all of whom could have added a level of factual and contextual complexity to the reports, received much less attention. Because it focused on victims, television made somewhat more use of citizens as sources whereas the prestige press, particularly the *New York Times*, gave scientists more prominent play. This was a change of degree rather than of general emphasis. Clearly, the people who had the power to act as information brokers in the Bhopal tragedy were themselves affiliated with institutions.

Institutions, in turn, were portrayed as the powerful actors. Forty-three percent of the television reports, 56% of the elite press coverage, 38% of what the wires sent out, and 35% of what the magazines wrote, portrayed governments and corporations, or those who represented them, as the most powerful actors.

A thematic tone of helplessness (Levin, 1977), which also pervaded most media reports, restricted the potential mitigation strategy in yet another way. More than 50% of what was printed or broadcast about Bhopal was judged to have some thematic content of helplessness, and such a tone was present in more than 80% of the television reports. The visual content of television news, analyzed without direct reference to scripts, scored somewhat higher on the scale.[2]

Of course, the media's preoccupation with immediate events influenced these findings. Although helplessness may be a predictable reality when "normal" accidents are the issue, it leaves much to be desired as a mitigation strategy, and certainly as a mechanism of societal adaptation. Such a view is even more noteworthy when coupled with a portrait of elites as the only actors capable of instituting change.

This emphatic view of who—or what—had power in the tragedy, one that crossed medium and varied only a little among media outlets, conveys a significant political message. The individual without ties to corporate or governmental influence adapted only as a victim or as a potential victim. When information possession became an indicator of political power, the political value pyramid, as reflected through media reports, tilted away from individual safety and deference and toward the economic apex.

THE CULTURAL MYTH OF BHOPAL

> Catastrophes are possible where community and regional interests are not mobilized or when they are overridden by national policy, where the economic costs of the disaster can be displaced from the private or governmental organization in charge to the rest of society, and where superorganizational goals, such as the economic health of an industry deemed vital or the control of outer space, are served. No one wants disaster, and better design, safety measures and regulations can help redress their likelihood. But as long as national goals are served by risky systems, we will continue to have them and their catastrophes. (Perrow, 1986, p. 356)

Media reportage of Bhopal provides the latest example of modern Western culture's attempt to give meaning to society's knowledge of its ability to create widespread death and destruction through technology. In this sense, media coverage represents an expansion of societal extinction myths that are part of the Judeo-Christian heritage and present in other forms of Greek and Roman mythology. These basic myths have several common elements. First, they attribute extinction to forces beyond humanity's control. Second, individual helplessness is a primary dramatic component, and institutional preparedness, either in the form of church or of government, seems to make little difference.

But human history is changing such a view. The invention and use of poison gas as a weapon of war began to fundamentally alter the existing myth structure. Gas, as it was used in World War I, and later in German concentration camps, and then in Vietnam by the United States and Afghanistan by the Soviet Union, has become an instrument of government policy. Bhopal's contribution to this mythical development may well be the addition of the notion of the "unintended accident that results from intentional national economic or political goals."

As a myth, media coverage of the Bhopal accident is the next step in the evolution of societal extinction myths. For good reasons, the Indian government had set a national policy of "feeding itself" and attaining economic self-sufficiency. The Bhopal Union Carbide plant, and what it produced, aided those goals, but scientists and engineers have known for decades that such technology is subject to "normal accidents."

This framework thus gives rise to the notion of the unintended, but predictable, accident resulting from national political and economic aims. Institutions assume a dominant role, and the individual citizen, caught in the maw of the policy debate between national goals and personal safety and health, loses a substantial amount of control. For such a view to take hold, the costs of technology must be economic, the loss of life "accidental." For such a view to sustain itself, reports of such accidents need to include a sense of individual helplessness reflected not only in terms of specific acts but in many more subtle ways; for example, the choice of a legitimate information source or the absence of any discussion of the larger political context of the event.

Certainly Bhopal news reports seem to support the latest development in the evolution of a myth of societal extinction. Visual images focused on victims and on gas. The powerful figures were institutions, and issues of long-range debate and historical and cultural context were largely ignored. Such reportage is truly knowledge without meaning, but it is not without a cultural construct. In this case, it is one that supports the notion of institutional superiority and individual absence from the policy debate. Such a heritage is profoundly undemocratic, but one that is unlikely to be the subject of creative reinterpretation in news reports, considering the media's already documented biases.

THE POLITICS OF RISK

The politics of the Bhopal disaster began long before tank #610 exploded. In some sense, the original political decision lay with the Indian government's eagerness to develop an indigenous chemical industry and to import technology to aid that goal. Political planners considered the subcontinent's ability to feed itself, while providing income to an extremely poor population, urgent. The political goals were found paramount when balanced against the certain knowledge that creations of technology wear out and cause inevitable accidents that take lives. This somewhat statistical view of risk was less politically central than the risks to economic health (and hence national security) involved in not importing such technology. In the most basic sense, the politics of Bhopal began with the politics of the Green Revolution, a story that, because it appeared not to be an aberration, was never really covered, least of all in an analytic and systematic way.

This was not the end of the politics of the story. The Indian government, in keeping with its drive to fortify the economic portion of the value pyramid, had demanded that the Indian plant be labor intensive. And a computerized safety system was omitted. To encourage economic development, local officials did not resist the creation of slums that mushroomed around the plant, a pattern firmly imbedded in a non-technological culture.

To the media, these fundamental political pressures were not news. Even specific events like a 1981 death at the plant went unreported. Only when the chemical pressure in the MIC tank built up and exploded did the media tumble to the story that by then had become a sort of horse race between technology and human safety. The result was media coverage that could have easily been predicted. It was a mediated politics of risk, long on surveillance of the event but short on almost everything else, including the notion that citizens have the power to suggest alternative options in the technological debate.

Hazard mitigation, and the assumption of societal risk, is one of several late 20th-century political issues demanding a collective choice from a political culture that views itself as individualistic and that some theorists have argued is dominated by elites. What is needed is a mediated reality that has as its fundamental goal the building of community, in addition to mere environmental surveillance.

Current media coverage of hazards undermines such a goal. First, it provides a lopsided form of environmental surveillance, one that points to an event as a random, unavoidable problem rather than as a problem of the social and technical system that produced it. As an adaptation strategy, media reports portray the individual as powerless and institutions as change agents capable of acting for the collective good.

Such a view does not build community. It hinders development of community by substituting a myth structure for discussion of issues that, at least in theory, are within the purview of a democracy and of collective decision making. When the issue is political decisions that led to collective risk assumption, mass communications needs at least to raise the issue of collective choice. If it does not, communication, as reflected in the mass media, may not lead to discussion of collective choice but to its opposite—a pseudo-community that will ultimately founder under the weight of a mediated reality that diverges significantly from genuine shifts in the political value pyramid.

ACKNOWLEDGMENT

Funding for this study was provided by the National Science Foundation, grant number CEE-8412067 and the Institute of Behavioral Science, University of Colorado, Boulder. The opinions expressed here are those of the author and do not reflect NSF policy.

I would like to thank my colleague Philip Patterson, Oklahoma Christian College, for his comments on the first draft of this chapter. The improvements that resulted were largely the result of his clear thought; the deficiencies remain my responsibility.

NOTES

[1] The findings described here are the result of a content analysis conducted on reports in 13 media outlets from the 2 months after the disaster, December 3, 1984 through February 3, 1985. Those outlets studies included the three American television networks, the Associated Press, United Press International, Reuters, the *New York Times*, the *Washington Post, Time, Newsweek*, and *U.S. News and World Report*, the *Times of India*, and the *Manchester Guardian*. Television coverage was acquired from the Vanderbilt Television University archives, print reports, with the exception of the *Times of India*, were acquired through the Nexus data base. Those items coded included: story source, dateline, general story subject, the three most frequently cited sources, primary and secondary foci, and so on.

For a more detailed account of the study, readers should see Wilkins (1987).

[2] All stories were ranked along a helplessness scale ranging from extreme—that is, an item in which a central figure is presented in such a way as to suggest a complete inability to have affected the outcome—to mild—that is, an item in which a central figure is presented as having had a good chance of affecting outcomes but some reason is unable to do so. A "not relevant" segment also was added to the scale.

3
The Sound and the Fury:
Mass Media and Hurricanes

John A. Ledingham
University of Evansville

Lynne Masel Walters
Houston Area Research Center

Galveston, Texas, is typical of many Gulf Coast communities. Each June hurricane season begins. During the season that runs through September, storms are routinely tracked, and residents are attuned to their possible danger through several channels, including the media. How well does this information process function? The answer to this question is related to many variables, including information source and credibility, media use, perceived media accuracy, differing functions of different kinds of communication, the effect of past experience, evacuation decision making, and ethnicity. Not only do these issues need clarification, but a conceptual framework for future research needs further development. In addition, those charged with responsibility for alerting and advising residents of a disaster-threatened area need communication guidelines.

What is known about the mass media's role, function, and use in times of disaster comes from a body of literature bridging the fields of sociology, psychology, and communication. Sociologists and psychologists have used floods, hurricanes, earthquakes, and other natural disasters to examine the ways individuals and populations react to danger and calamity. In their reports that list the greatest problem associated with natural disasters as persuading residents to evacuate, sociologists have tangentially examined the role of mass media. Additionally, mass-media researchers have used assassinations, industrial accidents, hostage situations, and other man-made disasters as settings to examine media coverage and information diffusion. Generally, logistical and medical problems have been the focus of governmental agencies, relief organizations, and forecasters.

From this broad range of research, a good deal is known about media use, message effects, and decision making in a disaster environment. The mass media are seen as a tool for surveillance of the environment, as information channels, and as purveyors of official positions (Rogers, 1980; Larson, 1980). The media are the pervasive first source of disaster warnings (Greenberg, 1964, pp. 225-232; Moore, Bates, Layman, & Parenton, 1963, p. 23). Residents are reported turning to the media to gain insight into events and for rumor confirmation (Ostland, 1973, pp. 601-610). Message credibility has been found to influence perceptions (Harolde & Harvey, 1979, pp. 771-775), whereas excessive warnings have been reported to desensitize residents to the scope of a threatened disaster (Turner, 1976, pp. 753-774). Some residents are said to cope with warnings of an impending disaster by minimizing danger or by belittling the information source (Janis & Feshback, 1953, pp. 78-92; Perry & Mushkatel, 1986). According to others, warning messages may have little effect unless residents are predisposed to act (Ledingham & Masel-Walters, 1985, pp. 50-58)). Those who choose to evacuate are reported to consult media and interpersonal channels in arriving at their decision (Quarantelli & Dynes, 1972, pp. 67-70). Disaster victims are said to be more likely to be predisposed to future evacuation (Moore et al., 1963, p. 23), and some research suggests this is also true for those who heard a previous warning but were not actual victims (Killian, 1953). When officials disagree as to appropriate defensive action, residents are reported to increase their use of interpersonal channels (Fritz & Williams, 1957, pp. 42-51). Ethnicity has been suggested as a predictor of disaster impact because ethnic groups attach low predicitibility to the dominant media outlets and because of geographic factors (Perry & Greene, 1982; Perry, Greene, & Mushkatel, 1983).

Other relevant research has focused on the communication process. Consider early flow models of communication that viewed audience members passive recipients of messages, rather than active participants in the communication process. Later models emphasized the two-way nature of the communication process by adding a feedback loop. Both of these focused on originators, disseminators, and receivers.

The agenda-setting perspective is within this tradition. Agenda setting is seen as a function of the mass media. That function is not to tell audiences what to think, but what to think about (McCombs & Shaw, 1972, pp. 176-187). According to this view, residents could be expected to report the media as their source of news about a threatened disaster, while turning to their own experience or to other sources for confirmation and to decide an appropriate response to the news reports.

Also significant is the uses-and-gratifications paradigm. This is concerned with how media meet individual and social needs. The emphasis is on an active audience, one that uses media. In effect, uses and gratifications is concerned with media sources of satisfaction, the kind of media attended to, media content, and the social environment of the media. Among others, those functions include surveillance, diversion or escape, and functions pertaining to personal identity of social relationships (Katz, Blumler, & Gurevitch, 1974, pp. 11-35). In this view of the interaction of audience and media, audience members can be expected to be active information seekers in the process of surveillance of the disaster-prone environment. The uses-and-gratifications model assumes that audience members are largely responsible for media selection and that other sources compete with or augment the mass media.

Chaffee (1981), as well as others, has examined the question of whether mass media and interpersonal channels complement or compete. The consensus is that media and interpersonal channels serve complementary roles, with each acting, at different times, as a prelude or as support for the other while also fulfilling unique roles.

The disaster-threatened environment offers the opportunity to examine these interrelated issues. Do the mass media, as bearers of news, serve as a surveillance tool for residents? Does the news provided by the media fill the public's plate or is the process more complicated and, perhaps, less direct? What is the role of interpersonal communication? How large a part is played by past experience and by societal factors?

The disaster environment, with its heightened awareness and sensitivity, provides a backdrop against which to look for answers. The history of Gulf Coast hurricanes is a tale filled with dreadful statistics. In 1900 more than 6,000 people died when hurricane-whipped waters flooded Galveston, Texas. Nine years later, 350 perished when a storm swept along the Louisiana coast. In 1915, residents ignored repeated warnings to evacuate in the face of a storm that struck the Mississippi Delta—and 275 died. Four years later, some 500 perished when a storm made landfall in Corpus Christi, Texas. In 1928, 1,800 lives were lost when a storm drove the waters of Lake Okeechobee over its banks in Florida. Nearly 30 years later Hurricane Audrey killed nearly 400 people when it hit the Texas-Louisiana coast in 1957. A few years later, in 1969, Hurricane Camille killed more than 300 and caused widespread destruction in Pass Christian, Mississippi. In 1979 Hurricane Frederick ravaged Southern Alabama. The following year Hurricane Allen, described as the most powerful Carribbean storm ever recorded, hit Brownsville, Texas (Paths of Glory, 1980, p. 360). In 1983, Hurricane Alicia hit Galveston, then moved on to Houston, Texas. The storm took 21 lives and caused an estimated $2 billion in damage (*Houston Post*, 1985).

Against this historical backdrop, residents were alerted to the buildup of Hurricane Allen in 1980 and were told that Galveston was the probable point of landfall. Because Allen was thought to be of a force seldom seen, Galvestonians were properly concerned. Many decided to leave in advance of the storm. This evacuation proved anything but orderly, resulting in a traffic jam that stretched nearly to Houston, 50 miles north. Ironically, Hurricane Allen missed Galveston completely. Nonetheless, it left its mark on the island community.

In 1983, Galvestonians were alerted to the probable landfall of Hurricane Alicia. Mindful of the cry-wolf experience with Hurricane Allen, and, with local and state officials offering conflicting advice, most residents opted to stay. Unfortunately, Alicia proved to be a major hurricane that left a trail of death and destruction in its wake. Given the storm's magnitude, the fact that relatively few lives were lost was nothing short of miraculous.

Just 2 years later, island residents were again alerted to the buildup of Hurricane Danny. Danny proved somewhat elusive, dancing offshore, moving first toward Galveston, then the Louisiana coast, then again toward the Texas island. Although it appeared certain for a time that Danny would hit Galveston, it finally made landfall in Louisiana, and Galveston residents were spared.

To see how Galvestonians reacted and how the media performed, interviews were conducted in 1983 after Hurricane Alicia and in 1985 after Hurricane Danny. In the first instance, a telephone survey gathered information regarding media use and other behavior preceeding the landfall of Hurricane Alicia at Galveston. The Galveston telephone directory served as the sample frame with a list of potential respondents generated by selecting every nth number. (Galveston has less than 2% unlisted telephone numbers.) Interviews began 10 days after Alicia struck; within 18 days after the storm 172 interviews were completed. The data from those interviews were then analyzed (see Ledingham & Masel-Walters, 1985, pp. 50-58 for a complete account).

Two years later, Hurricane Danny provided an opportunity to test findings. Again, a telephone survey was chosen. A list of random suffixes and weighted prefixes was computer generated to provide a sample of telephone numbers in anticipation of the opportunity to re-enter the field. A survey questionnaire based on the results of the Alicia was constructed, pretested, and revised. Interviewing of Galvestonians began 2 days after the storm struck Louisiana, when it was apparent that there was no danger to Texas. To identify response to hurricane warnings, residents were called for 10 days. Efforts to reinterview Alicia study respondents resulted in 81 completed surveys, and 278 interviews were completed with new respondents. Data from these 359 interviews were analyzed. The findings from both phases of the study are similar, increasing confidence in appliciability of generalized results to the larger Galveston population (see Table 3.1).

Demographically, respondents are slightly older than 40 years of age and have resided in Galveston for an average of about 10 years. There were slightly more males than females. About 33% reported high school as the highest educational experience, whereas about 20% hold a college degree. Although ethnicity was not asked in the first phase (Alicia), Danny phase respondents reported the following

TABLE 3.1
Comparative Responses of Respondents to Surveys Concerning
Hurricane Alicia and Hurricane Danny

	Hurricane Alicia (N = 170)	Hurricane Danny (N = 359)
Age	±38.4	±45.4
Years living in Galveston	±10	±8
Male	54%	52%
Female	46%	48%
Education		
High School	35.0%	32.3%
Some College	23.0%	21.7%
College Degree	23.5%	17.3%
Post Graduate Study	13.0%	10.1%
First source of hurricane warning		
Television	60.0%	61.3%
Radio	17.0%	25.3%
Newspapers	2.4%	1.7%
Other Media	12.0%	7.5%
Other Person	10.0%	7.5%
Media credibility		
The media are accurate in their account of events:		
Most of the time	62.9%	66.1%
Some of the time	32.9%	28.0%
Seldom	2.4%	3.5%
None of the time	1.8%	2.2%
The media are accurate in forecasting hurricanes:		
Most of the time	63.5%	76.3%
Some of the time	23.5%	21.3%
Seldom	7.1%	2.9%
None of the time	5.9%	.1%
Talked with others living in Galveston during the warnings about Hurricane Allen	50.6%	80.4%
Did those you talked with evacuate in advance of Hurricane Alicia?		
Yes	32.9%	20.9%
No	67.1%	79.1%
Was that discussion important in your decision about what to do for Hurricane Danny?		
Yes	78.3%	56.8%
No	21.7%	43.1%
Did you hear any statements by public officials during the warning period concerning the hurricane?		
Yes	57.1%	44.9%
No	42.9%	55.1%
Were the statements by public officials important in your decisions about what to do?		
Yes	60.6%	44.1%
No	55.9%	39.4%

(Continued)

TABLE 3.1 — Continued

Where did you learn what to do to prepare for the hurricane?		
Media	25.5%	14.8%
Past experience	66.4%	80.1%
Other people	8.0%	4.9%
What was the most important source of information to you during this period?		
News events	40.7%	52.8%
Past experience	38.5%	37.7%
Other people	19.2%	4.1%
Public officials	1.4%	5.3%
Evacuated during warning period of Hurricane Alicia		
Yes	32.9%	20.9%
No	67.1%	79.1%

percentages: White, 68.9%; Black, 20.8%; Hispanic, 8.2%; and Asian-American, 2%.

As source of the warning message, television was the medium through which most respondents learned of possible danger. Radio was the next most often mentioned. About 10% said they were alerted to the possibility of a hurricane from another individual. The majority (62.9 to 66.1%) agreed that the media are accurate most of the time, and relatively few (2 to 3%) said the media are seldom accurate. A majority (63 to 73%) said the media are accurate most of the time in forecasting hurricanes. Twenty percent to 25% said hurricane forecasts are accurate some of the time, and less than 10% said the media are seldom accurate in hurricane forecasting.

Other channels of communication were opened when the warning was issued. More than 50% of the respondents said they talked with others after they learned of the hurricane threat. A majority of those they talked with lived in Galveston during Allen, the hurricane that missed. More than 50% of those interviewed said the interpersonal discussion played an important part in their decision about response to the warnings (see Table 3.1).

Information on previous hurricane experience and the impact of that experience was sought from the respondents. All respondents in this study were living in Galveston during Hurricane Alicia, 75% were residents in Galveston during Allen. Twenty percent to 33% said they evacuated for Alicia. Of the Danny respondents, 25% said the Alicia experience influenced their decision about what to do in advance of Danny. Nearly half (44.4%) of those able to identify Alicia's influence said the storm influenced them to be more cautious in the future, 23% said their experience with Alicia led them to plan to evacuate in advance of future storms. Nearly 20% said they planned to be better prepared for hurricanes as the result of Alicia, and 14% said they planned to take hurricanes more seriously in the future. Nearly 75% of those interviewed in connection with Danny resided in Galveston when Allen was forecast, and almost 38% said Allen influenced their decisions regarding Danny. However, only 9.4% of the respondents said they evacuated in the face of Danny forecasts, whereas another 7.5% said they stood ready to evacuate and were prepared to do so. The vast majority (81.6%) boarded up and bought supplies.

Galvestonians received more than media messages; they also were the intended targets of messages by public officials. Yet, only about 50% of those interviewed recalled statements by public officials. Of those interviewed in connection with Danny who recalled specific information, 51% said public officials told them to be ready to evacuate. More than 20% recalled being advised to stock supplies and somewhat fewer (17.3%) remember being advised to prepare their homes for the storm. Few (8.6%) recalled being told to listen for further advisories. A clear majority (60.6%) said the statements were important in their decisions on what to do. On the other hand, less than half (44.1%) of those interviewed in connection with Alicia described statements of public officials as important. When asked where they learned how to prepare for the hurricane, an overwhelming majority in both phases cited past experience, followed by media, and then other people (see Table 3.1).

In addition, respondents were asked which constituted the most important overall source of information during the warning period: "information from the media, from public officials, from other people, or from your own past experience." More than 50% of the Danny respondents cited the media, whereas slightly more than a third mentioned their own experience. Respondents in the earlier Alicia phase split more evenly, with less than 50% selecting the media; only slightly fewer citing their own experience. Other people's decisions were given by 19.2% of the Alicia respondents but constituted only about 5% of the Danny respondents (see Table 3.1).

Additional questions regarding media and interpersonal sources were asked of Danny respondents. A majority (71.9%) said their newspaper reading remained "about the same" during the warning period. Nearly the same said they read the newspaper more often (12.8%) as said they read it less (11.7%).

Regarding television, its use increased for 15.8% of the respondents, whereas 44.2% said their viewing time remained the same. Some 39.9% said they watched television less. With regard to specific use of the pervasive medium, 61.5% said they used television to monitor the storm's progress, 16.2% said they watched television weather forecasts, and an additional one fifth (18.8%) commented on the good television coverage of the storm. A few (3.4%) said they kept the television on throughout the warning period to make certain they did not miss news of the storm.

When asked about spending time with people during this period, a majority (67.7%) said they spent "about the same" amount of time with other people. One fifth (19.4%) said they spent less time, whereas fewer (12.8%) said they spent more time with other people.

Despite all this exposure to the media and warnings from several channels, many respondents did not become convinced Alicia or Danny would hit until late in the development of the respective storms. Nearly 25% of the Alicia respondents were not convinced the storm would hit until it actually arrived. Of those in the Danny survey, 68% never were convinced the hurricane would strike Galveston.

With regard to evacuation, respondents were asked what they would do if another hurricane were forecast. In the aftermath of Alicia, 56.5% said they would leave. Conversely when Danny was forecast, less than 10% actually evacuated, whereas an additional 7.5% made ready to leave. Most people (81.6%) boarded up and bought supplies to ride out the storm. After Danny lost its force, 24.7% said they would evacuate if another hurricane were forecast, half the percentage who gave a similar answer after Alicia. Another 20.5% said they would evacuate "if necessary." On the other hand, 18.4% said they definitely would stay for the storm, 5.4% said they would "prepare for the storm," and 8.6% said they would listen for instructions and act accordingly. Some 12.2% gave miscellaneous other responses. Respondents who initially mentioned some action other than evacuation were then asked specifically if they would evacuate. One third (33.4%) said they would. Clearly, evacuation was not their top-of-mind response.

A number of variables concerning media use, defensive behavior, past experience, and demographics were crosstabulated with other variables to uncover relationships. Unfortunately, the large number of cells thus generated, coupled with small numbers in some cells, made the search for statistically significant differences difficult.

Nonetheless, two crosstabulations proved interesting. The statistical procedure revealed that those who resided in Galveston during Hurricane Allen were considerably less likely to report they were ever convinced Hurricane Danny would hit Galveston (75% to 57.7%; Chi square = 11.6; $df = 4$; $p = .0206$). Also those who evacuated in advance of Hurricane Alicia were three times as likely to report they would evacuate in the event of a future hurricane forecast (51.6% to 15.2%; Chi square = 48.8; $df = 12$; $p = .001$).

The results of the Alicia and Danny studies support many of the findings of prior research. The media were found to be the pervasive first source of disaster warnings and those media, particularly television, served a surveillance function for the populace of the disaster-prone community. The media also enjoy reasonable credibility for their ability to forecast hurricanes. In fact, credibility in weather forecasting is greater than for news reporting in general.

Residents of the disaster-threatened environment differ somewhat in the time they spend with media during the warning period. Some increased the amount of time spent with media, whereas others spent less time. The majority said the time they spent with media did not change during the warning period. However, most reported using the media to track the storm's progress, to monitor weather reports, and to keep up with news of the storm. Those who spent less time with media usually said they were busy preparing for the storm. It appears that time was carved from entertainment programming rather than news. In addition to the surveillance function, residents reported the media as a major information source on how to prepare for the storm.

Clearly, the media set the agenda of the island's population. As the storm moved toward land, residents used the media to maintain awareness of storm activity and to develop a response to the warnings. Yet, the media were not the only information channels. Public officials were also a source for some Galvestonians. However, almost half those interviewed said they did not recall exposure to messages from these officials. For the other half of the respondents, either the efforts of public officials did not cut through the clutter of communication, or those messages were not important enough to be remembered.

Discussions with other people served as a complement to mass media messages. Most turned to interpersonal networks of friends and relatives to seek (and perhaps to give) advice during this period.

What emerges is a picture of far-from-universal behavior. Apparently, the warning messages triggered the formation of a kind of hurricane culture that may be part of the island's response to a threatening storm. In this environment, residents turned from the media to more personal communication channels, while maintaining environmental surveillance through the media. Behavior differed among population members. For some, the first warnings set in motion the process of surveillance—confirmation, advice giving and seeking, and decision making. Others were well into the warning period before that process was initiated. Still others remained unconvinced until the last moment. In the case of Hurricane Alicia, they guessed wrong. In the case of Hurricane Danny, their skepticism proved correct. The screen through which all this activity was filtered was the individual's own experience. Residents reacted in accordance with their own perceptions of the situation, and those perceptions drove, and were affected by, all they saw and heard.

As diverse and complicated as the reactions were, some shared characteristics do emerge. Historically, about 10% of the Galveston population reacts to hurricane warnings by fleeing the area. Nearly twice as many react to hurricane alerts by preparing to ride out the storm. Between these "chronic stayers" and "chronic leavers" fall the majority of the population, some 70% or so, who adjust with each new development. Within this group of undecided, a number are predisposed to evacuate (some additional 10%), whereas others remain either cautious, cynical, or somewhat fatalistic. If evacuation is the major problem associated with natural disasters, then efforts to urge evacuation must reinforce some predispositions and attempt to overcome others.

Still, should the media actually urge residents to leave? Sometimes this is a question of hindsight, because, as major sources of information, the media find themselves in a difficult situation, as do public officials and advisory agencies. If they prompt evacuation and the storm does not materialize, the impact of those warnings may be lessened when a new threat arises. Conversely, failure to unite in a call for evacuation may leave residents confused as to appropriate response, which could result in many injuries and fatalities if the storm actually hits.

Another quandry involves the correct theoretical framework for studies of future hurricanes. Respondent behavior demonstrates that residents turn to various systems in this disaster environment, which suggests that system theory might be an appropriate theoretical framework for additional study. Little doubt remains that the media set the agenda for Hurricane Danny and Alicia respondents, but the media also played a major role in behavior that followed the alert. For a goodly number of respondents, the media served as the most important source of information during the event. For many others, the media played an important secondary part in the process. Similarly, residents clearly used the media to help gratify certain needs pertaining to surveillance and decision making. Thus, at a minimum, when attempting to ascertain the media's impact, the effects view must be balanced with the uses-and-gratifications perspective. However, the process appears to be more complicated and interactive than comfortably provided for by either theoretical framework. With regard to media and interpersonal communication, respondents utilized both. Although media served to alert the population and to provide information on response options, discussions with friends and family were equally important in the options respondents ultimately chose.

As exhibited by the data on hurricanes Danny and Alicia, a methodolgical problem can arise in this type of research. That problem involves the relatively low numbers of respondents in specific characteristic categories. Evacuators, for example, make up a proportionally and numerically small portion of the sample. That fact, coupled with attempts to define behavior in as specific a way as possible, makes several analytical techniques difficult. Attempts to identify the effects of ethnicity were hampered in this manner. A larger sample size would help alleviate some problems, but funding surveys with more than 300 respondents raises a different set of problems.

There are other options. The data reported here might offer insight if many of the variables were recoded to fewer categories. Small group research, with its opportunity for in-depth analysis might also prove useful. And, a strategy of interviewing only evacuators in subsequent studies, then comparing the results to the Danny and Alicia data, might prove productive. Future studies could be designed to include an examination of the interaction of the media with other systems of the disaster environment as part of a systems analysis of the threatened area. Whatever the case, the Danny and Alicia data, in addition to providing comparative information from two points in time, provide a benchmark against which future efforts can be measured.

In addition, the Danny and Alicia data demonstrate that the media are crucial to a population threatened by imminent danger. Likewise, the messages of the media are also crucial. To some, they are a tale of sound and fury, signifying little. To others, they are the voice of a trusted ally in the decision-making process. To most, the media and their messages are the monitor of the environment and a source of potentially valuable information. As such, they not only help shape our perceptions, but are part of our behavior as well.

4
Communicating Threat Information for Volcano Hazards

Ronald W. Perry
Arizona State University

Michael K. Lindell
Michigan State University

As natural phenomena, volcanoes represent an interesting challenge to humans. Eruptions and associated hazards are a threat to human settlements largely in proportion to the encroachment of these settlements upon volcanoes. It is probably more accurate to characterize people as attracted to volcanoes than to portray them as invasive. Rich volcanic soil yields lush natural or cultivated vegetation that contributes to an ecosystem rich with fish, wildlife, and fowl. During noneruptive periods, such environments serve as a magnet to human development. Indeed, the high potential, coupled with the cycle of long dormancy that is interspersed with relatively short eruptive periods, captures both the allure of volcanoes and their special danger to humans.

Special characteristics that set them apart from other natural hazards heighten the danger posed by volcanoes. One of the most important of these lies in the relationship of time to local residents' perceptions of environmental risks. Historically, people are drawn to volcanoes during dormant periods. They may become established over many years, or sometimes many generations. Those who have spent their lives on the slopes of peaceful volcanoes tend to think of the mountain as part of a supportive environment, rather than a threatening one. They judge the volcano's behavior in terms of human time, a very small unit when compared with geological time. Such a perspective creates a complacency that exposes people to dangers that otherwise might be escaped.

Another feature of volcanic activity that sets it apart from other natural hazards is the idea of multiple or repeated impacts. During any active period a volcano may erupt dozens of times, and the magnitude and nature of each eruption may vary widely. Consequently, unlike floods, hurricanes, or tornadoes, a volcanic event is not clearly circumscribed by one pre-impact period of threat, a short-impact period, and a post-impact quiet time. Instead, the entire volcanic sequence, which may last for several years, is a time of threat during which there is an elevated probability of an eruptive event. The multiple eruptions constitute multiple impacts, a condition that places severe coping demands on both citizens and emergency managers.

Local residents must develop an understanding of volcanic and associated dangers while remaining vigilant against eruptive threats for extended periods of time. The first element of this vigilance involves attention to warning and preparedness measures devised by authorities, and the second is the adoption of personal protective measures that may alter daily living patterns. Emergency managers face the complicated task of continuously educating and motivating the population-at-risk, while maintaining a long-term close coordination with a large number of hazard-relevant agencies. There is the added constraint of capturing and retaining administrative and fiscal resources for these sustained operations.

To examine the issue of communicating threat information to citizens at risk from an active volcano the current eruptive sequence at Mt. St. Helens has been examined. Data were drawn from Toutle and Lexington, two communities situated near the volcano. Toutle is an unincorporated town of about 1,500 people. It is situated on a river of the same name, approximately 25 miles northwest of Mt. St. Helens.

Because the wind was blowing toward the volcano on May 18, 1980, few people reported hearing any noise from the initial cataclysmic eruption. For most citizens, the first evidence of the eruption was the huge, mushroom-shaped ash cloud that filled the horizon to the south. Residents reported feeling a dramatic increase in temperature; with it came the sounds of trees and automobile windshields cracking from the heat. The area experienced only a light ashfall, which reached Toutle about 90 minutes after the eruption (Korosec, Rigby, & Stoffel, 1980, p. 14). There was, however, serious damage from mudflows and flooding along the Toutle River that began a few hours after the eruption.

The situation in Lexington, only about 10 miles farther from Mt. St. Helens, was somewhat different. A community of slightly more than 2,000, Lexington lies along the Cowlitz River. The May 18 eruption produced significant flows of mud, ash, and debris down the north fork of the Toutle River. When this flow reached the Cowlitz River, some downstream flooding resulted, but the Lexington area was, for the most part, spared severe damage. Although ashfall affected the area, it was only a light dusting. Thus, the magnitude of consequences of the May 18 eruption for Lexington was significantly less than that incurred at Toutle.

CURRENT VOLCANIC DANGERS

Since the explosive eruptions of 1980, Mt. St. Helens has engaged in a process of dome building through effusive eruptions of thick, "doughy" lava extruded into the crater. These effusive eruptions are adding approximately 35 million cubic meters of material each year and, over a long period of time, could completely refill the crater (Gillins, 1985). By May 1985, the dome had grown to 800 feet in height and 2,700 feet at its base, with the side of the dome nearly touching the walls of the crater.

It would be inaccurate to interpret these "gentle" effusive eruptions as an indication that Mt. St. Helens has fallen into a nonviolent, though active state. Although most eruptions have been effusive, the dome building eruptions that have occurred since 1981 have been interspersed with smaller but more explosive steam-and-ash eruptions. Ash and other light ejecta (e.g., pumice) continue to fall periodically on communities within a 50-mile radius of the volcano.

Although Findley (1981) has indicated that most of the eruptions in the near future will continue to be of the effusive type, Mullineaux has argued that the increasing size of the dome will be accompanied by a renewed threat of violent eruption. "The larger it grows, the larger its potential for collapse with mudflows down its flanks.... The mountain's history is one of moderate to major eruptions...periods when activity is less strong, followed by another significantly voluminous eruption" (p. 4).

Consequently, the idea that Mt. St. Helens will again pose an eruptive threat to nearby communities cannot be realistically eliminated.

There is also a significant noneruptive threat from Mt. St. Helens caused by a debris dam on Spirit Lake. After the May 18 eruption, ash, boulders, timber, and other debris completely blocked Spirit Lake's outlet channel. As a result, the reservoir increased from 123,000 acre feet to 275,000 acre feet in less than 2 years (Swift & Kresch, 1983, p. 2).

By the summer of 1982, officials determined that the dam was considerably less stable than previously thought; unexpected erosion suggested the possibility of a breach. Depending on the severity of the breach, such an event could produce serious flooding in communities along the Toutle, Cowlitz, and Columbia rivers. An explosive eruption, earthquake, or mud or debris flow into Spirit Lake could produce an overtopping or complete collapse of the dam.

In the face of the danger, Washington Governor John Spellman declared a state of emergency on August 2, 1982. Seven days later, following the governor's request, President Ronald Reagan issued a Presidential Emergency Declaration for the State of Washington (General Accounting Office, 1982, p. 51). This declaration directed the Federal Emergency Management Agency, in coordination with the Forest Service, Geological Survey and Army Corps of Engineers, to develop and to implement a plan to reduce the flood danger associated with possible failure of the debris dam.

The threat mitigation plan involved creating an outlet channel from the debris dam to the north fork of the Toutle River and, in the short run, pumping water from Spirit Lake into the outlet. The Army Corps supervised construction of 3,800 feet of 5-foot diameter pipes connecting the lake with the Toutle River (General Accounting Office, 1982, p. 53). Beginning in November of 1981, a pumping barge was used to siphon water out of Spirit Lake to stabilize the lake at a volume of 275,000 acre-feet (Swift & Kresch, 1983, p. 2).

More permanent measures for creating drainage proceeded concurrently with the pumping. After considering several alternative solutions, the Army Corps adopted a plan to create a tunnel through rock to South Coldwater, which empties into the north fork of the Toutle River. Work was begun in the summer of 1984 by a private contractor to re-create a permanent outlet for Spirit Lake, and the temporary pumping operation continued until the new tunnel was completed in the spring of 1985.

The resolution of the debris dam threat did not end concern with noneruptive flood threats. There remains a danger to the Toutle, Cowlitz, and Columbia rivers from long-term sedimentation as ash and soil from Mt. St. Helens' slopes are introduced into the river systems. As the river beds rise, the flood threat increases. Initially, dredging the Toutle River combated the problem, eliminating the sediment before it could move into the Cowlitz and Columbia. In late spring of 1984, a plan was adopted to handle long-term sedimentation by means of a series of dams. Each was to be built as needed to trap sediments escaping from dams previously constructed.

The Cowlitz County Department of Emergency Services (DES), a division of the Sheriffs' Office, handles emergency management of flood and eruption threats associated with Mt. St. Helens. The DES coordinates the efforts of all federal, state, and local agencies that pertain to threatened residents of the county. In general, two strategies dominate plans to preserve public safety: development of an elaborate warning and evacuation system and enforcement of a policy of restricted access to danger areas around the volcano.

Nearly 5 years after the eruption, the towns around Mt. St. Helens still occupy somewhat precarious positions both demographically and economically. The population of the area has declined very slightly. In 1982, Congress established a 110,000-acre volcanic National Park at Mt. St. Helens. By 1985, the U.S. Forest Service had established several visitor centers, information centers, and viewpoints for the volcano, the closest just more than 3 miles from the crater. Several hundred thousand tourists visited the centers in 1984 and larger numbers are projected for the future, some 3 million annually by the year 2000 (Connelly, 1985).

An increase in tourism would go far toward restoring economic viability to the area, and some movement in that direction has occurred. With the 1985 season, the area around Mt. St. Helens finally began to experience the resurgence that had been predicted, but not materialized, in previous years. In any event, further reduction of the restricted zone would again open up recreational facilities and hunting and fishing areas. This would create an opportunity for an even stronger local economy than that which was evident before the eruptions.

With this background, probability samples of Toutle and Lexington residents of size 122 and 120 were drawn, respectively. In-person interviews were conducted with 99 Lexington residents for a completion rate of 82.5% and with 103 Toutle residents for a completion rate of 84.4% (see Perry & Lindell, 1985, pp. 7-11 for a full discussion of methodology).

VOLCANO INFORMATION DISSEMINATION

As a land form, Mt. St. Helens has stimulated considerable interest for many years. Information about the volcano's beauty, resources associated with it, and its periodic eruptions has appeared in Indian folklore, depictions by explorers, missionaries, and settlers, and in the more recent systematic writings of naturalists and scientists. Indeed, for a person who looks for it, there has traditionally been much descriptive information. Even before the present volcanic sequence began, considerable technical data existed regarding the threats posed by Mt. St. Helens for 20th-century inhabitants of the region surrounding the volcano (cf. Crandall & Mullineaux, 1978).

The current eruptive sequence is distinguished by being the first to occur since (a) settlements became larger and characterized by high population densities; (b) local governments developed; (c) the technological growth of "modern" earth science; (d) the rise of emergency management as a profession; (e) and the growth of modern mass media, particularly telecommunications.

When combined, these factors created an environment in which many citizens and much economic activity are at risk. Fortunately, there is substantial threat-relevant information that is available or can be created, as well as a capacity to distribute that information. And, local residents have time available in which to take action on the information. The beginning of volcanicity in March 1980 may be seen in this context as providing the impetus to begin the process of producing and disseminating information about threats associated with Mt. St. Helens.

Whatever the natural hazard, there are many reasons for disseminating threat-relevant information. From the standpoint of authorities, dissemination programs are undertaken to develop *hazard knowledge* so that citizens recognize and understand threats. These programs also help develop *salience*—to help citizens appreciate the importance of the threat. Finally, dissemination programs seek to develop *coping skills* that provide people with protective notions and strategies. In all, the hope is to induce citizens to "realistically" appraise environmental dangers and to integrate them into their social world in a way that minimizes probably negative outcomes.

Although the goals of dissemination may appear clear and straightforward, the practice—and even the study—of dissemination is beset with problems (cf. Knott & Wildavsky, 1979). Technical specialists ponder what information should be disseminated, in what form, by whom, and how frequently (Douglas, Westley, & Chaffee, 1970; Meltzner, 1979; Travis & Reibsame, 1979). All of these questions influence information-handling strategies.

With respect to Mt. St. Helens, the problems of dissemination can be focused on two categories of content. The first consists of messages about short-term status of the volcano: eruption warnings, flood warnings, and other announcements of immediate danger. For the most part, such messages are products of detection or prediction technology designed to provide an assessment-current (or imminent) level of volcano threat and to elicit an immediate response from citizens. The second category includes information of a longer range nature describing the evolution of threats, or warning systems and hazard management programs generally, or explaining protective strategies or tactics available to citizens. These are the types of information of interest here.

Pertinent to this discussion are not only message content but the target and sources of information. Hazard information is directed at the technically defined population-at-risk; in this case, residents of Toutle and Lexington, Washington. A variety of sources, which may or may not coordinate content, style, or timing of dissemination among themselves, make information available about Mt. St. Helens. The sources include private groups such as the Red Cross and mental health centers, the news media, and government agencies at all jurisdictional levels such as the Sheriffs' Office, county and state emergency services, the U.S. Geological Survey, Army Corps of Engineers, and the National Weather Service. Other important sources are friends, relatives, and neighbors. Obviously, both the nature of information routinely provided and the technical authority or expertise of these sources differs radically.

To examine systematically the environment in which volcano-hazard information is disseminated, a focal source must be designated to provide a structuring mechanism. In this case, that focal source is the county-level emergency manager. At Mt. St. Helens, the county unit has more resources than the municipalities to direct hazard management, and the county is directly responsible for the safety of most citizens. From its perspective, the goals of information dissemination remain the development of hazard knowledge, salience, and coping skills in the target audience, the residents of Toutle and Lexington.

4. COMMUNICATING VOLCANO THREAT INFORMATION 53

Multifacted sources of information create a problem. These sources can be divided into several groups: (a) the county as the focal organization, (b) state and municipal organizations interested in public safety that have a "local" orientation, (c) agencies with technical expertise charged with monitoring or administering some aspect of the threat or response to it, and (d) interested citizens.

Within certain political and technical constraints, the county has complete control of the information it disseminates, some influence possibly through coordination over the information that state, municipal, and technical agencies disseminated, and limited influence over that which citizens disseminate. Because all these sources may be "transmitting" simultaneously, the problem becomes one of determining how the local emergency manger can operate to insure timely passage of accurate information to the public-at-risk.

A review of the research literature provides some guidelines to insure adequate, accurate passage. One is to develop a proactive dissemination program based on accurate threat data that includes periodic contacts with the public-at-risk (Perry, 1985; Quarantelli, 1977). Another is to coordinate with other information disseminators to achieve some consistency of content-across messages (Perry & Nigg, 1985). Careful coordination, coupled with monitoring of messages delivered by others, also permits a local emergency manager to provide interpretation or qualification of information within the scope of his or her own dissemination efforts. A further suggested practice involves disseminating information through a variety of modes or channels to enhance coverage of the population-at-risk. Finally, the local emergency manager should build credibility as a source by maintaining visibility in the community, establishing channels that permit citizen-initiated contacts, and making public the basis of the agencies' knowledge about the threat (Dynes, Quarantelli, & Kreps, 1972).

Such guidelines are especially useful because they apply to threat information management in many settings. Because they are not hazard specific, they should apply to volcanoes as well as to riverine floods, earthquakes, tornadoes, or hurricanes. Of course, the test of their utility is what happens in practice, and the Mt. St. Helens eruptive sequence provides an excellent opportunity to do so with respect to two important aspects of the pattern of citizen information receipt: usual and preferred communication channels and citizen assessments of source credibility.

One caveat must be made: remember that these data reflect communication patterns that prevailed slightly more than 3 years into Mt. Helens' current eruptive sequence. So these patterns are contacts between citizens and sources that have become routinized.

Information receipt patterns have clearly changed over the years. In April 1980, at the beginning of the sequence, there was heavy demand for volcanic threat information. At that time, more than 50% of the residents of three communities near the volcano reported that they *received* information from some source more than four times each day (Greene, Perry, & Lindell, 1981). These levels of information receipt declined slightly over time, but increased again following the cataclysmic eruption of May 18, 1980 (Perry, Greene, & Lindell, 1980). In turn, this increase was sustained during the frequent explosive eruptions from May to August, 1980, but gradually decreased with declining eruption magnitude and frequency, decreasing mass media attention, and apparent information saturation of the local residents. Within this context, our data represent exchanges derived from the systemic efforts of agencies and organizations with an emergency management mission to keep the population informed and interchanges among citizens, generally aimed at clarifying, interpreting, or simply relaying information.

CHANNELS FOR INFORMATION RECEIPT

Are the communication channels through which citizens report that they usually receive information the same as the ones through which they prefer to receive information? This is an important question when conducting an investigation of communication patterns for hazard information. And, by documenting channels through which people remember hearing threat information, it is possible to identify those channels that actually reach citizens. When coupled with data on channel preference, this information allows an emergency manager to target effective channels when designing a dissemination program, enhancing the probability that the messages will reach the intended audience.

Sometimes it is difficult to separate information source from communication channel when dealing with hazard information. The concept of information source concentrates on the person or agency that constructs the information forming the message. A communication channel is a mechanism through which a message is transmitted. Emergency management authorities, police, firefighters, friends, and neighbors are all clearly sources. Messages developed by these sources may be delivered through a variety of channels, including personal conversation (either face-to-face or by telephone), in a public meeting, as a brochure, or using mass media (newspaper, radio, or television). The distinction between source and channel is clear analytically, but can become blurred in practice. Indeed, certain channels are commonly used by certain sources. Information from friends, relatives, or neighbors is likely to come via personal conversation. Emergency management authorities are more likely to use a range of channels.

The mass media can be conceived both as a channel and a source. Radio, newspapers, and television form channels through which information can be passed to citizens. An emergency manager may formulate a threat status bulletin and choose to disseminate it by releasing it to the mass media with the request that it be reproduced. Mass media can also become sources, particularly with chronic environmental threats or multiple- or extended-impact disasters. In such cases, mass

4. COMMUNICATING VOLCANO THREAT INFORMATION

media fulfill their "normal" news function regarding the environmental threat. A quantity of information is gathered by reporters, assembled, interpreted, and disseminated. Such information may include data from emergency managers or agencies, but it is also likely to include a variety of other material subject to the interpretation of writers and editors. In this situation, the channel becomes a source, a constructor of messages.

This distinction between mass media as channels and as sources bears upon the analysis of Mt. St. Helens data. Table 4.1 shows the usual and preferred channels for information receipt for Toutle and Lexington, the two study communities. Respondents were asked to select the single channel through which they usually, or most commonly, received threat information regarding Mt. St. Helens. In Toutle, the largest percent (41.7%) identified radio as the usual channel. Newspapers were the usual channel for 27.2% and 17.5% cited personal conversation. About 10% mentioned television and only very small numbers cited brochures and public meetings. In Lexington, virtually all of the respondents selected some mass medium as the channel through which information was usually received. Newspapers accounted for 42.4% of the selections, televisions for 36.4%, and radio for 17.2% Only 3.0% cited personal conversation and one person mentioned brochures.

TABLE 4.1
Usual and Preferred Channels of Information Receipt

	Toutle		Lexington	
	N	%	N	%
Usual Channel of Receipt				
Personal Conversation	18	17.5	3	3.0
Television	11	10.7	36	36.4
Radio	43	41.7	17	17.2
Newspaper	28	27.2	42	42.4
Brochure	2	1.9	1	1.0
Public Meeting	1	1.0	0	0.0
TOTALS	103	100.0	99	100.0
Preferred Channel of Receipt				
Personal Conversation	0	0.0	3	3.0
Television	1	1.0	18	18.2
Radio	22	21.4	13	13.1
Newspaper	54	52.4	37	37.4
Brochure	20	19.4	15	15.2
Public Meeting	6	5.9	13	13.1
TOTALS	103	1200.0	99	100.0

Channel use in Toutle emphasized radio, with the newspaper and personal conversations serving important secondary roles. Perhaps this reflects a perceived need among Toutle residents for quick response. Because of the town's close proximity to the volcanic cone, Toutle residents are sensitive to mudflow/flood threats that could reach Toutle relatively quickly. As a continual broadcast medium, radio can provide very current information, and Toutle residents may have gravitated toward this medium with the expectation of maximizing their lead time. In addition, there are no local television stations serving the area closest to the volcano. So those who wish to hear locally relevant information more frequently than daily (from the *Longview Daily News*) must use radio. In Lexington, the most common channels for information receipt were newspapers and television, followed by radio. Personal conversations were cited as the usual channel for receiving threat information by fewer respondents in Lexington than in Toutle. Not surprisingly, this reflects previously reported data in which the use of friends and neighbors as a source in Toutle exceeded that in Lexington, particularly in light of the fact that personal conversation tends to be the channel when the source is friends or neighbors (cf. Perry et al., 1980, p. 211).

The channels through which citizens preferred to receive hazard information differed from those cited as most commonly used. In Toutle, there was a clear preference for newspaper transmitted information (endorsed by 52.4% of the respondents). The next most frequently selected channels were radio (21.4%) and brochures (19.4%). Very few Toutle residents selected public meetings or television as preferred communication channels and none endorsed personal conversation. The largest single proportion of Lexington residents (37.4%) also preferred to receive threat information through newspapers. When newspapers are excluded, respondents are evenly spread across the remaining channels. Among these selections, television was most often endorsed (18.2%); followed by brochures (15.2%), radio (13.1%), and public meetings (13.1%). Again, very few selected personal conversation as a preferred channel.

Both sites showed a preference for channels transmitting information in written form. Nearly three-quarters of Toutle respondents and more than half from Lexington who were given a choice elected to receive information via newspapers or brochures. This finding is not surprising. It is consistent with other research showing that people with White ethnic backgrounds opt for written threat information. (Minority groups vary from this pattern; see Perry & Mushkatel, 1986, p. 182.) One explanation for this perhaps rests in the fact that written information may be kept for future reference.

Similar comparisons can be made for other channels. A preference for radio was evident in both towns, particularly Toutle. About 20% of Lexington respondents preferred television; only 1% in Toutle. In Lexington 13% of the residents endorsed public meetings compared to 5.9% in Toutle.

4. COMMUNICATING VOLCANO THREAT INFORMATION

Beyond comparison, these data emphasize the diversity of citizen channel preference. By doing so, they underscore the importance of using multiple channels in connection with threat information dissemination programs.

ASSESSMENTS OF SOURCE CREDIBILITY

Research has shown that source credibility influences behavior in at least two contexts. First, during the emergency response phase of a specific impending threat, citizens are more likely to promptly comply with warning messages from sources perceived to be credible. Second, during nonemergency times when environmental dangers are present but not imminent, citizens apparently attend more carefully to information and preparation suggestions disseminated by credible sources.

Consequently, source credibility affects the way the public acts on hazard information in different contexts. So emergency managers, as one of many potential sources, must attend carefully to credibility issues to insure effectiveness in providing information.

The Mt. St. Helens case provides an opportunity to identify patterns of credibility attributions and to link these attributions with specific rationales underlying the designation of sources as reliable. Table 4.2 shows the sources nominated

TABLE 4.2
Most Credible Source by Reason Chosen
(Frequency Only)

Site	Reason Chosen	County DES	Sheriff	USGS	Army Corps	Friends/ Neighbors	TV/ Radio
Toutle							
	Concerned for citizens	2	0	0	0	0	0
	Special skills/information	8	35	5	2	0	3
	Past reliability	3	36	0	0	2	0
	Integrity	3	4	0	0	0	0
	TOTAL	16	75	5	2	2	3
Lexington							
	Concerned for citizens	4	0	0	0	0	1
	Special skills/information	14	14	0	2	0	3
	Past reliability	5	38	1	0	0	0
	Integrity	2	7	0	0	4	4
	TOTAL	25	59	1	2	4	8

by our respondents as "most credible" crosstabulated by the reason offered by justify that selection. In both cases, respondents were asked, using an open-ended question format, to first name the single most credible (trustworthy and reliable) source for volcano information and then to explain the basis of their confidence.

The range of sources named as most credible was narrow when compared to the number of sources available. Only six were named: County Department of Emergency Services (DES), County Sheriff, U.S. Geological Survey, Army Corps of Engineers, friends or neighbors, and local television or radio. And only a small number of respondents mentioned the last four sources. The majority in both communities identified the County Sheriff as the most credible source. Seventy-five Toutle residents (72.8%) and 59 Lexingtonians (59.6%) selected the Sheriffs' Department. The County DES was next in frequency, accounting for 15.5% of the Toutle and 25.3% of the Lexington sample. Taken together, the Sheriff and County DES account for approximately 85% of the nominations for most credible source made by respondents from both communities.

In Toutle, people who believed the sheriff was the most credible information source cited two primary reasons for this choice. Thirty-five people (46.7%) said that the Sheriffs' Department had personnel with special skills and access to technical information. The second basis centered on experience. Thirty-six respondents (48%) cited reliable information received in the past. Only a small percent of the Toutle respondents (5.3%) listed department "integrity" as a reason for selecting the sheriff as most credible.

Similar reasons were given by Lexington residents who identified the Sheriffs' Department as most credible. The majority (64.4%) focused on past reliability when selecting the Sheriffs' Department. Fourteen people (23.7%) mentioned special skills and access to technical information, and 11.9% said that Sheriffs' Department integrity formed the basis of its credibility.

The reasons given for placing high confidence in the County Department of Emergency Services covered a wider range than those cited for Sheriff. In Toutle, 50% mentioned special skills and information, 18.8% cited two skills (past reliability and integrity), and 12.4% cited DES' "concern for citizens." The majority of Lexington respondents mentioned special skills and information (56%), followed by past reliability (20.2%), concern for citizens (16%), and integrity (8%). What stands out from these results is that the possession of special skills and information is by far the most common basis for a credibility attribution in either community.

What becomes clear from the data is that residents have defined the two local emergency authorities, the County Sheriff and Department of Emergency Services, as being the most reliable sources of information regarding the Mt. St. Helens threat. This has positive implications for citizen attention to, and compliance with, hazard-related information and protective measures. For, although credibility attributions are an often-cited goal for emergency managers, they are difficult to achieve in practice (Perry, 1985). In riverine floods, relatives and friends are sometimes defined as credible sources almost as often as local emergency managers (cf. Perry, Lindell, & Greene, 1979). And, during the nuclear reactor incident at Three Mile Island, the mass media dominated citizens' nominations for most credible source. Only 2% of those surveyed identified local emergency management authorities (Barnes, Brosius, & Mitchell, 1979, p. 14).

For the most part, credibility attributions are subjective judgments made by the public. The data relative to Toutle and Lexington provide a glimpse of this judgment process, identifying two principle dimensions by which such attributions are made. These are past reliability and access to skills and information. When the Toutle and Lexington residents named a source they believed to be highly credible, large percentages justified the choice in terms of the extent to which the organization possessed these characteristics.

These dimensions are consistent with considerations in previous discussions of credibility in communicating risk information. Lindell and Perry (1983) noted that experimental research on persuasive communications has suggested two principle components of source credibility relevant to hazard situations: expertise and trustworthiness. *Expertise* is what has been described here as special skills and information. *Trustworthiness* refers to a willingness and ability to communicate information without bias. This attribute corresponds to the categories of concern for citizens and integrity listed in Table 4.2. The emphasis by Toutle and Lexington residents on past reliability can be interpreted as referring to the basis upon which an inference of credibility is made, rather than to specific aspects (expertise and trustworthiness) of credibility.

More generally, there are three different bases on which a source can be judged to be credible. The first is the source's "credentials," usually a job title such as geologist, meteorologist, or hydrologist. Each of these three examples conveys an image of expertise resulting from credentials. Inferences about trustworthiness can also be made from credentials. A university professor is likely to be considered disinterested, whereas a representative of a corporation whose timberlands might be closed is likely to be considered less than completely trustworthy. A second basis of source credibility is the way in which the source is treated by others whose credibility has already been established. The public is likely to accept a source of unknown credibility if it is treated with respect by sources that have already established their credibility. The third basis is past job performance. The 3-year series of volcanic eruptions at Mt. St. Helens had provided the County DES and Sheriffs' Office with an opportunity to establish their credibility through continuing job performance tests.

Emergency managers should be aware of factors that influence public perception of their agencies' credibility. The objective is not to create unwarranted visions of reliability; it is probably impossible to make a basically unreliable system appear competent over any significant period of time. Rather, the idea is to communicate accurately both the strong points and limitations of technical emergency management systems, so that citizens can compare information from these systems with that derived from alternate sources. Essentially, this gives a clear basis for rejecting inaccurate or inappropriate protective action recommendations generated by sources with faulty or incomplete information.

In disseminating information, local emergency managers must strive to provide data that are as technically accurate as possible. A chronic problem in emergencies is that hazard monitoring systems break down, data are misinterpreted, and conditions rapidly change, rendering data no longer representative of the actual situation. When an emergency manager disseminates information that turns out to be unreliable for any of these reasons (basically outside the department's control), an effort should be made to disseminate follow-up information that corrects the inappropriate messages and provides a brief explanation of how incorrect information was disseminated in the first place. The goal here is to avoid permitting an incorrect or misleading forecast of status report to simply stand. By providing an explanation, the emergency manager helps the public to interpret apparent "unreliability" by understanding its genesis.

Such treatment converts what would otherwise simply be remembered as an instance of unreliability into an opportunity for the emergency manager to educate the public regarding the limitations of available technology. In effect, such performances demonstrate to the public that emergency managers exercise control over the situation in that errors can be identified, explained, and corrected.

Another avenue for enhancing agency credibility can be derived from citizen concern with the special skills and information that may be used by a source in generating threat information. In all dissemination efforts, emergency managers should seek to educate the public about not only environmental threats, but also about the process and practice of emergency management. When threat information is disseminated, emergency managers are describing and interpreting the state of the environment and asking citizens to accept that view. In the special case of disaster warning messages, authorities not only ask citizens to accept their view of the environment, but also to undertake specific actions consistent with their view. It is well documented that citizens infrequently accept on faith the judgments of emergency managers (cf. Quarantelli & Dynes, 1972). Instead, receipt of threat information—from any source—stimulates individuals to observe the environment (that is, collect information) and devise a personal "definition of the situation" that may or may not agree with the view promoted by the information source. So it is important for an emergency manager to present interpretations and conclusions as well as to share the bases that underlie them. This includes establishing ethos by describing the kinds of expertise in the form of specialized equipment and personnel available to the emergency manager that were used in evaluating the relevant environmental threat.

4. COMMUNICATING VOLCANO THREAT INFORMATION

This tactic has two effects. First, it communicates information about the decision process used by the authorities, which, in turn, increases the chance that citizens will focus their own decision making on similar issues and adopt a similar point of view (Perry, 1985, pp. 65-72). Second, it publicly describes special resources available to emergency managers that uniquely qualify them to make pronouncements about environmental threats. The volcano data indicate that citizens are particularly attentive to such qualifications when making judgments about source credibility. It is important to emphasize that establishing credibility is a long process that is difficult to short-cut. Perceptions of credibility flow from many experiences or source-citizen interactions over a sustained time period.

Volcanic threats are marked by special characteristics, particularly prolonged eruptive periods, that tend to set them apart in some respects from other natural hazards. To use risk characteristics proposed by Slovic, Fischhoff, and Lichtenstein (1980), volcanic activity has the potential for catastrophic consequences, and neither science nor people exposed to the threat understand the threat well. Moreover, the risk of a dangerous eruption continues and changes over time.

These threat characteristics result in high levels of citizen information seeking and pose special communication demands. There are three types of information routinely required in connection with volcano threats. First, citizens need current monitoring information on the status of volcanicity. Traditionally, emergency managers have met this information need by devising warning systems that send a signal (a siren, for example) or a message by phone or mobile loudspeaker directly to individuals. As an alternative, citizen preference data suggest that radio can also serve this function well, particularly in volcano threats where very large geographic areas may be endangered.

A second type of communication demand is the need for information about the status of hazard management efforts undertaken by public agencies. At Mt. St. Helens, agencies like the U.S. Geological Survey are engaged in an ongoing process of assessing the nature of the eruptive threat, which changes over time. As both eruptive and noneruptive threats change, agencies charged with hazard reduction, like the Army Corps of Engineers, must adapt their programs to new conditions. From a public safety standpoint, citizens must be aware of changes in the threat, as well as changes in government programs to mitigate the associated dangers. Although these information needs have been addressed with public meetings and brochures, our data suggest that citizens also find newspapers an appealing source because of their written form, easy accessibility and retrievable nature.

Finally, people exposed to volcano threat have a need for continuing information regarding the types of personal protective measures they can adopt. Citizens face a constellation of eruptive and noneruptive dangers such as sedimentation dams, some of which must be abated on a large scale, usually undertaken by governments. There are also a variety of personal measures that may be used to enhance safety: acquiring breathing masks, learning about evacuation routes and shelters, reinforcing buildings, and so on. These measures also change as the nature of the threat changes. Again, although such information is traditionally communicated via public meetings and brochures, our data suggest citizens have a preference for finding such protective information in newspapers.

Perhaps one of the most important implications of our research is that emergency managers need to re-evaluate the nature of communication channels used to provide hazard information. Technically, any single communication channel cannot meet the information demands associated with a volcanic sequence. Our data on citizen preferences suggest two important conclusions. First, a mix of channels should be used to send messages. Second, the news media need to be systematically incorporated into this mix. The relationship between emergency managers and the news media has not been traditionally close. Yet, to incorporate media into hazard warning and information-dissemination plans demands closer ties to insure the accuracy of messages and appropriateness of timing and coverage. Our data show that citizens do rely on, and in some cases prefer, media for all types of hazard information. Thus, it would seem that the development of an ongoing relationship marked by careful coordination between emergency managers and the media represents an important avenue to increased public safety in volcano threats.

5
TMI: *The Media Story That Will Not Die*

Sharon M. Friedman
Lehigh University

In December 1986, almost 8 years after the accident at the Three Mile Island (TMI) nuclear plant, the editors and broadcasters who subscribe to the Associated Press voted the continuing saga of TMI the sixth most important story in Pennsylvania that year ("Casey Victory," 1986).

Both the local and national media have chronicled extensively the events at TMI. It seems safe to speculate that TMI has collected more column inches in the nation's newspapers and more hours of television coverage than any other technology-related story. Only the Chernobyl accident in 1986 has lessened the media's use of their almost mandatory description of TMI as the "worst commercial nuclear accident." And despite the severity of Chernobyl in comparison to TMI, the Pennsylvania accident and its multiyear ramifications continue to receive more media attention and to stimulate more controversy than the Soviet accident, at least in Pennsylvania.

Media coverage of TMI not only has been extensive, but that coverage has been extensively studied. Because there was so much confusion during the 1979 TMI accident, many people charged that lies, coverups, and media sensationalism abounded. To investigate these matters, President Jimmy Carter's Commission on the Accident at TMI set up the Task Force on the Public's Right to Information. Task force members studied numerous topics including past media coverage of nuclear accidents, how well reporters and information sources functioned during the accident, and information flows for specific accident events. They also analyzed media coverage for content, quality, and tone.

One prime task force conclusion was that a major communications breakdown occurred during the accident due, in great part, to lack of planning. This lack of planning was present with all players in the TMI drama—Metropolitan Edison (Met Ed), the utility that operated TMI; the U.S. Nuclear Regulatory Commission (NRC); and the media. Its roots, however, began far before 1979, so that pre-accident policies and actions of these three groups functioned like blueprints for failure. They ensured the communications crisis that was to come during the accident (see Friedman, 1981; U.S. Government Printing Office, 1979a).[1]

PRE-ACCIDENT INFORMATION EFFORTS

The Utility

Met Ed had three main programs for providing information about TMI to the media and to the public: a general public information program about all utility activities, a public relations effort specifically about TMI's plant status, and a community relations program directed at local residents.

Four public relations professionals in Reading, Pennsylvania, which is about 60 miles from TMI, carried out the general information program. This overburdened staff handled numerous tasks ranging from issuing press releases to preparing an internal newsletter to devising advertising copy for the entire Met Ed system. The staff members had no scientific training, and all but one had little time on the job. At the time of the accident, their average tenure was about 7 months. In addition, the staff dealt only with local rather than national media. All of these factors hindered these four individuals in providing accurate and adequate information to reporters during the accident.

Engineers in the utility's generation department directed the public relations program specifically about TMI's status. The trained public relations personnel in Reading participated only minimally. Because the engineers had little idea of what media needs were or could be during an accident, they did not include any information on how to inform the public or the media about an accident in their emergency plan. This lack of public information planning led to communications chaos during the accident's first days.

Despite this omission, the engineers did provide a great deal of information about TMI to the media and the public. This took the form of weekly press releases on the status of the plant's two nuclear units, 1 and 2, and the events or problems the engineering staff had reported to the NRC that week. Although these weekly releases could have been an excellent tool for keeping the public informed about successes and concerns at TMI, they suffered from many problems. Chief among these was the technical jargon used by the engineers, involving terms such as *deenergized power generation buses*. The releases also failed to describe the significance of events so reporters could decide whether something was important and needed to be followed up.

They confused the media about the timing of events, because the releases did not report when problems had actually occurred, but rather when they were reported to the NRC. For example, something that happened on March 29 was reported in a press release on May 5 (Metropolitan Edison Press Release, May 5, 1978). This was because the NRC required many reports, some immediate, some weekly, some monthly, and Med Ed lumped information from all these reports into its weekly press releases.

Although these releases did not lead directly to the many problems during the accident, they indirectly contributed to the communications breakdown. First, because reporters could not understand the releases, they were not often used. So readers did not get a picture of how the plants were operating. Second, if a reporter did call about a problem highlighted in a release, he or she usually was told it had been corrected. It often had because what the reporter was inquiring about had happened weeks earlier, but had just been reported to the NRC. These time lags gave the local media the impression that everything was running smoothly at the plant, which was not the case with TMI-2 as Med Ed brought it through the start-up phase in 1978. Third, the releases set up a tradition of engineers handling media information about TMI, something that would continue into the accident and eventually backfire.

The last aspect of the utility's information effort, its community relations program, was the most successful of its public relations activities. This effort to convince audiences that TMI was completely safe was perhaps too successful. Customers and neighbors were so assured that when the accident happened, they were not prepared, and Met Ed suffered a serious loss of credibility that contributed to the communications chaos during the accident.

PRE-ACCIDENT MEDIA COVERAGE

The utility was not the only element involved in the public information flow about TMI in the local regions. Six daily and one weekly newspaper served the four major cities or towns within 25 miles of TMI—Harrisburg (the state capital), Lancaster, York, and Middletown. Between 1978 and March 1979, when the accident occurred, they had printed 158 articles on TMI, most of a positive nature, frequently based on press releases from Met Ed's Reading office.[2] Few paid much attention to the engineers' weekly press releases about plant status or questioned events at the plant. Most reporters covering TMI were general assignment or business writers, who had a superficial, if any, understanding of how a nuclear reactor worked. Regional radio and television coverage of TMI before the accident also was lacking, with very few stories on the nuclear plant.

Because of this flaccid coverage, readers did not learn about problems at TMI-2, and the local media lulled themselves into a complacent state, not learning more about how the reactor functioned and discarding all those weekly press releases, so they could not be used as references during the accident.

On the national scene, a number of reporters, particularly those who specialized in science or energy coverage, were familiar with the nuclear debate, both pro and anti. In fact, a study by the Battelle Human Affairs Research Center estimated that there had been a 400% increase in print media coverage of nuclear power issues between 1972 and 1976 (U.S. Government Printing Office, 1979b, p. 1). The Battelle study also showed an increasingly negative treatment of nuclear energy in four national periodicals, including the *New York Times* during that time period (Rothman & Lichter, 1982, p. 51).

Despite this increased coverage, most reporters were not familiar with technical aspects of how a nuclear plant worked. And even the most experienced had not covered a nuclear accident in progress. They had only covered incidents after they had happened, such as the fire at the Browns Ferry nuclear plant in Alabama.

The NRC

The NRC had a policy of not monitoring or even advising utilities on public relations activities. It had no requirement for utilities to have an emergency public information plan, and, in fact, did not have one itself.

It too had a small information staff, 10 professionals in all, 5 in Washington, DC and 5 scattered in its regional offices. The agency did not enjoy good media relations. Reporters said the NRC was timid in dealing with the press, and technical staff members frequently hid behind technical jargon. Although the commissioners themselves were somewhat more effective, they often told the media one thing and members of Congress something else. Later, these conflicting statements got back to the media and into print.

So the stage was set for the communications crisis. Met Ed had a small, inexperienced public relations staff with engineers in charge of reactor information. The local media were complacent and not well prepared to cover TMI, and some of the national media were not much better off. The NRC's information staff was understaffed, and the agency was not skilled in media relations.

THE ACCIDENT ITSELF

The accident was a test for Met Ed and the NRC to inform the public effectively under crisis conditions (accident review abridged from, Summary of Report of Public Information Task Force, 1979b).[3] It was a test for reporters to cover a nuclear accident as it was happening. It was a test that everyone failed.

The accident began at 4 a.m. on March 28, 1979, and by 7:24 a.m., Met Ed had declared a general emergency. A general emergency is the most serious level on the emergency scale, and means that off-site radiation is present. At 9:00 a.m., the Associated Press sent out a report over its national wire announcing that a general emergency had been declared. Shortly thereafter reporters began to flood Met Ed and the NRC with phone calls for information. (See U.S. Government Printing Office, 1979c; Ford, 1982; Gray & Rose, 1982; and Stephens, 1980, for more complete chronologies.) Since neither the utility nor the NRC had emergency information plans, much of the communications breakdown that occurred could be traced squarely to their bumbling, ineffectual efforts.

Met Ed and NRC Efforts

Met Ed and the NRC were the prime information sources for the media about what was happening during the accident, but they provided very little useful information during the first few days. Because neither had emergency public information plans, their responses to media queries were confusing, conflicting, and disorganized. On the first day of the accident, no one even knew who was in charge of informing the public. Met Ed issued statements from three different places, all saying something different about off-site radiation.

The NRC's Region I information officer in King of Prussia near Philadelphia could respond to initial media queries, because he had been notified about the accident. However, because he was not kept up to date, he could only give the media old information.

This confusion among the major information sources mirrored that in the Unit 2 control room during the first day. Yet, reporters would not accept that the experts were confused. They kept looking for a coverup to explain the lack of coordination, and, in doing so, they missed the biggest story about that accident—that the experts really did not know what was happening in the reactor at that time (Sandman & Paden, 1979, pp. 48-49).

At the accident's beginning, Met Ed dominated the information scene, with its vice president for generation serving as chief spokesman. The four public relations people in Reading were all busy answering reporters' phone calls and trying themselves to find out what had happened. They played a very minor role throughout the accident. The engineers took charge. Because of their inexperience in dealing with national reporters, they made several mistakes.

One mistake was an attempt to play down the amount of radiation being released in the air. This resulted in Lt. Governor William Scranton stating in a press conference that the utility was not telling everyone all that it should. Such mistakes continued for several days, culminating in a disastrous blunder. Right in the middle of the nation's most serious nuclear accident, the vice president for generation told the press that he did not know why he had to tell reporters each and every thing Met Ed did. This lost the utility whatever credibility it had managed to retain at that time.

Although the NRC tried to distance itself from Met Ed by refusing to participate in Met Ed press conferences, it did not do much better in serving as an information source. One problem was that the NRC spoke with multiple voices. The first voice was the Region I information officer who had come from King of Prussia to Harrisburg; the second was the engineers at NRC national headquarters in Bethesda, Maryland, particularly in the Incident Response Center. The third was NRC engineers at TMI, and the fourth was the NRC Commissioners themselves.

What resulted was confusion. Often conflicting information came from engineers in Bethesda and TMI. On the fourth day of the accident, those at Bethesda told the media that a hydrogen bubble might explode in 2 days. NCR engineers at TMI quickly denied that possibility. And the commissioners, in direct contrast to their engineers, made every effort to downplay the accident's severity. They even took pains not to call it an accident for the first few days.

Media Activities

Adding to the confusion was a large influx of reporters, most of whom knew next to nothing about nuclear plants and how they worked. By the end of the first day, there were 100 reporters at the site. As the accident dragged on, this number grew to between 300 and 500, including reporters from all over the world.

These reporters had deadlines. Yet, they could get little information from Met Ed or the NRC, and what they did get often conflicted. Although some newspapers sent their science writers, many others sent general assignment reporters who were good at handling emergencies. Others were represented by journalists who just happened to be present in the newsroom when the TMI general emergency was declared.

The reporters were almost immediately confronted with nuclear terms. A simple question on whether the core was uncovered got complex answers concerning ruptured fuel pins, pinholes in the cladding, failed fuel, and core melt. Some reporters went to libraries to search out explanations; others called sources at other utilities and elsewhere for help. Still others turned from the technical aspects and talked to local residents for "color" stories on the frightened populace.

For the accident's first two days, Met Ed and the NRC gave almost no organized help to reporters. Normally, public information operations aid reporters by

5. TMI: THE MEDIA STORY THAT WILL NOT DIE

returning phone calls promptly, setting up press conferences and press centers, providing background explanations, and if necessary, having people available to explain technical details. Because of this lack of planning, none of this was available. At the start of the accident, the media inundated utility and NRC phone lines and calls often were not returned, or they were returned too late and with too little information. As a result, reporters began calling anyone they could, leading to more confusion. The situation was so bad that the mayor of Harrisburg said he found out about the accident when a reporter from a Boston radio station called him for information.

Not until the third day of the accident, Friday, March 30, did Met Ed set up a press center, and then it was in Hershey about 20 miles from TMI and only for phone calls. The NRC did not set up a press center until the following Monday, 6 days into the accident. The lack of a press center meant no central place for reporters to gather information, few public relations aides, and even fewer technical personnel to explain the complex technological aspects of the accident.

Confusion mounted. It became very bad on that Friday, after a 1,200 millirem radiation release from the plant led to a discussion of a possible meltdown. This confusion was not the media's alone. Pennsylvania's governor was getting confusing reports from the NRC about the danger and whether to evacuate the populace. So were the NRC commissioners.

Finally, at the governor's request, the White House stepped in, centralizing communications and limiting the number of people who could speak about the accident. Harold Denton, a high-level NRC engineer, became the prime spokesman at the site, and he cut through much confusion. Still, because he frequently used technical terms, reporters said that they were petrified that Denton would announce a meltdown in technical language and they would not know it.

Although many of the media's problems could be blamed on the confusion and lack of planning by the information sources, the media were not without fault. Because of their own lack of planning, many did not have reporters or editors familiar with nuclear technology and terminology.

The media did many things incorrectly. They mirrored the confusion of their sources, further confusing their readers and viewers. Reporters quoted sources who said that the 1,200-millirem burst of radiation on Friday morning was both planned and unplanned, controlled and uncontrolled, and expected and unexpected. What was a reader or viewer to think?

They also missed or delayed coverage of several important stories, such as that on the core being uncovered and seriously damaged. They did not report during the first week that Met Ed cleared the control room of unnecessary personnel because of high radiation levels, or that a coolant pump had not worked on the first day. They even missed political stories, including one on a battle between the state and the NRC over who would take responsibility for allowing industrial waste water to be dumped into the Susquehanna River.

More seriously, reporters used information that readers and viewers could not understand or interpret. They did not explain the significance of a general emergency. Nor did they provide background or contextual information about radiation releases at the plant or their potential health effects. In fact, the radiation issue was about the worst covered because the reporting was almost always incomplete.

Although the media missed some stories and failed to provide context for others, they were not as alarmist about the accident as most people believed. An in-depth analysis by the President's Public Information Task Force showed the media offered more reassuring than alarming statements about most aspects of the accident. The possibility of a meltdown was the only directly accident-related item about which the media were more alarming than reassuring, and this was based on alarming information from the NRC. Nor were most media sensational in their headlines, photos, or graphics. A survey of 43 newspapers showed that, other than the *New York Post* and *New York Daily News*, the newspapers did not sensationalize or overplay the story. Some television commentary did adopt a more sensational approach.

The Clash of Different Worlds

Throughout the accident, the clash of the different worlds of the engineer and the reporter took its toll. Reporters were confronted with complex explanations in which engineers made various distinctions based on technical information reporters could not understand. Although such distinctions were real for the engineers, they only confused the main issues for reporters. Engineers found press ignorance frustrating. They were particularly concerned about having to give short, simple answers to complicated questions and about having to deal with "what if" questions that led to meltdown scenarios.

Yet media needs proved as baffling to engineers as reactor technology did to reporters. The engineers did not realize that the media needed to have information on a regular basis because newspapers do not print blank pages and television news programs cannot run 30 minutes of recorded music. They also could not understand the media's tight deadlines and reporters' need for something new. The engineers wanted time to solve reactor problems, while the media and citizens were concerned about potential health hazards and possibilities of evacuation. So although the accident at TMI was unique, it can be seen in a large context as a classic example of the clash between technology and the media.

LESSONS LEARNED FROM THE ACCIDENT

The Utility and the NRC

Due to, among other things, studies of the accident, Met Ed and the NRC made many improvements in their public communications efforts. General Public Utilities Inc., the parent corporation for Met Ed and TMI, created a new operational unit, GPU Nuclear, to run TMI and relegated operation of non-nuclear power plants to Met Ed. GPU Nuclear hired a new and enlarged group to staff the TMI information operation, which moved to the island from Reading. Drawn from newspapers and television stations, these new communications staff members had an understanding of media needs, and, in some instances, were former colleagues of local reporters and editors.

A 1983 survey of local reporters and editors found they were generally satisfied with the personnel and activities of the new TMI information operation (Friedman, 1984a, 1984b, 1985). Most of the 21 reporters and editors questioned said GPU Nuclear communications staffers were well versed in the issues, helpful, and very accessible during 1981-1982. They felt that TMI press releases were accurate, understandable, and did not include much technical jargon. On the negative side, a majority of news personnel had a few reservations and believed that they were only being told the utility's view of events.

The credibility lost during the accident proved somewhat hard to regain. Most local media personnel said that, although the GPU Nuclear communications staff had not misled or lied to them during 1981-1982, their questions were not always fully answered. According to one reporter, "Depending on the criticality of the situation, they would either be vague or not convey as much information as they were holding. If reporters didn't ask the question, they didn't feel the need to provide the information" (Ryan, personal communication, June 30, 1983).

Among other things, the NRC responded to criticism of its public information operation by requiring detailed emergency public information plans for itself and for all nuclear plants. In addition, these plans are tested each year as part of every plant's emergency drills. NRC public information officers evaluate the public information aspects of the drills and offer suggestions for improvement.

The Local Newspapers During 1981-1982

The local media, too, made some changes. Reporting about TMI in the region's six daily newspapers made some strides during 1981-1982 (Friedman, 1984a, 1984b, 1985).[4] During these 2 years, the 6 newspapers published 1,897 TMI articles, compared to 155 they had run in 1976-1978. This more-than-tenfold increase demonstrates the extensive coverage by the local papers especially when compared to 172 TMI stories in the *Philadelphia Inquirer* and the 102 in the *New York Times* during 1981-1982.

In covering the issues, the local newspapers expanded their purview from featuring "good news" stories to reporting on a wide range of events, including technical details of the cleanup of the damaged reactor, funding for cleanup activities, or plans for restarting the undamaged Unit 1 reactor. They also reported on many related issues, including lawsuits resulting from the accident, a cheating scandal involving plant operators, and the development of evacuation plans.

Rather than the heavy dependency on Met Ed, many more sources appeared in the local coverage during 1981-1982. However, this increase was not due to inspired newspaper performance. It was mostly because there were more actors involved in the drama. Besides the utility, these included pro- and antinuclear groups, the NRC, federal and state courts, various financial institutions, numerous state and federal government officials, and representatives of the nuclear industry. While no one source dominated the coverage because events were too diverse, some desirable sources were missing, particularly scientists and engineers from universities or scientific societies who could have provided objective evaluations.

Although several improvements in coverage occurred, other aspects showed little change. Four of the six regional newspapers had a part-time TMI beat staffed by general assignment or business reporters, whereas the other two either used any available general assignment reporter or depended on the wire services. This was not much different than before the accident, although part-time beat reporters said they spent between 20% and 40% of their time covering TMI during 1981-1982. Five of the newspapers had one or more opportunities to replace the reporter covering TMI after the accident, but none had chosen to hire a journalist with a scientific or technical background.

Local reporters covering TMI in 1981-1982 had only slightly more technical background or training than those in 1979 who covered the accident. One had taken a few civil engineering courses in college, and another had taken a graduate course in nuclear plant operations after being assigned to cover TMI. Two reporters said they had learned about some technical issues by covering the accident itself. All reporters and editors felt their understanding of nuclear plant operations was better than it had been before the accident, but they admitted their understanding was still superficial and that they relied heavily on the utility and other sources for technical explanations.

Although extensive in 1981-1982, the coverage itself was reactive, consisting primarily of hard news stories on events at TMI or reports of announcements by the utility, the NRC, antinuclear groups, other government officials, federal or state judges, or financial institutions. The quality of that hard news reporting varied with the newspaper and over time, but it appeared to be adequate or better in all but one newspaper. As before the accident, very few articles contained in-depth explanations or put events or issues into perspective for readers, although occasional "perspective" pieces did appear in the Harrisburg newspapers.

People who had served as news sources for the local press complained that the six newspapers did very little digging and did not follow through on stories. They accused them of being event oriented and not reporting anything beyond the latest happening. A number of local reporters and editors agreed that the majority of their articles reacted to events and that they did not often initiate their own articles. One reporter said he did self-initiated stores about six times a year, while another said about two or three stories a year, primarily wrapups on where things stood (Kirkpatrick, personal communcation, July 21, 1983). Another noted: "I share some of the day-to-day boredom with TMI. I don't go out of way to generate story ideas. I've never sensed any concerns from my editors about it. In-depth stories about the cleanup haven't interested me, and no one's pushed me on it" (Myers, personal communication, May 11, 1983). By contrast, another reporter declared, "We've got a good track record. We explained Unit 1 repairs and the treated water. We didn't wait for an incident. We tried to step backward and explain the situation" (Kozak & Eyerly, personal communication, May 4, 1983).

Charting the number of TMI articles printed each month for each newspaper confirmed an event-oriented coverage pattern. For almost every coverage peak, a corresponding event could be identified. This type of reactive reporting, combined with lack of interpretive or investigative coverage, does not speak well for the quality of *overall* TMI local coverage during 1981-1982 (not to be confused with the quality of hard news reporting). With all the many points at issue at TMI during this period, such inadequate coverage could confuse readers, perhaps misleading them, given the complexity of issues such as whether the cleanup was proceeding safely and whether the undamaged reactor should be started. It was hard enough for readers to understand just one aspect of the TMI story, let alone all the issues involved, unless such complex information was put into perspective. These reporting deficiencies occurred even though they had been roundly criticized in the accident coverage by the President's TMI Public Information Task Force.

Some reasons that editors gave for this lack of in-depth reporting included size of the reporting staff, little direct access to TMI technical personnel, and sources' inclinations to take major stories to the national media. According to the editors, another important factor was concern that their audience would not take the time to read long, involved interpretive stories. Consequently, they did not assign many of them.

Half of the news personnel felt that local TMI coverage had improved since the accident because it was more evenhanded, consistent, technically better, more sophisticated, and quoted more diverse sources. On the other hand, some felt their colleagues were relying too much on the wire services or blanket press releases without delving into issues or checking things out.

Press sources were split on whether the local coverage had improved. Those who felt it had gotten better credited increased coverage plus more knowledgeable reporters. But even these people had reservations. "Quality has improved," said one, "but not markedly. They are still heavily reliant on sources. But they are no longer befuddled by some technical words" (Sholly, personal communction, June 13, 1983).

Despite the problems with in-depth coverage and event orientation, most press sources agreed that the local newspapers did a far better overall job on TMI than did most of the national media, including such newspapers as the *New York Times*, the *Washington Post*, and the *Philadelphia Inquirer*. The sources said was this was because the local reporters lived with the TMI story every day and had more general knowledge and background about the issues involved. "The national media blow in and out and make no effort to keep track of what's happening," said one GPU Nuclear communications official (Fine, personal communication, April 5, 1983).

Even local news personnel closed ranks in accusing the national media of "hyping" stories, saying the farther away the media were situated from TMI, the more sensational the stories were. Press sources felt that local reporters were more sensitive to regional needs and concerns, particularly concerns over psychological stress caused by fear of another TMI accident. Because there have been no statistical studies of national media coverage of TMI during this time period, data are not available to support or refute these viewpoints.

MEDIA COVERAGE FROM 1983-1987

Not only were studies not done of TMI national media coverage during 1981-1982, but none seem to have been done since that time on TMI coverage, either local or national.

A review of selected issues of the six local newspapers, daily scanning of the *Allentown Morning Call* (a major regional newspaper 70 miles from TMI), and selected newspaper clippings supplied by GPU Nuclear and Three Mile Island Alert (one of the leading anti-TMI groups) during 1983-1987 shows little letup in the amount of detailed coverage of the TMI saga, particularly in the region surrounding the nuclear plant and Eastern Pennsylvania.

Nationally, TMI also did not appear to lose its appeal, although perhaps it was not covered as frequently as it had been immediately following the accident. In 1983, the *New York Times* carried at least 49 articles that dealt primarily with TMI in the headline and lead paragraph. There were many additional stories that mentioned TMI, particularly in comparison to problems at other nuclear plants or in discussions of nuclear power in general. TMI was even discussed in reviews of a book of poems and a photo essay. On television, in addition to reportage on news shows, TMI was featured by "NOVA," the hour-long public broadcasting science program, in *Sixty Minutes to Meltdown*. "NOVA" dramatized the 1979 accident, taking viewers through it step by step, while explaining various technical terms along the way. The program painted a very negative picture of the utility and suggested that its operators could not think through the situation that confronted them at the start of the accident.

Other important stories that made media headlines during 1983 included a suit by GPU Nuclear against Babcock and Wilcox, the builders of the TMI-2 nuclear reactor; whistle blowing on "unsafe" cleanup operations by four TMI engineers; a decision by the U.S. Supreme Court that psychological fear could not be a factor in evaluating restarting Unit 1; considerable questioning by the NRC, state officials and local groups about the ability and integrity of TMI and GPU Nuclear leadership; revelations about falsifications of leakage rates by Met Ed personnel before the accident; the start of a study by former Admiral Hyman Rickover of the integrity of TMI's management; the eventual resignation of the president of GPU Nuclear; and, finally, the NRC urging the limited restart of Unit 1.

The fifth anniversary of the TMI accident drew heavy regional coverage in 1984, with most newspapers putting together three- or five-part retrospectives looking at the accident and what had happened since. Management integrity issues still drew headlines and long, drawn-out hearings on the restart of Unit 1 claimed hundreds of column inches in local newspapers. A number of presidential candidates proclaimed that TMI should be shut down forever, and the Rev. Jesse Jackson even held a demonstration at the site. Class action suits against TMI were settled, protestors at the site were arrested, radioactive fuel was removed from the damaged reactor, and more than 340,000 tourists came to view the site.

In 1985, came the event GPU Nuclear had been working toward since 1979. The NRC gave TMI-1 the go-ahead to restart. However, this was not before a bitter conclusion to the restart hearings in 1984. During these hearings, more than 200 witnesses had been called, 33,000 pages of transcripts generated, and the administrative record grew to more than 100,000 pages. An appeal to the U.S. Third Circuit Court of Appeals stayed restart for a while, and a further appeal by the governor of Pennsylvania and others took TMI once again to the U.S. Supreme Court. In October, the court handed down its decision, and a limited restart operation began.

National and local media chronicled these major events in great detail. There were articles on residents' reactions, on demonstrations, and on every little step or problem in the restart process. Besides this coverage, the *Philadelphia Inquirer* published a three-part series in February, accusing GPU Nuclear of sloppy and unsafe cleanup practices (Detjen & Fitzgerald, 1985a, 1985b, 1985c). On June 6, ABC aired a 3-hour program called "The Fire Unleashed," which included a segment on nuclear power and TMI.

After the momentous year of restart, 1986 was relatively tame in coverage, although local and Eastern Pennsylvania newspapers kept readers up-to-date on

TMI-1 obtaining 100% power in early January, various problems at the plant, progress in the cleanup, health concerns and studies in the region, fines by the NRC, and charges that Admiral Rickover's study was biased because GPU Nuclear contributed money to a fund that Rickover had controlled. Nationally, TMI frequently was mentioned retrospectively, and comparatively, in coverage about the Chernobyl nuclear accident.

In 1987, positive media coverage focused on a report that called TMI's radiation protection program "particularly successful," on the 8-year, $1 billion cleanup of TMI-2, during which more than 160,000 pounds, or 55%, of the debris from the wrecked core had been removed, and on a new 12-month high for GPU common stock. On the negative side, the media reported about "dangerous" design flaws; problems with cooling leaks that forced shutdowns; positive drug tests for 10 employees; allegations of on-the-job sleeping by reactor staff; attempts to stop a train loaded with radioactive waste from TMI from crossing St. Louis; and a study that showed that citizens in the region still suffered from above-normal stress due to the accident. A major controversy, heavily covered by the local media, centered on citizens' objections to GPU Nuclear's plan to evaporate 2.1 million gallons of radioactive water left from the accident and cleanup acitivities.

COMMENTARY ON LATER TMI MEDIA COVERAGE

Although no formal studies have been done of the later TMI media coverage, there have been some articles about it, as well as a number of statements made by journalists.

In a 1983 article on page 1 of the *Wall Street Journal* entitled, "High-Technology Age Causes New Problems in Coverage by Media," the subhead read "Press Becomes a Big Factor in the Continuing Fight Over Three Mile Island" (Machalaba, 1983.). According to this article, reporting on TMI was especially difficult because each side had its own experts bolstering its arguments, particularly on the restart issue. The executive editor of the Harrisburg newspapers claimed he was caught "in a cross fire of conflicting claims and scientific evidence as utility officials attempt to assuage public fears and debunk their opponents' claims that operating the plant is dangerous" (p. 1). Said one journalist, "A reporter trying to walk the median line is hard-pressed to get accurate information not colored in some way" (p. 15). Digesting and conveying complex information was another problem. One television reporter told the *Wall Street Journal* that GPU officials "show you charts, all of that stuff, but it's very hard to condense so a guy at home drinking beer and eating spaghetti can understand" (p. 15).

In 1984, Hodding Carter, host of PBS' "Inside Story," was reported to have said of TMI coverage during a broadcast on "Nuclear Power and the Press:"

5. TMI: THE MEDIA STORY THAT WILL NOT DIE

> The accident at Three Mile Island put the news media on notice: nuclear power was more than an occasional story. Five years later, reporters know more about nuclear technology, and editors are more aware of the importance of covering nuclear power. But there are still too few news organizations willing to put the time and resources into understanding and then explaining the baffling, complex subject of nuclear energy. (Notes On, 1984, p. 5)

Many other comments on the coverage of nuclear power and TMI appeared in *AIF Press Info*, a newsletter published by the Atomic Industrial Forum, a major trade association for the nuclear industry. In a frequently published section called "Notes on the Press—By the Press," the newsletter's editors reprinted short excerpts of articles, editorials, and other publications mostly favorable to nuclear power and often critical of various press actions. As an example, the October 1985 issue had excerpts from the *Wall Street Journal, Barrons,* and the *Macon* (GA) *Telegraph and News* that respectively talked about antinuclear hysteria and its connection to media coverage, the handling of TMI-1's startup by the media being fairer than most previous media coverage, and why media coverage led people to rate risks related to nuclear power plants very high (Notes On, October, 1985b, pp. 4-5).

Criticism of media coverage also found its way into many letters to editors and news directors sent out by GPU Nuclear officials. They mounted an aggressive campaign to attack coverage they thought was unfair, inaccurate, or incomplete. In December 1982, GPU Nuclear complained to CBS about a broadcast on the morning news by Jane Wallace that labeled the area around the plant "radiation alley" and presented what a utility official called "farfetched claims" about the effects of TMI on animals "that have been extensively rebutted" (Gifford, January 17, 1983).

GPU Nuclear officials sent other letters of complaint about media coverage in 1981 to the *Elizabethtown* (PA) *Chronicle*, the *Lancaster Sunday News*, WGAL-TV, WHTM-TV, the *Philadelphia Daily News*, the *Philadelphia Bulletin*, the *Philadelphia Inquirer*, United Press International, and the *Harrisburg Patriot-News*. In 1982, the *Inquirer*, the *Patriot-News*, the *Lancaster Intelligencer-Journal*, the *Latrobe* (PA) *Bulletin*, the *York Daily Record*, WHP Radio, the *Middletown Press and Journal*, the *National Journal*, the *Roseburg* (OR) *News-Review*, the *Reading Eagle*, and the *Pennsylvania Beacon* all heard from GPU Nuclear about some aspect of their TMI coverage. In 1983, the *Bulletin of the Atomic Scientists*, *Bryn Mawr Now*, the *New York Times*, the *Wall Street Journal*, and the *Inquirer* and *Patriot-News* received letters of complaint from GPU Nuclear's communications officials.

GPU Nuclear and the Atomic Industrial Forum were not alone in their criticism of some media coverage. Others criticized it as well. Academicans, private citizens, and even media personnel also had complaints. A 1982 study claimed that key science journalists were far more skeptical of nuclear energy than scientists. This was especially true of science journalists at major national media outlets including the television networks, the *New York Times*, and the *Washington Post*. The authors of the study also found that leading journalists who were not science writers but who reported for the prestige press were less supportive of nuclear power than the science journalists. The authors implied that these negative views influenced the reporters' nuclear power coverage (Rothman & Lichter, 1982, p. 51).

Many citizens also were not pleased. Relative to the TMI story, a high school teacher told the *Wall Street Journal*, "If you are looking for perspective, the media aren't the place to go" (Machalaba, 1983, p. 15). Disagreeing with TMI reporting, one local resident said, "The media are presenting the issues on a subjective basis, that is their personal views—and relinquishing their responsibility and accountability to the public interest at the expense of the public's health, safety, and best interest in violation of their responsibility to the First Amendment" (anonymous, Personal Communication, October 15, 1985).

Writing in a 1983 column, Robert Giles, editor of the *Rochester Times-Union* and the *Democrat and Chronicle*, questioned how four major news services covering a press conference on the first televised look at TMI's damaged nuclear core could come up with such different views. As Giles (1982, p. 21) wrote, the key element was whether the nuclear fuel had melted. The leads from the four news services he quoted were:

> AP: A camera lowered into the crippled Three Mile Island reactor revealed severe damage to the top of the nuclear core, but found no evidence that fuel had melted, officials said today.... However, they said, the television camera showed no visible damage to internal components above the reactor fuel and no indication that the core melted during the accident.
>
> UPI: Officials at Three Mile Island said today a camera inspection confirms a partial meltdown occurred in the March 1979 accident at the nuclear plant.
>
> *New York Times*: A camera lowered into the reactor of the damaged Three Mile Island nuclear power station showed that the center of the reactor core was shattered, with the top of it lying in a "bed of rubble." But officials of the company that owns the reactor said today that there was no indication that the nuclear fuel had melted.... William Hamilton, one of the scores of technicians here for the television examination, said at a news conference that there was no evidence of melting.
>
> *Los Angeles Times/Washington Post:* Scientists...concluded that an almost complete meltdown had taken place in the center of the core. William Hamilton, head of the technology assessment and advisory group that planned the inspection, said the two-hour look at the central region of the core showed that "uranium oxide fuel had melted." (Giles, January 29, 1982, p. 21)

How the different leads came about was explained in a letter from a GPU Nuclear official to Giles. According to the official, the reporter from the *Washington Post* had been unwilling to wait for a full-scale briefing GPU Nuclear had scheduled for the morning after the television inspection. Instead, the reporter called William Hamilton, chairman of the Technical Assistance and Advisory Group for TMI-2, and "obtained comments on the core damage that he apparently misunderstood." GPU Nuclear said the report of an "almost complete meltdown" originated in the *Post* and was picked up by UPI. The Associated Press and the *New York Times* stories were accurate (Bedell, 1983).

Two major 1985 coverage pieces, the *Philadelphia Inquirer* series and ABC's "The Fire Unleashed," also drew great criticism. GPU Nuclear was so upset about the *Inquirer* series that it spent $95,000 on double full-page ads in the *Inquirer* and 10 other Pennsylvania newspapers to refute specific points ("GPU Replies," 1985).

This battle was particularly heated, partially because the utility and the *Inquirer* bumped heads over TMI coverage. The *Inquirer* had won a Pulitzer Prize for its coverage of the TMI accident and had followed later events at TMI very closely. According to a notice about the series, two reporters had worked 21 months on it, interviewing 225 TMI workers, scientists, and government regulators. They reported that hundreds of workers had been contaminated needlessly by radioactive particles and that the Nuclear Regulatory Commission had predicted two to six workers would die of exposure to radiation during the cleanup. Using the Freedom of Information Act, they gained access to radiation and inspection records kept by the NRC "after the government and GPU Nuclear refused to cooperate" (The Right Words, 1986).

On Sunday, February 10, the series began:

> Six years after the nation's worst nuclear power accident, tons of deadly radioactive debris still contaminate Three Mile Island. For cleanup workers, contact with radiation is still a constant peril. A 21-month investigation by The *Inquirer* shows that for TMI workers facing the dangers of contamination and the long-term threat of cancer, the March 1979 accident has never really ended. (Detjen & Fitzgerald, 1985a, p. 1A)

First-day headlines included: "The lethal legacy inside TMI; From worker's clothes to their bodies, nothing is immune from contamination in the cleanup; Uncertainties about radiation's dangers; Federal inspectors have found 60 instances of lapses in radiation protection since the cleanup began; The krypton gas has been vented, but tons of radioactive debris still contaminate the plant." The first day's coverage, with illustrations, occupied about four and one-half pages (Detjen & Fitzgerald, 1985a).

On the second day, headlines read: "At the crippled plant, workers face invisible dangers; They're 'the grunts' of the cleanup job, called upon to scrub and hose away the radioactive debris; Without a registry of cleanup workers, little will be learned of the radiation's long-term effects; He refused to give up his respirator, and he was fired." Two and one-half pages of coverage was devoted to part two (Detjen & Fitzgerald, 1985b).

Part three included these headlines: "TMI critics who paid a price; The former Navy engineer saw a pattern: In job after job, he says, safety rules were disregarded; Over and over again, Gischel's bosses asked that he submit to psychological testing to keep his position." Again two and one-half pages were devoted to the coverage (Detjen & Fitzgerald, 1985c).

The series won acclaim from some. It received the Edward J. Meeman Award, one of the Scripps Howard Foundation National Journalism Awards in 1986. This award is given "to encourage newspapermen and newspaperwomen to help educate the public and public officials to a better understanding of conservation" (The Right Words, 1986).

GPU Nuclear's double-page ad against the series was headlined: "The Inquirer gave you its view of TMI in 30,000 words—Here's some of what was left out." It charged that from the beginning the *Inquirer*'s editors and reporters were "not looking for evidence that might suggest the cleanup was progressing, or that the workers and management were doing a good job under difficult circumstances." The ad accused the *Inquirer* of misrepresentation and leaving out "big chunks of factual information, all of which was available," while "reaching into the farthest fringes of scientific opinion." It took the series to task on 12 specifics, one of which was that the experts quoted by the *Inquirer* had little credibility among the majority of radiation scientists ("The Inquirer Gave," 1985, pp. 10-11A).

On another front, most of the nuclear industry and many television critics joined GPU Nuclear in protesting ABC's "The Fire Unleashed." This June 6 ABC "Closeup" focused on the unleashed power of the atom in four separate areas: nuclear proliferation, nuclear power, nuclear waste, and nuclear weapons. Although an ABC advertisement in San Francisco quoted *Newsday* as calling it, "...the most important documentary of the year," the Atomic Industrial Forum's newsletter reported in its June issue that the documentary drew mixed reviews.

Printing brief excerpts from several reviews, the newsletter quoted the Associated Press' TV critic who wrote:

> Nearly one-third of the segment devoted to atomic power is taken up by the claims of people who live near the Three Mile Island plant in Pennsylvania that the March 1979 accident has caused widespread incidences of cancer and genetic mutations. People shunned by such mainline antinuclear groups as the Union of Concerned Scientists get an ABC platform for stories of milk-dry cows, giant dandelions, a spastic cat and informal surveys of neighbors reportedly stricken by TMI-caused cancers. Years of research by the Nuclear Regulatory Commission, the federal Centers for Disease Control in Atlanta and the Pennsylvania Department of Health—all finding no link between the accident and cancer figures in central Pennsylvania—are dismissed as "official disclaimers." (ABC Nuclear, 1985, pp. 2-4)

The July *AIF Press Info* detailed official AIF and GPU Nuclear protests. "The Fire Unleashed" landed at the bottom of the ratings and fared poorly at the hands of the major critics, a "richly deserved" fate, according to AIF Vice President for Public Affairs Paul Turner (AIF, GPU, Protest, 1985). Saying that it was "panned by reviewers" for the *Wall Street Journal, New York Times*, and Associated Press, the newsletter printed four more brief excerpts about the show. Among them were:

> "The Fire Unleashed" was high drama with its eerie music and ominous photography. But it was lousy science and still lousier journalism, reported the *Richmond Times-Dispatch*.
>
> The show comes out sounding like a one-sided attack on nuclear energy. Though described as a "documentary," it treads close to advocacy, said the environmental writer for the *Chicago Tribune*. (AIF, GPU Protest and Notes On, 1985, p. 6)

And so the disagreements over media coverage of TMI and nuclear power in general continue. The media story, if not the accident, seems without an end. Local and national media have become key participants in both the Three Mile Island story and the general debate over the safety of nuclear power. As noted by GPU Nuclear's chief spokesman, "the future of this technology is wrapped up in the way in which the media report and the public perceive it" (Machalaba, 1983, p. 1).

CONCLUSIONS

In some ways, the recent coverage of Three Mile Island provides some grounds for optimism. Local media outlets particularly appear to have recovered from some of the initial media mistakes in the TMI story. Although few truly prepared reporters now cover the plant, the nuclear industry and TMI in particular have been the subjects of significantly increased coverage. The local media are doing a better, and a more thorough job, of reporting on the plant. TMI is a story that, appropriately, will not, and should not, die. It continues to teach the world an important lesson—that recovery from a nuclear accident is a drawn-out and expensive process. It is a story of struggle: struggle for a utility's survival, for new methods to clean heavily contaminated buildings and for a community's adjustment to perceived and real danger within its midst.

On another level, however, there is somewhat less ground for optimism. Coverage improvement has been spotty and national outlets, arguably able to employ more sophisticated reporters, remain capable of making mistakes or omissions. A recent study of coverage by 5 U.S. prestige newspapers and major networks of the Chernobyl accident found that these organizations did not provide enough radiation or risk information for their readers and viewers (Friedman,

1987). Further, the chasm between the worlds of the scientist/engineer and the journalists still looms, although it is not as deep or as wide as it was in 1979. Although the nuclear industry has made major efforts to train key technical and information employees on how to deal with journalists, the media, unfortunately, have not encouraged training for new and inexperienced reporters on nuclear power technologies or issues.

So, although it could be argued that coverage of Three Mile Island and nuclear power is better today than it was 8 years ago, the improvement may not be enough for the media to credibly perform their role as watchdog of the public safety regarding nuclear power. This is particularly true for smaller media outlets located near nuclear facilities. Based on what has happened to TMI coverage over time, it is probable that when another serious nuclear accident occurs in the United States, on-going events will be reported in an improved fashion, but in-depth analytical and explanatory coverage will once again be lacking, leaving readers without the perspective they need to judge their long-term risk and the overall safety of nuclear power.

ACKNOWLEDGMENT

Parts of this chapter first appeared in A case of benign neglect: Coverage of Three Mile Island before the accident, in S.M. Friedman, S. Dunwoody, & C.L. Rogers (Eds.), *Scientists and journalists: Reporting science as news* and are reprinted with the permission of the American Association for the Advancement of Science.

NOTES

[1] As a member of the President's Public Information Task Force, I studied the plans and activities of Met Ed and the regional media before the accident. As a consequence, they are described in more detail than information on pre-accident activities by the national media and the NRC.

[2] Articles from the *Harrisburg Patriot and Evening News* were from 1978 to March 1979. Those from the *Middletown Press and Journal, Lancaster Intelligencer-Journal, York Daily Record,* and *York Dispatch* were from 1976 to 1978. These were subpoenaed Met Ed files, which may have been incomplete. There were no files for the *Lancaster New Era* or *Sunday News*. The short time span for the 1979 study precluded reviewing clippings from all but the Harrisburg newspapers in library files

[3] Most of the information I describe about the accident is taken from the 13-page summary of the TMI Public Information Task Force report. Task force findings are presented here in the broadest terms, omitting many caveats and qualifiers

in the written report. Another review of the accident media events based on the task force summary is Cunningham (1986).

[4]The six newspapers studied for 1981-1982 were the *Harrisburg Patriot, Harrisburg Evening News, Lancaster New Era, Lancaster Intelligencer-Journal, York Daily Record,* and *York Dispatch.* Early in 1984 the *Patriot* and the *Evening News* merged. They were treated in the study as they appeared in 1981-1982, as separate entities. The weekly *Middletown Press and Journal*, which was included in the 1979 study, was not included in the 1981-1982 study due to its small circulation and its perceived lack of influence in the community.

6
Preventive Journalism and AIDS Editorials: *Dilemmas for Private and Public Health*

Gene Burd
University of Texas at Austin

How the press assigns personal and public responsibility for social problems and how it suggests such problems be solved provides clues to press responsibility in society. Preventive journalism has been suggested as a means to solve problems and prevent crises before they develop (Burd, 1978). The former editor of the *New York Daily News*, Mike O'Neil, said, "We need to put more emphasis on what I call preventive journalism—deliberately searching for the underlying social currents that threaten future danger so that public policy can be more intelligently mobilized" (Keir, McCombs, & Shaw, 1986, p. 7).

For those responsible to "avert these catastrophic dangers," there is "clear and present need for a positive politics of preventative therapy" that can be used by "policy advisers and decision-makers" (Lerner, 1980, p. 392). For individuals making decisions, "The recipient of a therapeutic journalistic effort will find in it *counsel* and information. As for *diagnosis*, the reader will be helped to recognize when a recommended action is appropriate for himself or for others" (Joslyn-Scherer, 1980, pp. 72-73).

It seems understandable why preventive journalism has been tied to the analogy, metaphor, and practices of health and the suggestion that communication functions operate on levels like the health-care system (Burd, 1980). In the latter, the first level is called one of primary prevention. This is where we remove a hazard that may impinge upon that client's safety and well-being. For example, if we view a disease condition as growing out of the interaction of man and environment, as we do in the field of epidemiology, then we must intervene in that interaction to change it from one of negative to positive valence. (Josylyn-Scherer, 1980, pp. 72-73)

Traditionally, working journalists have been assigned the task of reporting and revealing issues and problems, whereas editorial writers are providing persuasion and points of view toward a solution. "As reporters, we've been taught answers are what publishers write in the editorial pages" (Jackson, 1977, p. A4-5). Because editorials are designed to persuade and often appear at the peak of priorities and public issues, they seem a logical place to examine advice, counsel, and proposed solutions to remedy problems and prevent future ones. Because the notion of preventive journalism has been examined on how a newspaper *reports* about health and nutrition, the next step would be to examine how newspaper editorials *recommend* action to prevent disease (Burd, 1981).

NEWS COVERAGE OF THE CAUSES OF AIDS

Between 1981 and mid-1986, more than 11,000 Americans, mostly male homosexuals, died of Acquired Immune Deficiency Syndrome (AIDS). Medical experts reported public health efforts had failed to stop the spread of the disease, which is transmitted by a virus exchanged in body fluids such as blood and semen during anal and vaginal sexual activity and during the sharing of needles among drug addicts (Vaughan, 1986, p. A5).

Many medical authorities warned against any delay getting information to the public. According to Dr. June E. Osborn, dean of the University of Michigan School of Public Health, public officials were not acting fast enough to warn potential AIDS victims and to give them explicit, practical instructions on how to lessen their risks (Eckholm, 1986). "It's amazing how much ignorance is still out there," said Jeffrey Levi of the National Gay Task Force. Press reports cited the most important task as making "more detailed information about risky behaviors swiftly available" (Eckholm, 1986, pp. 19-20). Dr. Peter Mansell, of M.D. Anderson Hospital and Tumor Institute in Houston, Texas, said, "There's a tremendous public reaction against things that need to be talked about openly and plainly," because half the 20,300 people with AIDS are not changing their sexual behavior and thousands more carry the virus and millions are expected to contract it (Vaughan, 1986, p. A5). This is unfortunate, because AIDS is "essentially preventable, not by medical means as yet, but by changing how people behave," according to Mathilde Krim, board chair of the American Foundation for AIDS Research and former head of the interferon lab at the Sloan-Kettering Institute for Cancer Research (AIDS: What is, 1985, p. 44).

There has been some debate on how specific the mass media should be in discussing graphic details on the apparent causes of AIDS, which might be used as preventive advice to stop its spread. In mid-1983, Arthur Kaplan of the Hastings Institute noted the media's "mincing of words" on actually what goes on during the transmission of the virus. He suggested that explicit description was more relevant in reporting than terms like sexual "intimacy" and "close contact" (Nightline, 1983). At about the same time, homosexual leaders in California were accused of a "conspiracy of silence" because they obscured vital information on how the disease is spread, including omission of reference in educational pamphlets on the role of anal sex (Collier & Horowitz, 1983, p. 54).

Although the mass media have been warned that negative news hampers public education about AIDS (Stein, 1985, pp. 16-17) and have been accused of irresponsible sensationalism (Streitmatter, 1984, pp. 22-26), "perhaps the most common problem is a squeamish lack of specificity" and omission of reference to "breakage of rectal lining through anal sex" which is "probably how the vast majority of the cases have been transmitted" (Alter, 1985, p. 25). The mass media have hidden behind polite euphemisms like "intimate sexual contact" and "exchange of body fluids" whereas smaller, special audience publications have been more graphic. For example, *The Whole Earth Review* in the fall of 1985 published a detailed list of "safe," "possibly," and "unsafe" sex practices. Compiled by Bay Area physicians, these included a warning against oral sex, anal intercourse, and use of sex toys (Herron, 1985, pp. 34-53).

A less sympathetic, but also specific reference, to prevention of AIDS appeared in *The National Review*, which reported that, "The main method seems to be anal intercourse, a primary mode of homosexual conduct: The walls of the anus are delicate and easily broken, allowing infection to occur" (Sobran, 1986, pp. 22-26+). Although the *New York Times* magazine mentioned the likelihood of AIDS transmission by oral–anal contact in 1983, "it wasn't until comparatively recently that the words 'anal intercourse' made their way into general news stories or editorials" (Stokes, 1985). One reason for this inclusion, suggested by ABC Medical News Editor Dr. Tim Johnson, was the widespread coverage and details on President Reagan's rectum when "full disclosure was needed to forestall an undue social or political reaction" (Stokes, 1985).

In terms of media responsibility, one suggestion is that, "reporting of AIDS and other health hazards will come of age when such grown-up materials can be presented in depth and with care on the evening newscasts" (Diamond, 1983, p. 8). Another is that newspaper obituaries should tell the public who is dying of AIDS. "It might encourage more people at risk not to go on courting death. A good scare might be beneficial" (Sanford, 1985, p. 18).

EDITORIALS ON PREVENTING AIDS

High standards of editorial writing often have been identified with calling attention to problems and taking positions to solve them or prevent them from occurring in the future. A good editorial, we are told, does not just view with alarm or point with pride or direct attention to a problem's existence. Instead, a good editorial makes a point clearly, providing facts and arguments in its support (MacDougall, 1973, pp. xii, 28).

Methodology

To examine editorials on AIDS in the 5-year period since the disease was first discovered in mid-1981, this study used *Editorials on File*, an illustrative, but not necessarily representative, sample from U.S. newspapers.[1] Editorials in the file are selected from 122 U.S. newspapers with a total daily circulation of 27,895,000—more than 45% of the total daily U.S. newspaper circulation. Thirteen Canadian newspapers are included in the database but are not included in this study (see Table 6.1).

The major question asked was *whether the editorials provided advice and information to prevent the transmission and contraction of AIDS*. To make that assessment, the editorials were evaluated using a composite criteria of qualities and criticisms adapted from Edelstein's (1956) model, Kreighbaum's (1956) synopsis of problems with editorial writing, Maury and Pfeiffer's (1960) advice on how not to write an editorial, Goldschen's (1965) list of editorial writing virtues, and Burd's (1983) application of the technique in evaluating editorials on government policy.

A composite yardstick was abstracted from those sources into three tests of editorial quality in preventive journalism on AIDS:

1. *Origin, Timing, Quality, Volume, Perspective, Position, Range, and Selectivity.* (Was there reasoned response in number, space, frequency, and time relative to public opinion? Were significant positions taken on news, both controversial and silent issues? What were news pegs, dates, and publications?)

2. *Defense of Position, Truth, Clarity, Accuracy, Persuasion, Logic, Judgment* (Were the arguments factual, consistent, convincing, fair, relevant, with specific preventive advice to solve the problem posed and the position taken?).

3. *Style, Tone, Self-Interest, Partisan* (Were evasive, provincial, self-righteous, scolding or courageous, unpopular positions taken? Were editorials pontifical, ambiguous, bland and dreary, bookish? Did they point with pride or cry without suggesting an answer to the problem posed?)

Editorials provide a chance for giving advice to prevent crisis at the peak of alarm and persuasion. In this case, specific information on the cause and preven-

TABLE 6.1
United States and Canadian Newspapers
Represented in Editorials on File

Akron (Ohio) Beacon Journal (164,000)
Albany (N.Y.) Knickerbocker News (42,000)
Albuquerque (N.M.) Journal (90,000)
Anchorage (Alaska) Daily News (47,000)
Anchorage (Alaska) Times (45,000)
[a]Ann Arbor (Mich.) News (46,000)
[a]Atlanta (Ga.) Constitution (211,000)
[a]Augusta (Ga.) Chronicle (59,000)
Baltimore (Md.) Afro-American (20,000)
[a]Baltimore (Md.) News American (137,000)
[a]Baltimore (Md.) Sun (183,000)
Billings (Mont.) Gazette (62,000)
Biloxi (Miss.) Daily Herald (39,000)
[a]Birmingham (Ala.) News (164,000)
[a]Birmingham (Ala.) Post-Herald (66,000)
Bismark (N.D.) Tribune (29,000)
(Boise) Idaho Statesman (57,000)
[a]Boston (Mass.) Globe (511,000)
Boston (Mass.) Herald (228,000)
[a]Buffalo (N.Y.) News (331,000)
Burlington (Vt) Free Press (51,000)
Casper (Wyo.) Star-Tribune (39,000)
[a]Charleston (S.C.) News & Courier and Evening Post (107,000 comb.)
Charleston (W. Va.) Gazette (54,000)
Charlotte (N.C.) Observer (172,000)
Chattanooga (Tenn.) Times (46,000)
Chicago (Ill.) Defender (15,000)
Chicago (Ill.) Sun-Times (652,000)
Chicago (Ill.) Tribune (758,000)
Christian Science Monitor (Mass.) (145,000)
[a]Cincinnati (Ohio) Post (143,000)
[a]Cleveland (Ohio) Plain Dealer (458,000)
[a]Columbia (S.C.) State (108,000)
Columbus (Ohio) Dispatch (204,000)
El Sol de Texas (Dallas) (125,000)
[a]Dallas (Texas) Morning News (317,000)
Dallas (Texas) Times Herald (269,000)

Dayton (Ohio) Daily News (125,000)
Denver (Colo.) Post (256,000)
Denver (Colo.) Rocky Mountain News (322,000)
Des Moines (Iowa) Register (266,000)
Detroit (Mich.) Free Press (632,000)
Detroit (Mich.) News (643,000)
Edmonton (Alta. Canada) Journal (173,000)
Emporia (Kans.) Gazette (11,000)
Fall River (Mass.) Herald-News (40,000)
Fargo (N.D.) Forum (56,000)
Fort Worth (Texas) Sar-Telegram (103,000)
Gary (Ind.) Post-Tribune (79,000)
Grand Rapids (Mich.) Press (132,000)
[a]Hackensack (N.J.) Record (146,000)
Halifax (N.S., Canada) Chronicle-Herald and Mail Star (75,000 comb.)
[a]Hartford (Conn.) Courant (214,000)
Honolulu (Hawaii) Advertiser (83,000)
Houston (Texas) Post (376,000)
Hutchinson (Kans.) News (44,000)
Indianapolis (Ind.) News and Star (362,000 comb.)
[a]Kansas City (Mo.) Star and Times (526,000 comb.)
[a]Las Vegas (Nev.) Review-Journal (98,000)
Lexington (Ky.) Herald-Leader (103,000)
[a]Lincoln (Neb.) Star and Journal (78,000 comb.)
(Little Rock) Arkansas Democrat (68,000)
(Little Rock) Arkansas Gazette (128,000)
London (Ont. Canada) Free Press (125,000)
[a]Los Angeles (Cal.) Times (1,053,000)
[a]Manchester (N.H.) Union Leader (67,000)
Memphis (Tenn.) Commercial

(Continued)

TABLE 6.1 – Continued

[a]Miami (Fla.) Herald (417,000)
[a]Milwaukee (Wisc.) Journal (307,000)
Minneapolis (Minn.) Star and Tribune (363,000)
Montreal (Que. Canada) Le Devoir (35,000)
Montreal (Que., Canada) La Presse (1982,000)
[a](Nashville) Tennessean (125,000)
[a]Newark (N.J.) Star-Ledger (424,000)
New Orleans (L.A.) States-Item and Times-Picayune (278,000 comb.)
Newsday (N.Y.) (516,000)
[a]New York Daily News (1,544,000)
New York Post (960,000)
Norfolk (Va.) Virginia-Pilot (136,000)
[a]Oklahoma City (Okla.) Times and Oklahoman (270,000 comb.)
Orlando (Fla.) Sentinel (208,000)
Ottawa Citizen (Ont. Canada) (179,000)
Philadelphia (Pa.) Inquirer (561,000)
(Phoenix) Arizona Republic (264,000)
[a]Pittsburgh (Pa.) Post-Gazette (182,000)
[a]Pittsburgh (Pa.) Press (260,000)
[a]Portland (Me.) Evening Express and Press Herald (90,000 comb.)
[a]Portland (Ore.) Oregonian (308,000)
[a]Providence (R.I.) Journal (84,000)
Quebec (Que., Canada) Le Soleil (119,000)
Rapid City (S.D.) Journal (33,000)
Reno (Nev.) Evening Gazette and Nevada State Journal (57,000 comb.)
[a]Richmond (Va.) News-Leader and Times-Dispatch (1248,000 comb.)
Roanoke (Va.) Times & World News (71,000)
Rochester (N.Y.) Democrat & Chronicle (133,000)
Rockford (Ill.) Register Star (75,000)
[a]Sacramento (Cal.) Bee (220,000)
[a]Saginaw (Mich.) News (56,000)
St. John's (Nfld. Canada) Evening Telegram (34,000)
St. Louis (Mo.) Globe-Democrat (261,000)
[a]St. Louis (Mo.) Post-Dispatch (236,000)
St. Louis (Mo.) Review (98,000)
[a]St. Paul (Minn.) Pioneer Press (104,000)
St. Petersburg (Fla.) Times (247,000)
[a]Salt Lake City (Utah) Deseret News (70,000)
[a]Salt Lake City (Utah) Tribune (112,000)
[a]San Diego (Cal.) Union (217,000)
[a]San Francisco (Cal.) Chronicle (538,000)
San Francisco (Cal.) Sun Reporter (9,000)
San Jose (Cal.) Mercury and News (228,000 comb.)
Santa Ana (Cal.) Register (253,000)
[a]Seattle (Wash.) Times (254,000)
[a]Sioux Falls (S.D.) Argus-Leader (43,000)
Springfield (Mass.) Union (71,000)
Syracuse (N.Y.) Herald-Journal (106,000)
Tampa (Fla.) Tribune (191,000)
Toledo (Ohio) Blade (163,000)
Topeka (Kans.) Capital Journal (69,000)
Toronto (Ont., Canada) Globe & Mail (330,000)
Toronto (Ont., Canada) Star (486,000)
Tulsa (Okla.) World (130,000)
Vancouver (B.C., Canada) Province (132,000)
Vancouver (B.C., Canada) Sun (228,000)
Victoria (B.C., Canada) Times-Colonist (76,000)
Wall Street Journal (N.Y.) (1,926,000)
Washington (D.C.) Post (726,000)
[a]Washington (D.C.) Times (86,000)
Wichita (Kans.) Eagle-Beacon (122,000)
Wilmington (Del.) Morning News and

(Continued)

TABLE 6.1 — Continued

News Journal (117,000 comb.) Winnipeg (Man. Canada) Free Press (178,000)	Winston-Salem (N.C.) Journal (72,000) [a]Worchester (Mass.) Evening Gazette and Telegram (143,000 comb.)

Note: The total daily circulation of the U.S. newspapers from which editorials are selected is over 27,895,000 — over 45% of the total daily newspaper circulation in the United States. The combined daily circulation of the Canadian newspapers used in Editorials on File is over 2,340,000 — over 44% of the total dialy newspaper circulation in Canada.

[a]Carried AIDS Editorial, April 25, 1984-November 29, 1986

tion of AIDS was searched for in editorials, although news on AIDS can provide preventive information. An effort was made to cull evidence of any editorial advice urging any changes in social and sexual behavior, which are tied to the *acquired* aspect of AIDS. In addition, the editorials were examined to see if they dealt with preventative measures and causes in a more specific physical and scientific manner.

An effort was also made to assess the balance between personal and social rights and responsibility and between rational/scientific arguments as opposed to emotional/social persuasion. The editorials were also examined for their balance between public and private aspects of health, and the wider, larger issues involving minorities, discrimination, jobs, medical benefits, and the nature of public awareness and response (see Table 6.2).

Discussion/Conclusions

In the 5-year period of 1981-1986, there were 66 editorials in newspapers in 51 U.S. cities. Thirty-six newspapers had one editorial each; 14 had two, and 1 had three. All editorials appeared in cities over 100,000 population except for 10 below that, with a town of 60,000 the smallest in the sample. The largest circulation daily was the *New York Daily News* and the smallest were the Sioux Falls (SD) *Argus-Leader* (43,000) and the Ann Arbor (MI) *News* (46,000). A wide geographic area was covered, including large and small cities, urban and rural regions, including most of the affected and infected cities (except Chicago, which is one large U.S. city without a typical big city epidemic of AIDS).

TABLE 6.2
Analysis of Editorials on AIDS 1984-85; Findings

Date/Newspaper	News Peg	Position	AIDS Cause	AIDS Prevention
April 25, 1984 Los Angeles *Times*	Virus is Discovered; HTLV Test	"remarkable progress" to find cause & prevent spread	"Intimate sexual contact"	Vaccine to be created by scientific research
April 25, 1984 Pittsburgh *Post-Gazette*	Virus is Discovered; HTLV Test	Discovery will defuse fears and public hysteria	None given	Vaccine
April 25, 1984 Worcester MS *Evening Gazette*	Virus is Discovered; HTLV Test	Discovery means better life for everyone	Homosexual promiscuity lifestyle is "rhetoric"	Vaccine "in a few years"; test in months
April 25, 1984 Milwaukee *Journal*	Virus is Discovered; HTLV Test	Research brings hope, relief; science "conquers the unknown"	None given	Vaccine "discovery of prevention and treatment" in 2-3 years
April 26, 1984 Cincinnati *Post*	Virus is Discovered; HTLV Test	"significant breakthrough" in research	"associated with homosexual men"	Screening test "is not a cure
April 27, 1984 Hartford *Courant*	Virus is Discovered; HTLV Test	Hopeful news, but AIDS "can neither be cured nor prevented at the present time".	"medical mystery"	Scientists will find "sure means to detect cure and prevent"; educate public; treat, counsel victim caution with risky "sexual behavior".
April 29, 1984 Louisville *Courier-Journal*	Virus is Discovered; HTLV Test	"faith in medical science"; pride in the "solution"; AIDS "crumbling"; research "paid off".	"affects" homosexual/bisexuals; "bodily fluids" i.e. blood	Vaccine, but "long way to go in solving the AIDS puzzle".
April 30, 1984 Baltimore *Sun*	Virus is Discovered; HTLV Test	"better diagnosis, treatment or prevention"	"blood borne" mostly gay males	hypotheses on transmission "none yet proven".

April 30, 1984 Seattle *Times*	Virus is Discovered; HTLV Test	"astonishing skills of medical science" "utterly remarkable"	"identified principally with homosexuals"	Discovery "opens door to a preventive vaccine"
April 30, 1984 Richmond *Times-Dispatch*	Virus is Discovered; HTLV Test	"worth cheering"; "should help end the hysteria on blood transfusions"; race to find cause of disease brings fame, prizes etc.	"mystery disease" has "terrorized (principally) homosexual communities"; virus "probably is guilty".	Vaccine in two years
August 6, 1985 Hartford *Courant*	AIDS spreads	AIDS not curse or punishment for homosexuals' sins; "malfunction of body"; public & govt. should not be judgmental.	Cause "unclear"; most patients homosexuals & drug abusers.	Medicine can cure like leprosy, TB, syphilis; research education.
August 7, 1985 Baltimore *News-American*	Hudson ill; Reagan calls.	Homosexuals and drug addicts are "victims" of AIDS; "pariahs .. lepers" of 1980s.	"mystery disease"	public sympathy; train nurses; homes for victims
August 8, 1985 Portland *Oregonian*	Hudson ill	President should fight "nation's No. 1 health problem" with speech.	Not just homosexuals & dope addicts; now is spreading to heterosexuals	Faster research for a vaccine;
August 17, 1985 Portland, ME *Press-Herald*	AIDS death in state	Need to battle "national health threat".	Virus (no mention of homosexuals *et al*)	Vaccine education, public money for research; "medical responses"

(Continued)

TABLE 6.2—Continued

Date/Newspaper	News Peg	Position	AIDS Cause	AIDS Prevention
August 18, 1985 New York *Daily News*	Epidemic in New York; public fears, problems of victims	Public should not be afraid and should provide care for AIDS victims.	Not discussed other than "the virus".	"cure is nowhere in sight".
August 18, 1985 Oklahoma City *Oklahoman*	Hudson ill	AIDS is threat to general public like past epidemics; no vaccine to prevent it yet.	"no reason for circumspect people to panic" but "can be transmitted to normal heterosexuals and unborn children".	"'could stop this epidemic?' if we stop drug abuse and "stop the exchange of bodily fluids'."
August 20, 1985 Las Vegas *Review-Journal*	Decline in VD rates	Less VD due to herpes and no cure for AIDS	"sexual promiscuity"	Less pre- and extra-marital sex
August 20, 1985 Cleveland *Plain-Dealer*	Indianapolis man with AIDS arrested for theft, given 1-way ticket to Cleveland; police wear masks/gloves	Irrational fears, half-truths, myths, paranoia ignorance re AIDS; Most not need worry.	Blood of drug addicts, hemophiliacs, "exchange of body fluids through certain sexual acts".	"massive informational campaign"; "more public awareness"; more "resources" to find cure; hospital treatment
August 21, 1985 Miami *Herald*	AIDS spreads to general public; job problems and medical cost	Government should provide policy, leadership, research; Keep AIDS test result private; Let victims keep jobs, stay in schools.	"first was closely identified only with homosexual sodomy" and drug needles. AIDS not victim's problem.	No advice other than take test
August 23, 1985 Birmingham *News*	AIDS spreads; no cure yet.	"We are confident that science will eventually find a cure or a control.	"sexual contact"; "one is relatively safe in other normal contacts with carriers."	"the prudent person" should "avoid promiscuity and any avoidable exposure"

94

Date / Paper	Topic	Commentary	Recommendations
August 23, 1985 Ann Arbor *News*	Hudson ill	Alarm about panic, fears, hysteria, ignorance, misinformation, half-truths, backlash against gays.	"very hard to transmit"; AIDS only one of 25 STDs; not divine retribution.	"search for a cure, prevention or treatment"; education; research.
August 25, 1985 Denver *Post*	State to list those with AIDS antibodies	"medically desirable" but "socially unacceptable"; gays would lose jobs, homes, friends, insurance etc. would not take test.	"primarily confined to male homosexuals"; not all with virus get AIDS; test not always reliable.	counseling, treatment, vaccine.
August 25, 1985 Milwaukee *Journal*	Series on AIDS	Provide information to lead to understanding & action.	Spread by "sexual contact", (gay males and bisexuals to female) drug needles and transfusions; such sex not choice of gays or bi-sexuals.	Abstinence "the surest — preventative", monogamy; condoms; tests; vaccine and "safe sex" (no details)
August 27, 1985 Sioux Falls SD *Argus-Leader*	Hudson ill	Must change public idea it's a gay disease; others are in danger.	"body fluids, mainly blood and semen"; Africa AIDS "heterosexual contact" is main transmission; MD says AIDS "somehow" got introduced in gay lifestyle "tends to spread" AIDS.	None, except to prevent public from being lulled into indifference
August 29, 1985 Washington *Times*	Law to ban discrimination for victims of AIDS.	Public needs right to protect self (until vaccine or cure) with "obvious precautions"; gay lobby delays control of epidemic.	No "scientific certainty" on how to avoid its spread.	Vaccine, cure, "unstinting support for research"

(Continued)

TABLE 6.2 – Continued

Date/Newspaper	News Peg	Position	AIDS Cause	AIDS Prevention
September 1, 1985 Hackensack NJ *Record*	AIDS kids in school prohibited	"unreasoning terror" and panic; not much chance children get AIDS in class; unfair to ostracize them as "lepers"	Caught by "sexual contact", "acts", transfusions, drug needles.	None, except AIDS kids in school "risk fatal infections from flu colds, or earaches and harassment.
September 1, 1985 St. Louis *Post-Dispatch*	Kokomo hemophiliac in school with AIDS	Unfounded, unreasonable, hysteria; violates civil rights of ill.	Not caught by casual contact; "disease remains a mystery"	None. "Let us hope" for vaccine as with polio.
September 4, 1985 Nashville *Tennessean*	CDC says AIDS kids should be allowed in school	Public fear of AIDS is a "menace"; threatens privacy and rights of victims	Not spread by "casual contact"; only a few "likely to contract" AIDS.	Stay calm, informed; treat victims "with compassion and not scorn"; a "mysterious disease" "too long ignored" by govt; scientific "cure" "no cure at this time"
September 4, 1985 Birmingham *Post-Herald*	Kokomo hemophiliac kept out of school; CDC rule	Hysteria, fear of public adds to AIDS victim problems; "does not make sense" to treat them as lepers; Not spread by casual contact.	Caused by sexual intercourse and "other intimate contact involving the exchange of body fluids or injections" not normally in a school setting.	

September 9, 1985 Boston *Globe*	Local AIDS victim to attend school	Hysteria, widespread anxiety, misunderstanding, "does not legitimize irrational discrimination"; states that barred AIDS students "should be ashamed"; not spread by casual contact like a cold or measles.	"little understood new virus"; "manifestations of disease are hard for the public to grasp" . . spread mainly by "virus infected semen", blood, needles, transfusions; can be in "body excretions" . . tears, saliva, urine, feces	"all-out research effort"; "full-scale attack"; Reagan paid "little more than lip service. Keep out of school kids who bite, have incontinence or are not toilet trained.
September 9, 1985 Sacramento *Bee*	Kokomo hemopliliac kept out of school; fears of mouth-to-mouth resuscitation.	Easier to catch hysteria than AIDS; officials should "calm fears, not fan them"; painful stigma to keep kids from going to school.	"too much about it is still unkown"; can't get via casual contract, saliva, a sneeze or handshake, but via blood, semen; "the most intimate forms of contact" in "sexual relations", sharing needles.	"common-sense measures and clearing up misconceptions" as so far, cure is "beyond science's ability"; if less fear, greater chance to resist and understand AIDS. (no specifics)
September 9, 1985 Buffalo *Evening News*	Increase in AIDS	Fears of health workers, parents can't be dismissed since risks of transmission remain; must protect both victims and others.	Not spread via casual contact, but found in saliva, tears.	Blood tests; education on "risks facing" homosexuals, drug users; some teaching kids at home; since "no cure is in sight"; research on how transmitted and a cure.

(Continued)

TABLE 6.2–Continued

Date/Newspaper	News Peg	Position	AIDS Cause	AIDS Prevention
September 11, 1985 Seattle *Times*	Queens, NY parents protest AIDS kids in school	"cruel and unreasonable" to restrict "blameless" victims.	"mysterious killer"; "no evidence that AIDS is transmitted through casual contact".	Nothing suggested
September 11, 1985 Newark *Star-Ledger*	Queens, NY protest on AIDS kids in school	"disturbing" and "escalating hysteria that threatens to become epidemic"; "widespread public misperceptions and unfounded rumors that have grossly distorted factual information. . . ."	"complex, medical-social problem"; very little danger getting AIDS by "casual social contact".	None cited; "should be dealt with in a rational manner, based on medical research"; No references to homosexuals or to transmission specifics.
September 11, 1985 Providence *Journal*	Students with AIDS in school	AIDS victims should not be ostracized "untouchables"; not a "societal threat"; "not the black plague" greater risk in an auto, fear, confusion, uncertainty requires "clear heads and reasonable perspective".	"much about it that is not known"; cannot catch it being in presence; must be blood & "sexual contact"; homosexuals not mentioned	Develop vaccine; "only simple precautions need be taken to avoid virtually all danger of developing the disease. None listed

September 15, 1985 St. Petersburg *Times*	AIDS cases ostracized in schools and other places	"cruel", uninformed, unfounded fear, hysteria, misconceptions as "terrifying killer presents numerous social problems."	Spread only through "sexual relations", needles and transfusions, not "casual contact" like sneezes, handshakes, family or treatment; "new cases" "overwhelmingly affect drug abusers and homosexuals".	"some restrictions" on victims like toddler who drools, wear diaper or "exhibit such agressive behavior as biting". (no advice for gays), "calm public panic" with compassion, "medical evidence".
September 15, 1985 Burlington VT *Free Press*	Queens parents school boycott	Not hard to understand why parents upset; precaution should be taken to ensure healthy students do not get AIDS	"Researchers" not yet sure; possibly "transmitted by as yet undiscovered means"; MD say not through "casual contact but homosexual "contact", drug use, transfusion.	Monitor children who share food, drink, bite or have open sores; and whose "body fluids tend to flow freely."
September 15, 1985 New York *Daily News*	Queens boycott by parents fearing AIDS	Reaction of parents was "unjustified", "Mistaken but understandable"; "stop the plague panic before it turns into witch hunt against homosexuals"; "It's not a 'gay disease'".	"happened to break out first among gays"; then spread to heterosexuals via prostitutes and "casual promiscuity"; "tiny danger" kids can pass it on; spread by sexual, not casual, contact; blood, drugs, transfusions.	Fight (AIDS) "in the right places and in the right ways". No suggestions as to exactly how to do it.

(Continued)

TABLE 6.2 – Continued

Date/Newspaper	News Peg	Position	AIDS Cause	AIDS Prevention
September 16, 1985 Manchester *Union-Leader*	AIDS kids and food handlers	Danger posed; concern of parents not hysteria; homosexual activists make AIDS political, rather than medical issue; officials incite, rather than calm fears by "submerging rights of nonafflicted majority to those of the tragically afflicted minority".	Homosexuals	Isolate AIDS victims
September 16, 1985 Kansas City *Star*	NY school attendance by AIDS victims	To ostracize children is "abominable" lack of compassion; "terrified dread", "excessive"	No mention of homosexuals; Much "still unknown", still a mystery for scientists to unravel; not caught by casual contact; kids get it from mothers, and transfusions;	"dumb" and "irrational" not to think of prevention. Society is "clamoring for factual info and we have right to from it; Should heed warnings and take "precautions" humanely.
September 17, 1985 Sioux Falls, SD *Argus-Leader*	Kokomo, Indiana hemophilia case	Can't keep boy out of school because of fear of AIDS	"exchange of body fluids, mainly blood and semen", not casual contact; It's not a "gay plague"; AIDS victims "happen to be" gays & bi-sexuals.	"no cure for AIDS"; "hysteria spreading faster than disease", "let's freeze out the rabble-rousers who are too ignorant to keep their minds open to the facts about AIDS"; "fear does not justify panic".

September 18, 1985 Pittsburgh *Post-Gazette*	Queens parents boycott school	Parents "sincere", "angry & aroused", but "the mob" is "wrong", "irrational".	"never contracted through casual contact" & only theoretical danger from non-sexual contact; needle sharing/blood.	Need documented facts about causes; avoid fear; provide emotional support for victims of AIDS. Follow AIDS "case by case" as CDC suggests
September 18, 1985 San Diego *Union*	Students and food workers with AIDS	Be tough, tender, thoughtful, cautious, humane	Spread only via "sexual contact," needles, transfusions.	Education, "case by case" screening; develop city policy before "public panic and protests".
September 18, 1985 Atlanta *Constitution*	School policies on admissions	Cool, calm debate	"tremendous odds against its being transmitted by casual" nonsexual contact.	Follow CDC advice on separating only those with lesions & biters. Add AIDS pre-marital test; protect confidentiality of victims. Provide public funds for "treatment".
September 18, 1985 Saginaw, Mich. *News*	School kids with AIDS	Avoid panic; be rational, responsible for society but "Gay rights does not mean AIDS rights"	"total lack of evidnece that casual contact spreads AIDS"; transfusions, needles, "sexual contact" cause AIDS	Research, funding, public education; "sympathy and scientific assistance" for victims; make donation of AIDS blood a crime

(Continued)

TABLE 6.2 – Continued

Date/Newspaper	News Peg	Position	AIDS Cause	AIDS Prevention
September 20, 1985 Miami *Herald*	School kids with AIDS	Parents have right to know "precautions school authorities will exercise"	Not spread by classroom contact or "body secretions" exposed to health care workers. Caused by exchange of body fluids in sex contact and needles.	Displace fear with information.
September 20, 1985 St. Louis *Post-Dispatch*	General "wave of panic" on AIDS.	We must not be hysterical or lose our common sense.	"no one is quite sure of its cause"; "mystery disease"; "lack of knowledge"; "sexual contact" (needles, blood transfusions); Not toilet seats, door knobs, tears, casual contact.	Need education, "increased public awareness", "vaccines or cures will reduce hysteria"
September 21, 1985 Salt Lake City *Desert News*	Latest Utah AIDS count	"No need for public panic" although danger AIDS may "invade" general public but cases are still small & research is being done.	"sexual contact" among homosexuals; needles & transfusions; females infected by males; not by casual kissing, utensils, door knobs, toilet seats, family or doctor-nurse situations.	"the safest course for people in high risk categories is to adopt a more conservative life style".

September 22, 1985 Pittsburgh *Press*	Local teacher has AIDS; officials want to know who.	No evidence to support public panic, hostility or isolation of AIDS victims	"mostly spread by anal intercourse among homosexual men" & unclean needles, blood transfusions, female prostitutes; not casual contact (handshake, bathrooms, food).	"worries about AIDS are based mostly on deeply imbedded emotions rather than informed judgments"; panic also before vaccine for polio and diptheria; Changes for AIDS remote—like being struck by lightning.
September 25, 1985 Augusta, GA. *Herald*	AIDS kids in school	AIDS child could get an infection in school	Infections are widespread	School age children "have not yet acquired an adult level of precautions in hazardous contacts. . ."
September 25, 1985 Portland, Me., *Evening Express*	AIDS in school	Public fear based on uncertainty; need policy based on reliable info to deflect spread of fear	None given	"Medical science has not yet been able to come up with enough confident answers. . . to allay fears about its spreading through casual contact."

(Continued)

TABLE 6.2—Continued

Date/Newspaper	News Peg	Position	AIDS Cause	AIDS Prevention
September 26, 1985 St. Paul, Minn., *Press-Dispatch*	Kids with AIDS in school	Don't bar kids from school, but modify sex behavior of adults.	Not caused by casual contact: sneezing, mosquito bites, food or drinking glasses, running noses. Caused by "deliberately chosen behavior", needles, anal sex with multiple partners (bi-sexual and homosexual).	Facts to stop virus and fear; "Behavior is to be shunned, not victims"; Educate teens on "extreme hazards of promiscuity and of specific sexual practices". Homosexual behavior begins in the schools.
September 26, 1985 Lincoln, Neb. *Star*	School boycott, talk of quarantines.	Ignorance, prejudice winning; education & reason fail.	Not spread by casual contact (handshakes, food, sneezes, toilets, health care workers). For most, not highly contagious risk.	Education, knowledge needed; federal money for AIDS research; "more drastic precautions" by drug addicts and gays.
September 27, 1985 Charleston, SC *News & Courier*	Kids with AIDS in school	No AIDS threat posed in classroom, except protecting a child from infections.	AIDS "can only be passed on through blood or semen."	Federal money for education and research; "panic fanned by rumors, falsehoods and exaggerations".
October 4, 1985 Akron, Ohio *Beacon-Journal*	Death of Rock Hudson; increase in federal research	Hudson died with courage and dignity; death focused attention on AIDS	None cited	"Action is needed to halt its spread . . . greater powers to enforce preventive measures."
October 6, 1985 Boston *Sunday Globe*	Increases in AIDS; use and confidentiality of tests.	Punitive quarantine of gays will drive them underground and violate civil rights and will not prevent AIDS.	No specifics on method of transmission. Only by sexual, not casual contact.	"keep the public fully and accurately informed"; "premature to restrict the lives and behavior of people".

October 6, 1985 Manchester, NH *News*	Media ignore how Hudson got AIDS and role of homosexuals.	AIDS is "homosexual's disease" "misguided and immoral philosophy".	Promiscuity, multiple partners, prostitutes, tainted blood	Media oppose closing bathhouse or quarantine but want "quick miracle cure"
October 7, 1985 Atlanta *Constitution*	Plans to get list of previous sex partners	Benefits as well as perils for such a program, VD tracking "created scant fuss".	No specifics	"public education find carriers, but protect civil liberties and avoid outcasts and witch hunts."
October 10, 1985 Columbia, SC *State*	Hudson's death	Little or no risk in using or giving blood.	No specifics	Deal rationally with fear of AIDS to avoid panic.
October 19, 1985 Seattle *Times*	Tests for AIDS in military	Prudent decision by military	AIDS "can be transmitted by blood transfusions".	Avoid dangers of blood exchange in combat.
October 22, 1985 Houston *Post*	Tests for AIDS in military	Prudent if not hysterical or violates confidentiality	No specifics	Avoid AIDS blood exchange in combat, medical discharge for those with AIDS
October 28, 1985 Dallas *Morning News*	State official proposes quarantine	State has such power which could control AIDS.	No specifics	"AIDS isn't a civil rights issue; it's a medical issue."
October 28, 1985 Cincinnati *Post*	Tests for AIDS in military	Appropriate action for healthy military environment; Not way to remove homosexuals.	Need "more known and ways are found to cure or prevent it".	Insure healthy military: physical health, avoid AIDS blood exchange in combat; close sleep and eating conditions could spread it.
October 30, 1985 Charleston, SC, *News & Courier*	Indiana insurance co. may screen out AIDS cases	Makes understandable "economic sense".	No specifics	No specifics

(Continued)

TABLE 6.2—Continued

Date/Newspaper	News Peg	Position	AIDS Cause	AIDS Prevention
November 11, 1985 San Francisco *Chronicle*	Bath and sex shops remain & allow unsafe sex; violates city law	Places should be locked and closed; danger to health, not repression of gays.	"the transfer of body fluids"	Close gay places; no details on what is "safe sex".
Novbember 26, 1985 Los Angeles *Times*	Plans to regulate baths	Mistake, wrong to close all baths or quarantine; would violate individual rights.	No specifics	"public policy should combat AIDS, not homosexuals"; facts, not politics
Salt Lake City *Tribune* November 29, 1985	Spread of AIDS, including a local prostitute	Public hysteria "must be tempered with heavy doses of reason" to stop public misconceptions, irrational, insensitive reactions.	Not spread through "normal, casual contact". No specific details.	Research money; "correct, objective information to prevent panic while scientists try to solve AIDS mysteries".

Editorials were clearly concentrated in two periods in the 5-year time: April 25-30, 1984—10 during news on discovery and tests (HTLV) and HHS superlative on AIDS as the "Number One" health problem; and August 6-November 29, 1985—56 during news on Rock Hudson's illness and death, school admission protests, and general public fear over increase in AIDS cases. Although no editorials "pointed with pride" to AIDS (outside of potential Nobel Prizes for a vaccine or cure), editorials did "cry with alarm" over public panic, hysteria, ignorance, prejudice, and misinformation. Generally, the editorials showed more concern with information to prevent public panic than with advice to prevent the disease. In this connection, they frequently made calls for "facts," "education," "information," but with few exceptions, provided little specific, graphic preventive information (for example, use of condoms, "safe sex" practices, or even abstinence) and even less on the apparent causes (e.g., anal intercourse).

Even so, editorialists repeatedly assured readers that AIDS was not caused by "casual contact" (handshakes, toilet seats, sneezing, food, family and medical contacts, tears, sweat, and kissing), but they seldom included specific reference to things like sodomy, fellatio, fisting, oral and anal sex. Repeated references were made to addicts' drug needles but seldom to any mix with semen. Exactly how exchanges in body fluids took place was vague. But some editorials did try to negate potential dangers among school children exchanging blood through biting, scratching, toilet and diaper habits, drooling, sores, and lesions.

Overall, very little editorial persuasion was directed to change or alter social or sexual behavior directly related to the disease. There seemed to be more concern with physical mortality than with social morality. Despite considerable certainty about the cause of AIDS by mid-1986, there was a mysterious quality about this disease with unknown, uncertain, and incurable characteristics. The editorials' concern with calming public fears was not expressed through urging the changes in private social behavior that would lessen the disease, hence lessening those fears. Instead, there was a somewhat "fix-it" mentality, assigning to "education," "science," and "research" a public (often government) responsibility rather than personal, individual liability for the disease.

Early editorials in the study period had greater faith and hope in science to prevent AIDS via a vaccine or wonder drug, but, after a delay in such a vaccine and after Hudson's death, harsher editorial preventatives appeared in support for military tests, quarantines, closed baths, listing of carriers, and more intimate and graphic terms in sexual promiscuity. Except for four or five editorials harshly critical of homosexual behavior (for example, Washington *Times,* August 29, 1985; Manchester (NH) *Union Leader,* September 16, 1985; and Dallas *Morning News,* October 28, 1985), editorial writers generally supported and protected the civil rights of homosexuals and their right to privacy and were often critical of those who contended AIDS was a moral or social (homosexual) issue. The historical use of shame did not appear, except for its use to criticize those who would ban kids with AIDS from schools (Boston *Globe*, September 9, 1985).

The Manchester (NH) *Union-Leader* (September 16, 1985) blamed other media for not being critical of homosexuals, and the Dallas *Morning News* (October 28, 1985) said AIDS was not a civil rights issue and invited quarantine. Neither newspaper had editorials that provided specific, concrete advice on exactly how to prevent the physical transmission of the virus. Nor were the Lincoln (NE) *Star* (September 26, 1985) (use "only the obvious rules of hygiene"), or the Salt Lake City *Deseret News* (September 21, 1985) ("Adopt a more conservative lifestyle") very helpful with specific advice.

More admirable in their editorial performances were the Milwaukee *Journal* (August 25, 1985) in editorials pegged on its own news series on specific causes and prevention and the St. Paul *Press & Dispatch* (September 26, 1985) which suggested, "Behavior is to be shunned, not victims," as it described the specifics of "deliberately chosen specific behavior," including anal sex and bisexuality. Few editorialists recognized or criticized bisexual links between the gay and straight communities, but female prostitutes were more frequently mentioned, although their role in AIDS appears less significant at present.

A sympathetic attitude toward homosexuals pervaded most of the editorials. Despite the statistics on AIDS, editorialists argued that AIDS is not a "gay disease" and is a medical, not a moral, problem (Baltimore *Sun*, April 30, 1984). Those with AIDS were often presented as "victims," "blameless," with their sexual habits "not by choice, passively infected and affected rather than actively causing the disease." The virus itself is "guilty," said the St. Louis *Post-Dispatch* (April 30, 1984). The Pittsburgh *Post-Gazette* (September 18, 1985) lamented the "virus of fear and irrationality." Editorials were as concerned with a tolerant public attitude toward gays as with action to stop AIDS.

In efforts to assure the general public not to panic, editors seemed as upset over the reaction to AIDS as to the problem itself. Fear was often presented as the epidemic. There is more danger in an auto or being struck by lightning, said the Providence *Journal* (September 11, 1985). AIDS is not a moral curse, but a mere "malfunction of the body," said the Hartford *Courant* (August 6, 1985) when it argued that those with AIDS are "less the victims of the disease than of the attitudes of those around them." The St. Louis *Post-Dispatch* (September 1, 1985) argued that "the rights of the well do not supersede the rights of the ill," and the Baltimore *News-American* (August 7, 1985) said that AIDS is "not a matter of public morality but of public health."

In an effort to avoid being self-righteous or scolding and intolerant of lifestyles and sexual behavior that court AIDS, the editorialists may have neglected to emphasize the specifics of modified social and sexual behavior that might prevent the disease for which they show concern. As the gravity of AIDS increases, will editorial writers become more graphic and perhaps less intolerant in suggesting solutions? Such an editorial shift might be one reaction to the dilemma of a public, value-free medical science unable to deal with private behavior affecting public health.

AN UPDATE: COVERAGE BETWEEN FEBRUARY 1985 AND FEBRUARY 1987

Although the AIDS epidemic is projected to grow to 324,000 cases by 1991, editorials in Editorials on File (EOF) have continued to neglect detailed specifics of the physical and behavioral causes of the disease, and, with the exception of the recent discussion of condoms, editorials have not advised against specific sexual acts whose elimination might prevent AIDS (Chase, 1987).

In 1986, editorial writers failed to deal with the causes and prevention of AIDS despite editorial possibilities presented on June 30, when the U.S. Supreme Court upheld a Georgia law making sodomy a crime, and on July 9, when the Meese Pornography Commission suggested pornography affected social behavior.

Of 25 editorials on the sodomy ruling, 20 were critical of the court for invading sexual privacy, but only 2 or 3 even referred to AIDS, although sodomy is a major method of transmission of the virus. The Kansas City *Times* (July 2, 1986) feared the ruling would "ostracize AIDS sufferers," and the Denver *Post* (July 2, 1986) saw the ruling as "growing discrimination in the wake of" the AIDS epidemic. The closest to dealing with the causes and prevention of AIDS came from Salt Lake City's *Deseret News* (July 2, 1986), which argued that, "With the shocking increase in the incidence of AIDS, the Supreme Court just might be saving some lives as well as striking a blow for simple morality." The Santa Ana (CA) *Register* (July 2, 1986) went so far as to say that, "The sexual acts in question are not physically dangerous. The spread of disease and fear of AIDS are separate issues," as it castigated the sodomy ruling as a governmental threat to personal freedom by imposing morality.

When pianist-entertainer Liberace died in February 1987, allegedly of AIDS, eight newspapers had editorials (see EOF sample, February 6-7) but none dealt with the causes and prevention of AIDS. Even the word "homosexual" was missing. The Cleveland *Plain Dealer* said "rumors of his alternate sexual life-style" could be excused by his "indefatigable good nature," and the Boston *Herald* argued that whether he was killed by AIDS was "no longer relevant" because of "the pleasures he gave to millions of show goers." Editorial writers accordingly eulogized his successful, popular, money-making career (Nashville *Tennessean*, Newark [NJ] *Star-Ledger*, Raleigh [NC] *News & Observer*). The Pittsburgh *Post-Gazette* idolized the "flamboyant" entertainer who "cried all the way to the bank," and defended this "very special man" whose "private life was sometimes the subject of speculation." Liberace was the "man who dared to be really different"

(Detroit *Free Press*) with "unapologetic guilt-free excess" who had the "courage to love life and indulge it" (Cleveland *Plain Dealer*). The Miami *Herald* said the "fabulous, frivolous, fantastic" showman was probably in heaven "out flapping the angels."

At about the same time, U.S. Surgeon General C. Everett Koop endorsed the use of condoms along with monogamy and abstinence to prevent AIDS. When local television affiliates in San Francisco, Detroit, and Indianapolis began advertising condoms in January 1987 (advertisements that national networks had rejected), the issue hit the editorial pages. Although the causes of AIDS were veiled in vague, generalized, nonspecific terms, 20 of 27 newspaper editorials in the EOF period of February 4-26, 1987, criticized the television networks and advocated both the use of condoms and their ads. Suddenly, the condom (which editorialists had not previously advocated) became the technical solution and the resolution of the AIDS crisis.

Although newspapers had heralded Liberace's liberating lifestyle and his value as an entertainer with a gay image, television, the competing medium, was lambasted, even blamed by many editorials, for its entertainment with sexual themes that were possible causes of AIDS. For example, the Toledo *Blade,* which said it had accepted condom ads, made no reference to the AIDS virus, blood exchange, or anal sex, but shifted both cause and prevention to television. It lamented TV's focus on "orgasms, variations in homosexual and heterosexual behavior...the penis, clitoris, and other parts of human sexual anatomy." The *Blade* argued that "No single institution in American life has done more to promote sexual permissiveness.... The networks should abandon their hypocritical, self-righteous protests and accept advertisements that can be life saving for people who adopt the TV ideal of having sex outside marriage with multiple partners." Condom ads offer the "potential of preventing disaster and death," said the Rapid City (SD) *Journal*, and "That's more than can be said for (TV) miniseries." The South Dakota newspaper, which made no references to the AIDS virus or how it is transmitted, said television was already sexually offensive and seeking ratings, but, "When it comes to saving lives, they hate it."

The Sioux Falls (SD) *Argus-Leader* also suggested condoms as a preventive measure and said TV networks "promote promiscuity," while being the most specific of all 27 editorials on condoms and the cause of AIDS (which the *Journal* had referred to as "AIDs"). The *Argus-Leader* paper cited old news and did not explain exactly how the sexual acts worked, but did say that "Researchers think it (AIDS) is caused by a virus transmitted through body fluids mainly blood and semen" and "most commonly among homosexuals."

Ironically, editorial writers were convinced there was no connection between pornography and behavior in July and October of 1986. They called the causal factor in the Meese Commission report "sloppy scholarship and fussy logic" (Boise [ID] *Statesman*), "a joke" (Los Angeles *Times*), "a sham" (Detroit *Free Press*), and "absurd logic" in the Las Vegas *Review-Journal*, which also proposed that if pornography caused sex crimes, then Commission members who viewed live homosexual acts should be held in preventive detention.

In contrast, when TV opposed condom ads, editorial writers seemed quite certain that both TV programs and ads affected behavior as both the cause and able to prevent AIDS. The causes of AIDS were interwoven with harsh newspaper criticism of TV for being hypocritical in opposing condom ads while encourgaging sex, alias AIDS. Condoms, said the Sacramento (CA) *Bee*, are no less offensive than TV programs. TV "fills the nation's airwaves with violence sex...rape, incest, child abuse," said the San Francisco *Chronicle*, which also supposed that condom ads were no more offensive than ads for "diarrhea, menstrual cramps, genital odors, hemorrhoids and jock itch." AIDS is offensive to all life (Portland *Oregonian*), as TV provides a "steady diet of sex imagery and products" (Akron *Beacon-Journal*) and "sexual permissiveness" through bikinis and skin-tight T-shirts" (Hackensack [NJ] *Record*).

Despite newspaper enthusiasm for condoms as a preventive device, there was frequently nothing hinted at or described as the cause of AIDS in the 1986-1987 period, in contrast to references to "exchange of body fluids" in the 1984-1985 period. As condoms became the not-so-new prevention, casual phrases seemed to revert to old generalized cliches that might obscure any unique or distinct aspects of AIDS transmission. Thus, its causes were "sexually acquired" (Nashville *Tennessean*) through "casual sex" (Denver *Post* and Minneapolis *Star*) and "sexual contact, activity" by the "sexually active" (Philadelphia *Inquirer* and Baltimore *Sun*). AIDS was said to be caused by "sexual promiscuity" (Manchester [NH] *Union-Leader* and Boise [ID] *Statesman*); "unnatural acts" (Denver *Post*); "sexual roulette" (Des Moines *Register*); "unusual sex things" (Kansas City *Times*); "sexual appetites" (Richmond [VA] *Times-Dispatch*); "sexually transmitted" (Worcester [MA] *Telegram*); "encounters," "freewheeling sexual activity" (Portland *Oregonian*); "widespread immorality," "wrong life-styles;" and "drug abusers and those involved in casual and plural sexual relationships" (Birmingham [AL] *News*).

As the epidemic worsened in 1986-1987 and as the condom became news, editorial writers were not as defensive of gay civil rights as in the 1984-1985 period. Despite press advocacy of the condom as a specific device, there still was a lack of specifics on safe and unsafe sex, although the Madison [WI] *State-Journal* joked that safe sex was the "catch phrase of 1987" like "trade protectionism." The editorialists also did not specify what they meant by condom ads that would be tasteful, decent, and health-oriented, in contrast to what would not be. Generally, writers borrowed from Surgeon General C. Everett Koop's logic, saying that condoms were perhaps not 100% effective, but were more practical than abstinence and monogamy, would encourage sexual responsibility, and would provide public health value and education in a general (but AIDS-related) prevention of teen pregnancy.

Condoms, and their ads, provided editorial writers in 1987 with a fix-it solution in many instances as they "literally save lives" (Hackensack [NJ] *Record*), "prevent death" (Nashville *Tennessean*), affect "money and lives" (Des Moines [IA] *Register*), are "life saving" (Chicago *Tribune*), and are a "life and death matter" (Honolulu *Advertiser*). There was some qualified skepticism of the condom as the "one known prophylactic" short of abstinence (Portland *Oregonian*), the "best current defense" (Lincoln [NE] *Journal*) that can "help curtail" (Philadelphia *Inquirer*), "possibly stop" AIDS (Des Moines *Register*), and "slow down the spread" (San Francisco *Chronicle*). Some wondered if condoms would work (St. Paul *Pioneer Press & Dispatch*), whether those who should use them would use them, like smokers and cancer ads (Denver *Post*), and if they were a "useful maneuver as far as it goes" but a "paltry" effort while the White House remained silent and blundered (Boston *Globe*).

Although all but 2 or 3 of the 27 AIDS editorials in February 1987, pragmatically accepted condoms as a preventive for AIDS, the minority viewpoint opposing or offering modified social behavior as an alternative to the rubber device provided few specifics as to the cause of the disease. "Anyone who believes that the answer to AIDS is abstinence is living in Pollyannaland," argued the majority viewpoint (Nashville *Tennessean*). The moral-social-behavioral issue was made moot with the appeal to science and technology. In contrast, cause and prevention (without specifics) was suggested by the Chicago *Tribune* with "good, old fashioned moral behavior," and by the Birmingham *News* with a "return to morality" and "stern religious teaching and principles," and "common sense" rather than "condom sense" by the Richmond [VA] *Times-Dispatch*. The Richmond paper admitted that condoms "can slow the spread" of AIDS, but are "not the answer to the problem." The Manchester (NH) *Union-Leader* reprinted a February 13, 1987, editorial from *The Pilot*, the newspaper of the Boston archdiocese, that said the only way to stop AIDS is to stop promiscuity and that profit-making condom advertisers make anonymous sex with strangers safe and cater to "the sort of behavior that transmits AIDS."

Advice and information to prevent AIDS was presented in Editorials on File editorials in a somewhat fragmented and parochial linking of community, science, and behavior in the 1981-1987 period. A reader of the nearly 100 editorials on AIDS might have been able to deal intelligently and responsibly with the "bad news," but it is more likely that old fears and old theories, rather than new hopes and new theories, explained causes and provided solutions to prevent the crises of personal and public disaster. Perhaps the press depends on technology rather than behavior to solve disasters and dilemmas it is either unable or unwilling to understand.

ACKNOWLEDGMENT

An earlier version of this chapter was presented to the Association for Education in Journalism and Mass Communication, Norman, Oklahoma, August, 1986.

NOTE

[1] Editorials on File (EOF) is a basic reference in most libraries and from which all editorials were taken. It includes no titles and no page numbers for newspapers. Keep in mind that United States' newspapers do not generally index editorials.

7
The Hostage Taker, the Terrorist, the Media: *Partners in Public Crime*

Joseph Scanlon
Carleton University

In 356 B.C., a man named Herostratus set fire to the famous temple of Diana at Ephesus, totally destroying one of the greatest wonders of the ancient world. When interrogated under torture, Herostratus confessed that he harbored only a single motive: knowing he had no particular talent to make him famous, he reckoned that by an act of unprecedented crime, he could achieve his greatest aim of life, immortality (Esslin, 1982, p. 35).

On March 12, 1985, three men backed their rented truck up against the fence around the Turkish embassy in Ottawa, Canada's capital. Then, using the truck as a ladder, they hopped over the fence, exchanged shots with a security guard, and used explosives to force their way into the building. Once inside, the men rounded up everyone they could find and took them to one room. There, while two kept the prisoners under guard, the third man began to make telephone calls.

Using telephone numbers on a sheet of paper he had brought with him, the man called the Canadian Press, Canada's main news agency, several times. He also called the network morning television show, "Canada AM," a show similar to "Good Morning America." And, as other media began hearing of the situation, he answered their incoming telephone calls. One newspaper was so persistent that it kept three staff members repeatedly dialing the number in the hope they could get through.

For the next 3 hours, the man talked to the media as his companions and their prisoners huddled around a television set watching reports of their actions on TV.

By noon, the story had attracted not just Canadian media but the three U. S. television networks—CBS, NBC, and ABC. By evening, the story led the news on all English and French language radio and television network newscasts in Canada and the United States. Like Herostratus, these men had achieved their goal— fame—even if it was temporary.

A little more than 1 year later on April 1, 1968, an armed man did much the same thing. He forced his way into the Bahamian High Commission (the Commonwealth equivalent of an embassy) in Ottawa and took the sole occupant hostage. Then he, too, began telephoning the media to tell what he had done and what he wanted. Again the media listened and called back and, once again began to focus on that man, what he was doing, and why he said he was doing it.

Although this second incident did not top United States television news stories, it did, as before, become the number one story on all Canadian local and network radio and TV. In fact, in both cases, the media did almost the same things:

- They immediately began broadcasting news of the incident, disrupting programming in the process;
- They reported what the callers said;
- They sent reporters and camera persons to the scene; and
- They called the police.

To some extent, both incidents became media circuses. The media talked to the persons involved, in the first case over the telephone and in the second by shouts from the street below. Reporters even interviewed the female hostage in the second incident while she appeared at the window with a gun to her head, just as other media had done with the pilot of a hijacked TWA jet. They also televised what was happening and who was where, even if those inside did not know these things.

For example, during the Turkish embassy incident, the media reported that the security guard was dead and that the ambassador was lying injured under the eaves trough at the side of the building. Although the latter proved untrue, since the ambassador had escaped by jumping through an upstairs window, the men inside watching TV didn't know either of these things.

At the second incident, TV ran shots of Royal Canadian Mounted Police (RCMP) marksmen in the building across the street and showed pictures of members of the Explosive Disposal Units (EDUS) arriving with their equipment (presumably there in case it was necessary to force access to the building).

INCIDENTS REPORTED DIFFERENTLY

The embassy incidents in 1985 and 1986 were similar. Both involved armed invasions of foreign missions in Ottawa. Both led to the taking of hostages. In both cases, those who took the hostages immediately began calling the media. In both cases, there was an immediate police and media response. Yet, the media reported the incidents differently. The first was treated as international terrorism; the second as a criminal matter.

There were two main reasons for the difference. The 1985 incident was the third attack on Turkish diplomats in Ottawa. In the two previous incidents, one Turkish diplomat had been killed and another one left a paraplegic. To the media, that pattern meant terrorism. Conversely, there had been no previous attack on Bahamian diplomats.

The second reason for the coverage difference was a result of what the media was told. The men in the Turkish embassy said they were there to avenge the genocide of Armenians by Turkey in 1915. Their goal was to free Armenia. The man in the Bahamian High Commission said he wanted to turn a local Ottawa fire hall into a place for the homeless and be reunited with a buddy from Kingston maximum security prison.

The media did not know either the men who entered the Turkish embassy or the man who entered the Bahamian High Commission. They knew only what they were told. They simply reported what they were told. Based on that, they made the Turkish incident international news (terrorism) and the Bahamanian incident national news (a criminal hostage taking).

Normally, when the media are given information, they check it. When a dramatic criminal act is under way, this normal precaution is forgotten. After a killing, an anonymous phone caller claiming responsibility is sufficient for a news report. During a hostage incident, a statement by the person involved is accepted. Check and double check goes out the window.

As one United States newspaper has noted:

> Journalists don't let Presidents or members of Congress command or control air time or newspaper space; they don't let millionaires control them; they certainly shouldn't let terrorists control or manipulate them. We don't want our government telling us how to cover a story, but there are circumstances which, in effect, we allow the terrorists to do exactly that. (Trounstine, 1977, p. 15)

Just how much the rules can change was shown in March 1977, when Hanafi Muslims occupied three Washington, D.C. buildings, killing one man and taking hostages. CBS Chicago got a call just before evening news time from a man who said he was an Hanafi Muslim and was at the Chicago temple. Despite the fact that no one knew who he was or what he would say CBS news put the self-professed Hanafi on the air.

> The young man, who could have been Santa Claus for all the reporters knew, at two minutes after 6, was addressing nearly two million people.... As it turned out he had much to say, but it did not pertain to the siege in Washington. (cited in Jaehnig, 1978, p. 719)

CRIMINAL OR TERRORIST?

Some would argue that these differences in coverage are acceptable because terrorist and criminal hostage takings are quite different. The terrorist hostage taking is carefully planned by persons dedicated to a cause who are prepared to die for it. The criminal one is a chance happening: an inmate caught in an escape or a bank robber caught in the act. Even if that were true, the results, in media terms, are the same.

But it is not true. Many so-called criminal hostage takers take hostages for exactly the same reason as the so-called terrorists. They want attention brought to themselves or their cause. They cannot get it by normal means so they take hostages to get it. One Royal Canadian Mounted Police officer who dealt with a number of prison hostages incidents agreed with the notion that terrorists crave publicity while noticing "the same desire for publicity when prisoners take hostages" (Northorp, 1978, p. 2).

To put it another way: terrorists are persons who attack innocent parties, kill or maim them, and/or use them as pawns. Criminal hostage takers do the same thing. If a robber sticks a gun at you and says, "give me your wallet," you can do that and hope he will be satisfied. If a hostage taker points a gun at you, you can not do anything. He tells someone else—not you the victim—"If you don't do what I want, I'll hurt or kill my prisoner." If you are the hostage, you are in the same fix; it doesn't matter to you whether the hostage taker is a "terrorist" or a "criminal."

So the fact is that both criminal hostages takers and terrorists are committing a crime to get attention. Both are succeeding. And both probably hold the media in contempt. As one hijacker pointed out, "television is a whore. Any man who wants her favors can have them in five minutes with a pistol" (cited in Hickey, 1976, p. 11).

NOT ORDINARY CRIMES

Hostage takings therefore are not ordinary crimes. They are criminal acts committed mainly to attract attention. Hostage takers are people who, instead of picketing a meeting, or staging a protest march, or writing a letter to the editor or their congressman, bomb, kill, kidnap, and take hostages.

In fact, when a criminal takes hostages to see some goal—whether it is escape from a bank robbery or escape from prison or (as happened in one case) a reduced mortgage rate, he at least is asking for something those he is dealing with could, conceivably, grant. When a "terrorist" takes hostages and asks for something like a free Armenia, his requests are well beyond the power of those he is dealing with.

else interpret that. Well, the police are hoping we don't give out too many details of the tactics that they are using, but we do know that the task force are at points around the house. (Scanlon, 1984, p. 168)

The same sort of thing was broadcast in Indianapolis when Anthony Kiritsis held a hostage—and he was listening:

> The Army bomb squad that's there has begun to think of ways to somehow get in without setting off the explosives...if Kiritsis could be incapacitated somehow, they could get in and diffuse the explosives that are in the room. (Jaehnig, 1978, p. 726)

Assuming that meant he was being attacked, Kiritsis reacted angrily, threatening, among other things, to blow up his hostage and himself.

And it is not just the broadcast. There are also the media phone calls. One hotline broadcaster told a hostage taker $10,000 was too little to release some children, so the man promptly increased his demands. Another had agreed to be taken to a particular prison then changed his mind when a media caller said he could get a better deal.

Even reporters' questions to police can affect what happens. In one incident, reporters asked a police officer what demands the hostage taker had made. He replied. Then they asked, "Has he made any attempts to secure immunity from prosecution?" The officer replied, "No, he's not done that" (Scanlon, 1984, p. 160).

When that exchange was televised, the hostage taker saw it, liked the idea (he had never thought of it), asked for and got immunity for his wife and children, although all had been active participants in the incident.

Charles Fenyvesi, a journalist, was a hostage during the 1977 Hanafi incident in Washington, D.C. During that incident, one news medium filmed a basket being lifted by rope to the fifth floor where some people had hidden themselves. Then a radio reporter upset the hostage taker by telling him that the police were trying to trick him. He promptly flew into a rage and picked out 10 men he would hang out the window so the police could see he was serious. Fenyvesi (1977) concluded:

> Terrorist incidents involving hostages should be handled by the news media in ways analogous to kidnappings and wars. In a kidnapping, police and reporters usually have an agreement on what can be published and what must be withheld until the victim is safe. In war, there is censorship of one type or another, the objective being to deny the enemy information it may use. (p. 18)

WHY THE FASCINATION?

Why do such hostage takers have so much fascination with news reports? Why do they react so strongly when there is little evidence the media can create such effects at other times?

There are a number of reasons. One is simply the amount of coverage. Hostage takings have the most basic of all news values—immediacy and conflict. They involve life and death, the good guys and the bad guys. They are even cast in media terms, with deadlines. They are perfect for broadcasting. They are ongoing events with good sound (conversations with the hostage taker and hostages) and good visuals. Both the sight of armed men and victims under duress and the massive police response, with barricades and assault teams, make for good television. This gives the hostage taker a lot to listen to and look at and a lot of information he/she could not get in any other way.

When a hostage taking occurs, the police try to control the area. They do not want anyone coming or going without their knowledge. They also try to gain complete control of communications; they do not want anyone involved having contact with anyone other than themselves or someone they have approved. Then they take their time trying to negotiate an amicable and mutually acceptable solution to the impasse. They have a trained communicator (negotiator) talk to the hostage taker. That person—because he or she is skilled—can usually resolve the situation peacefully.

They do it because this relaxed, low-key approach allows a relationship, known as the *Stockholm Syndrome*, to develop between hostage and hostage taker and because, over time, the hostage takers will become more and more separate from whatever it was that got them started on the hostage taking. This reduces the chance that the hostage will be hurt. Even if the start involved violence, it will seem further and further away. Now widely used, the New York Police Department (NYPD) first developed this technique (see Cawley, 1974). The media, however, interfere with this process. Their nonstop coverage, their incredible attention, make isolation impossible.

This does not mean the authorities do not prepare for the use of force. Normally, an assault team is brought to the site and its presence made known to the hostage taker(s). The hostage taker(s) is told that if he does not harm the hostages, force will not be used.

THOSE INVOLVED KNOW THIS AND USE IT

Whatever the reason, it is clear that the media have an incredible fascination with such events. In incident after incident they have devoted almost unlimited attention to what was going on.

When mayoral candidate Peter Lorenz was kidnapped by the Baader-Meinhof gang in Munich in 1975, program schedules were adjusted so that the media could run the gang's statements (Rabe, 1977, p. 4). The Hanafi incident in Washington, DC topped all three networks 3 straight nights and, over those 3 days, coverage totaled 67 minutes 20 seconds on NBC, 65 minutes 50 seconds on ABC, and 70 minutes on CBS (Terry, 1978, p. 74).

This media willingness to dance to the tune of the criminal explains why those who do such things plan with the media in mind. It is also clear that they get what they want. A Rand Corporation study of 77 incidents found terrorists had "almost a 100 percent probability of gaining major publicity" (Jenkins, Johnson, & Ronfeldt, 1977, pp. 24-25).

Terrorists know this. It is why Algerian terrorists, upset because their systematic killings in the interior were not getting attention, moved the killings to Algiers where the media were already located and where they could tip off photographers when an event was about to happen. It is why Black September picked the Munich Olympics for their attack on Israeli athletes. The media were there. A hostage taking at the Olympics was guaranteed massive coverage; the satellites were already booked.

> How sophisticated the media strategy of the Red Brigades is can be inferred from the fact they choose Wednesdays and Saturdays as their preferred communication days knowing that on Thursdays and Sundays papers are thicker and have higher circulation figures. (Schmid & Graaf, 1982, p. 51)

The government of Iran understood the role of media during the prolonged incident involving United States diplomatic personnel in Tehran: "The regime paid meticulous attention to feeding the satellite TV channels from Tehran.... One crowd chanting anti-American slogans in English for a Canadian television team on request repeated the slogans in French for the benefit of Quebec stations" (Bagdikian, 1980, p. 19).

Of course, the media have reported the response to such incidents, too. When the Israeli commandos flew secretly to Ghana to recover hijacked passengers, the story was told and retold in books and films. When the British Strategic Air Services assaulted the Iranian embassy in London, the assault was hailed as a major British victory.

A similar situation occurred with the even more successful assault by the German commando unit, GSG-9, at Mogadishu (October 8, 1977), after a Lufthansa jet had been hijacked and its captain murdered.

> It was over in 10 minutes and three terrorists—including the leader—were dead and the fourth wounded and captured. The hostages were seized unharmed from the jaws of death. The rescuing forces—unlike the Israelis at Entebbe—suffered no casualties. International terrorism had been struck a deadly blow. (Cooper, 1978, p. 101)

Yet, even reports of such counterattacks have raised concerned. For example, although the Israeli commando assault took place before anyone reported it, news of the GSG-9 assault in Somalia leaked out beforehand. The news of tactical radio activity in the area where the plane was located had been heard by a ham radio operator and reported by Agence France-Presse before the assault took place. Fortunately, however, the hijackers did not hear any of the resultant news broadcasts.

In another instance, the dramatic pictures of the SAS assault of the Embassy in London were obtained because a camera had been smuggled through police lines and a tape was being fed to the network while the assault was underway. Fortunately the reports did not affect what happened later because those inside the building were not watching television.

Except in these cases, reports of such incidents are often one-sided. There are reports of the event, reports of the demands, reports of both persons or groups involved. Then, when the event ends—especially if it ends without physical violence—coverage slows and then stops. The agony of the hostages and the emotional scars do not get the same play as the original event.

> Being kidnapped is one of the most harrowing experiences a person can be subjected to. No matter how short the period of captivity, it may be worse than the lengthy imprisonment of a convict. The sentence of the hostage is indefinite; it may end in release or death—the outcome in unknown—....It is not simply being deprived of one's freedom for a few days; it is a game of mental Russian roulette. (Jenkins, 1976, p. 5)

COPY-CAT HIJACKINGS

There are other problems. For one thing, media reports of one event often inspire similar activities by others. The famed D.B. Cooper parachute hijacking at Portland, Oregon, close to the Canadian border, came 12 days after a similar Canadian incident. Cooper was a copycat. And the Cooper stunt—hijacking a plane, getting money, jumping out—was followed by 25 similar incidents. As Schmid and de Graaf (1982) concluded, "The evidence for media contagion is rather strong" (p. 220).

Even fiction can trigger copycatting. In Rod Serling's television drama "Doomsday Flight," a caller reports a bomb onboard an airline, a bomb designed to go off at low altitude. Unless the ransom is paid, the bomb will explode as the plane lands. In the drama, the pilot saves the plane by landing at a high altitude airport.

Before this hour-long program was over, one airline received an identical bomb threat. Four similar threats came during the next 24 hours and another eight during the following week. Exported to other countries, the show made one Australian criminal $500,000 richer thanks to Quantas Airlines' desire to protect

116 passengers en route to Hong Kong, whereas BOAC officials faced with a similar threat demonstrated familiarity with the script by arranging a landing at Denver rather than London (Bassiouni, 1981, p. 20).

In Calgary, Alberta, Canada, a man took hostages because of a grievance against his bank and its lawyer. Having studied other events (such as the incident in Iran) he had decided a hostage taking was the way to get attention. He was right. He even coerced the media into running apologies from his bank and lawyer.

Such events do get publicity, but it may not be the kind of publicity those involved with the event want. A Canadian study (Cale, 1987) suggests the participants become well known but their cause does not. Most of us, for example, can remember the Symbionese Liberation Army, the Red Brigades, the Baadher-Meinhoff gang, but not what they stood for.

It could be that sheer publicity is all that such groups need. The Palestine Liberation Organization apparently felt that way. Its chief observer at the United Nations is quoted as saying, "The first of several hijackings aroused the consciousness of the world to our cause and awakened the media and world opinion much more and more effectively than 20 years of pleading at the United Nations" (Hickey, 1976, p. 12).

OTHER PROBLEMS

The media are involved in such incidents in other ways. In many, reporters have acted as go-betweens, as, in effect, negotiators. A television reporter did this in the Hanafi incident. An AP reporter did it when the Washington Monument was threatened. Tom Wicker of the *New York Times* did it at the time of the massive hostage taking at Attica prison.

The available evidence suggests that journalists rarely refuse such roles and, if they do get involved, stop acting as reporters. Such journalists have even slanted their own news reports to minimize the possibility that they can exacerbate a situation (Scanlon, 1980b, pp. 11-12).

The media have also been asked to report or not to report certain facts. Sometimes this request is subtle. Sometimes the authorities make more direct requests, but it is clear they are asking the media to distort normal news values to help resolve a difficult situation. One common request is that the media print a "Manifesto." "One such example is the Croatian case of September, 1976.... The hijackers insisted...two propaganda tracts be published on the front pages of newspapers. The *New York Times*, the *Washington Post*, and the *Chicago Tribune*, to mention a few, complied" (Alexander, 1978, p. 48).

Sometimes the request can be more vicious. Kiritsis, in Indianapolis, agreed to surrender if he could talk to reporters first. He came out with a shotgun wired to the head of his hostage, his finger on the trigger.

> But, instead of surrendering, Kiritsis, clutching the shotgun, delivered a 25-minute diatribe, riddled with obscenities. The "cocksucker" had undermined his attempts to package a land deal. The "motherfuckers" held a shotgun in his ear for years. "I'm a goddamn national hero," he proclaimed. It was one of the most incredible spectacles ever played out on live television. At any moment, it seemed, by intention or by accident, Hill's (the hostage) head could be splattered. (Trounstine, 1977, p. 15)

Whatever the case, the media adds an air of legitimacy. As one negotiator noted:

> I can give my word to hostage takers that they will be allowed to surrender in total safety or assure them of something else. I have however found they are not likely to rely on it unless I have given it first to the media. In most cases, they will hear the guarantees or assurances by radio, however they often times want to see the guarantees or assurances in print. (Northorp, 1978, p. 4)

After every such incident the media go through soul searching. They debate the ethics of what they have done. They develop guidelines. Then, the next time, whether it is in their country or somewhere else, they do the same thing again. For example, the Canadian Broadcasting Corporation set guidelines that stipulate that they will neither make nor accept phone calls from hostage takers. Yet, a senior news editor was one of the first to call the Turkish embassy, and the tape of his conversation was used and reused on Canadian Broadcasting Corporation radio.

Media involvement is not confined to hostage takings. Terrorists kill people, often with bombs. They have done that in a night club in Berlin. They also kidnap people, people like Aldo Moro in Italy, Hanns-Martin Schleyer in Germany, James Cross (a British diplomat), and Pierre Laporte (a Quebec cabinet minister) in Canada. Some victims have survived. Others—Moro, Schleyer, Laporte—have been murdered. "Operationally the activities of terrorist groups largely fall into the categories of bombings, assault, assassination and hostage taking with a related category...consisting of threats and hoaxes" (Kellett, 1981, p. 13).

There is little purpose to such activity unless a group gets the credit; so usually the group informs the media (sometimes before it happens) and keeps in touch with the media during the event. Of course, as was true for hostage takings, the media do not know the callers. But, as usual, they run the story anyway.

During a kidnapping, those involved may communicate with the authorities through the media and expect the authorities to reply the same way.

> Photographs of several victims (e.g., Peter Lorenz and Hanns-Martin Schleyer) were issued to the press with a notice reading, "Prisoner of the Red Army Faction".... The same technique was used by the Red Brigades with Aldo Moro. Dr. Schleyer was made to give a filmed interview which appeared

on worldwide television before they killed him. (Clutterbuck, 1978, pp. 62-63)

Yet, when NBC used an interview of one of the Americans held in Iran, the media reacted as if the tactic of sending out such interviews and the media using them was new.

> On 22nd October, the *Messagero,* a Rome newspaper, received an envelope posted in Naples a fortnight earlier. The newspaper editor was horrified to find the envelope contained a lock of hair and a human ear....the ear belonged to Paul Getty (who had been kidnapped July 9, 1973) and had been expertly cut off while he was still alive. (The Getty Affair, 1975, p. 167)

The Getty affair shows how terrorists and criminal actions are different in their relationship to the media where kidnappings are concerned. Criminal kidnappers usually want their activities kept secret. Terrorist kidnappers want all the publicity they can get (Mark, 1976, p. 17).

This sort of situation can lead to problems. One kidnap victim who had been allowed to write letters reported he was furious when the media said his missives had contained hidden messages. They hadn't, but his captors did not know that.

THE MEDIA OFTEN COOPERATE

Often in such events the media have acted discretely even if not asked to do so. They did not, for example, report that an employee of a U.S. security agency was on board when Shiite Moslems hijacked a TWA flight. They did not report that some of the staff of the American embassy in Iran had fled and that, as some reporters knew, they were being hidden by Canadian diplomats. In 1977, the German media even observed an almost total blackout during the Hanns-Martin Schleyer kidnapping and Lufthansa hijacking (Alexander, 1978, p. 50). In return, the German government issued a detailed document telling the inside story of government response.

Yet, the media have also been fiercely competitive. They have kept after families of hostages close to the point of harassment. They have fought with each other for access to hostages who were clearly under great strain.

> Most reporters were shocked and ashamed by the treatment given...to Mrs. Matthews (one of the two IRA hostages) after her release in Balcombe Street. Bombarded by news-hungry reporters from all sides, with flashlights popping and microphones thrust in her face, she looked like a hunted animal. (Clutterbuck, 1978, pp. 126-127)

The media have also competed to stop each other from getting stories. The Public Broadcasting System flew Robin MacNeill of the MacNeill/Lehrer report to Tehran for an exclusive interview with the Ayatollah Khomeini. MacNeill planned to use a camera crew from the ABC staff. In return, ABC would get some of PBS' footage. When CBS' "60 Minutes" heard of it, an executive put in a call to Sedegn Gotzbzadeh, by then foreign minister, and said that he didn't mind public broadcasting's small audience getting to the ayatollah first, but, if ABC was the first major network to get the coverage, the foreign minister would have to choose between public television and the 50 million viewers of "60 Minutes." MacNeill went home empty-handed. CBS' Mike Wallace got an hour interview with Khomeini; ABC and NBC got 15 minutes each (Bagdikian, 1980, p. 19).

Not surprisingly, all these activities have led to some questions: Should the hostages, obviously under duress, have been interviewed? Should the development of the U.S. Army's counterterrorism unit Delta Force have been reported? Should so much time and space have been devoted to a single story? Should the families of victims be subjected to such heavy media attention? Should reporters act as surrogate negotiators (Genovese, 1986, p. 28)?

When the Public Broadcasting Service put these and similar questions to journalists in a superb piece of public affairs programming, many of the journalists admitted being worried about their conduct.

EXTRAORDINARY MEASURES NEEDED

What should the media do when such events take place, whether such events are apparently local criminal acts or are the carefully planned acts of well-known international terrorist groups? Unfortunately there are no easy or obvious answers. Schmid and de Graaf (1982) said it would help if the media publicized grievances before groups resort to terrorism. "A right to communicate for aggrieved minorities...is likely to stop them from having to resort to terrorist violence" (p. 225).

This may be a bit naive. Schmid and de Graaf to the contrary, the evidence is clear that the media do consider such events special. Both individuals and media outlets have put normal rules aside during a hostage taking or terrorist act. Reporters have concealed things from their editors. Publications have willingly withheld what would normally be dramatic news. Reporters have agreed to slant stories. Publications have agreed to publish or not publish material to assist authorities.

There are several examples of this. In one incident, a reporter, worried about his editors' ethics, did not tell them of police activities he observed. In another, a number of journalists agreed not to report a police officer's death. In still another, all the media in Canada agreed not to report that a man involved in a hostage taking was suspected in a sex murder. Quite obviously, the media can and will cooperate with the police if they think it is necessary.

And cooperation has gone far beyond just keeping a story on hold. Newspapers have published fake front pages to assist police in dealing with hostage takers. Television stations have run special news items developed with the help of the police. Newspapers have given stories special play because they have been asked to do so by the authorities. Radio networks have adjusted programs for one section of the country so as not to upset a hostage taker. American newspapers have almost always published "manifestos" when asked to do so, even though the press runs have often been very limited.

These things have happened in more than one country. In Canada, the Netherlands, the United Kingdom, and Germany, the press has cooperated with the police. In fact, it is rare for the media to refuse to go along with the authorities.

Despite the atmosphere of cooperation, there is concern that the media are exaggerating the extent of terrorism. In 1976, Walter Laquer noted:

> A year or two ago, anxious newspaper readers...were led to believe that the German Baader-Meinhof group, the Japanese Red Army, the Symbionese Liberation Army...were mass movements that ought to be taken very seriously indeed....Yet these were groups of between 5 and 50 members. Their only victories were in the area of publicity. (p. 102)

It might be argued that the solutions lie elsewhere, with the authorities not with the media. The authorities have thought of news blackouts.

> If it is felt the terrorist will kill hostages and choose martyrdom, a useful device might be to withhold the media from the terrorist, thus eliminating his ability to publicize his martyrdom. The Marxist view is that such a sacrifice without the cooperation of the press would be useless. The martyrdom of a comrade to the cause would not be broadcast around the world to inspire others.... It is the rare terrorist who is willing to make a private sacrifice of his life. (Hassel, 1975, p. 56)

Many others, both academics and police, fear blackouts will lead to escalation. Alexander (1978) argued, "any attempt to impose media blackouts is likely to force terrorists to escalate the levels of violence in order to attract more attention" (p. 51). One of the world's most experienced hostage commanders also spoke to this issue. Said Frank Bolz (cited in Crisis Cop Raps Media, 1977) of the New York Police Department:

> If you don't cover what they're doing—suppose you have a news blackout—they're going to do something so spectacular you're going to have to cover them.... So cover them. What's the big deal?... There are no circumstances I can see at this point where we would order a blackout. (p. 21)

Other techniques have been considered. Technical interference with newscasts is possible. This would be extremely difficult, because the technology required may also interfere with police communications. Power cuts have been used on a few occasions, but these have their limits, too. Battery-operated radios and television sets can make power cuts useless.

However, any solution would appear to need the media. The media have shown in the past that they can adjust news values. When it appears necessary, they do so. They have done this with demagogues; Senator Joseph McCarthy was ignored in his final days in the Senate. They have done this with terrorists; the IRA hunger strikers in prison in Northern Ireland gradually attracted so little media interest that they stopped.

Perhaps an answer can be found, perhaps not. After every major incident, journalists talk, write, or debate possible solutions. So far, no satisfactory ones have been found. One thing is clear: Past media actions suggest the problem is extraordinary. The solutions must be extraordinary, too. Some scholars think that if the media do not act, governments will.

> The media reject as unthinkable any suggestion that might curtail or limit their reporting. Such suggestions imply to most journalists a form of censorship and ultimately suppression. However, ...the growing empirical evidence of the volume and content of media coverage...may lead governments to attempt to put restrictions on the "theater of terror." In the meantime, the highly valued right of the free press and the right of the public to know will ensure the terrorists a stage on which to perform acts of violence thereby gaining international recognition and even sympathy. (Weiman, 1980, p. 443)

Even some journalists agree with this approach. As David Broder (cited in Genovese, 1986) stated:

> The essential ingredients of any effective anti-terrorist policy must be the denial to the terrorists of access to mass media outlets. The way by which this denial is achieved—whether by voluntary means of those of us in the press and television...or by government control—is a crucial question for journalists. (p. 30)

Certainly, terrorist incidents make news. It is also true that news values shift over time. Events that were news fade over time. Events that were not news, such as acid rain or environmental pollution, have gradually gotten increased attention. The media can, and do, adjust their approach to the coverage of events and patterns of activity. The coverage of so-called terrorism, where the aim is media manipulation, seems to call for a review of media practices, particularly if government control is to be avoided.

8
Reporting Chernobyl: *Cutting The Government Fog to Cover the Nuclear Cloud*

Philip Patterson
Oklahoma Christian College

INTRODUCTION

On Monday, April 28, 1986, Swedish scientists routinely monitoring levels of radioactivity in the atmosphere discovered a remarkable increase in certain isotopes. Prevailing northerly winds left no doubt that the source of the contamination was inside the Soviet Union. Within the next 24 hours, the world determined the source of the radioactivity was the nuclear power stations at Chernobyl, and despite a lack of Soviet confirmation, it became obvious to western European observers that a nuclear accident of unprecedented magnitude was underway.

The Soviet nuclear power station at Chernobyl provided power for Kiev, the Soviet Union's third largest city 80 miles south of the installation, and to the surrounding farmland that has been likened to America's bread basket. The plant, comprising four reactors completed in the late 1970s, produced electrical energy through nuclear reaction in a water-cooled, graphite core, a construction type abandoned in U. S. power plants in the early 1950s.

The Saturday night of the accident, Soviet technicians decided to carry out an unauthorized test while the reactor was shut down. The test was to determine how much electricity the high speed turbine generator would produce after the steam from the reactor was cut off. Similar experiments had been successfully conducted at other Soviet generating stations. However, at Chernobyl the safety systems were disengaged, and the loss of power decreased the amount of cooling in pipes that, strained past their limits, burst. The vaporizing water created an explosive mixture of hydrogen and carbon monoxide that escaped into the air above the reactor. The resulting explosion and fire destroyed the reactor, part of the reactor building, and killed two workers. The chain reaction had begun.

The winds that forced the fallout over Eastern Europe did what the raging fire in the core had failed to do—force the Soviets to disclose the accident. What the world heard was this:

- there had been an explosion
- one nuclear reactor was in danger of melting down, and the graphite fire was estimated to be burning at 4,000 degrees, belching radioactive smoke
- furthermore, the accident had occurred about 48 hours before official government word was released

As the world demanded information, the Soviets appeared reticent. The Western European community, facing an immediate public health hazard, relied on its scientific experts for information and advice. Across the Atlantic, sensing an immediate political windfall, an executive order authorized the creation of a special Presidential task force to unravel the disaster.

One task force goal, which was the product of the review of the U.S. government's response to the 1979 Three Mile Island accident (Friedman, 1981), was to provide a central clearinghouse for information to the news media. From the outset, the media gave the Chernobyl story tremendous play. During the first month of the coverage of the accident, the three national television networks provided 6 hours and 23 minutes of Chernobyl reports, more than 19% of the total air time. In the first week after the accident, all three networks devoted major portions of entire newscasts to the story.

THE THEORETICAL FRAME

The Chernobyl story, particularly as seen on U.S. television, varied in the eyes of its creators. Just as there were two kinds of fallout, political and nuclear, there were two governments willing to reinterpret the event—they provided the "real fiction" (Fisher, 1970, p. 132) that viewers were to come to as the Chernobyl story. To the United States, Chernobyl became an opportunity to tout technological and political superiority. To the Soviets, the issue was not Chernobyl itself, but the campaign of lies in the Western news media. In that larger context, Chernobyl had become a propaganda power plant.

The vision of two governments at war with each other over the "real" meaning provides one frame of analysis to examine television coverage of the event. Using agitative propaganda, the United States government sought to put information about the tragedy into a context that would enhance its own view of the Soviet Union. As such, it sought to tell a different story about Chernobyl than the one the Soviets broadcast using the propaganda of reassurance and integration.

Agitative propaganda is the "propaganda of subversion" (Ellul, 1965) the propaganda governments employ for revolutionary ends. In the Chernobyl disaster, the end that the U.S. government wished to achieve was to undermine world confidence in Soviet technology.

Even as the Reagan administration forwarded its own political agenda through the Chernobyl story, other institutional imperatives were at work. In the midst of news rating competition the three American television networks, with a "sexy" story on their hands and 22 minutes of air time to fill nightly, had individual versions of the news. These reports did not exist in isolation. As observed by Gans (1979), network coverage of events, including technological hazards or "technological disorder news" is imbued with shared cultural values. The values outlined by Gans, in turn, fit neatly within what Ellul has described as integrative propaganda: a long-term and subtle portrait of events that encourages citizen participation in various decisions only according to established patterns. "In many cases, such propaganda is confined to rationalizing an existing situation, to transforming unconscious actions of members of a society into consciously desired activity that is visible, laudable and justified," (Ellul, 1965, p. 75). News reports that constitute some of the integrative propaganda used by all modern societies would thus emphasize the virtues rather than conflicts within a given system.
Further, such propaganda is founded on myth, what Ellul (1965, p. 31) described as an "all-encompassing, activating image," funded by a single dominant worldview: a linear notion of historical progress abetted by science and technology. Just as a storyteller conveyed myths in Biblical times, that role has fallen to the mass media in the 20th century. In a mass society, with its competing values, individuals depend on these underlying myths to explain the interaction between technology and the larger culture. The Chernobyl story provided an almost ideal opportunity for the "retelling" of such a mythical tale—the integrative propaganda of the superiority of American technology disconnected from the risks such technology had just as obviously brought the Soviets.

THE QUALITATIVE STUDY OF TELEVISION NEWS

Any systematic study of television news—a medium that combines words and pictures—must deal with a number of methodological questions. State-of-the-art quantitative content analysis (Budd, Thorp, & Donohew, 1967), while able to document certain tendencies and developments, has yet to comes to grips with the issue of verbal and visual tone that is so much a part of broadcast reportage.

James W. Carey (1969) has asserted, with considerable support, "All journalism, including objective reporting, is a creative and imaginative work, a symbolic strategy; journalism sizes up situations, names their elements, structure and outstanding ingredients and names then in a way that contains an attitude toward them" (p. 36). Carey's view, one that was foreshadowed by Lippmann (1949) when he characterized news as "a report of material that has been stylized," calls for a more thematic approach. In addition, some tools of rhetorical analysis, such as the concept of "real fictions" and Nimmo and Combs' (1985) rhetorical view of crisis coverage, underlie much of the analysis. The goal is to provide the reader with an interpretive study—a description and analysis of events that explores interconnections and seeks to develop an "introspective capacity that produces formulations which accurately and substantively make compelling generalizations" (Christians & Carey, 1981, p. 359).

The verbal and visual content of the Chernobyl tapes was first analyzed to assess technical aspects of the coverage. Most of the visual code of the paper was done using "hard analysis" (Frank, 1973, p. 23)—simple frequencies of discrete and quantifiable variables. The unit of analysis in this coding was quite frequently a single word, or a phrase designed to establish network tendencies in the verbal content aired. Second, each story was looked at using what Frank called "soft analysis" (Frank, 1973, p. 23). Soft analysis uses the judgment of the coder to evaluate the news story and its surrounding context in the wholistic approach. The soft analysis looked for tone, theme, and context (such as the Challenger explosion which had shaken the American technological community) that affected the way the story was delivered by the networks.

Videotapes of the networks' news broadcasts were obtained from the Vanderbilt Television University Archives and span the first report of Chernobyl on network television on April 28, 1986, through June 1, 1986. This coverage represented more than 90% of the stories aired about the plant for the first 3 months after the event and is longer than many similar content analyses of news coverage due to the evolving nature of the story. The unit of analysis, except where noted in the text, is the individual story, although a number of the "stories" that comprised the networks' Chernobyl coverage were composed of multiple reports on various facets of the issue. Television scripts were coded separately from the visual portions of the broadcast, and standard content analysis methodology was used in coding both the visual and written elements. Both the visual and the verbal elements of the 61 stories aired about Chernobyl were coded by a graduate student and the author with an intercoder reliability using Holsti's (1969) formula of .94 for the visual code and .97 for the verbal code. Although there were percentage differences among the networks in the various categories in the "hard analysis," none of those differences reached acceptable levels of statistical significance. Consequently, network coverage, except where specifically noted, is treated as a unit.

TECHNOLOGICAL DISASTERS AND THE MEDIA

In 1986, two technological disasters, the explosion of the Challenger space shuttle and the explosion of the nuclear power plant at Chernobyl, topped the list of news stories for the year (The top ten, 1987). A look at recent years shows that technological disasters such as Three Mile Island or Bhopal frequently make the list of most newsworthy stories. However, technological disasters, although important events, cause major coverage problems for the networks that routinely get 75% of their news from predictable forums such as as news conferences, rallies, protests, and the like. Faced with the very real event of a nuclear power plant explosion or a chemical gas leak, the networks find themselves at a disadvantage. Because technological accidents are often hidden deep within a complex system, these disasters are hard to capture in "raw" form. Roscho (1975) called this the challenge of "routinizing the non-routine" nature of catastrophic events.

The result, according to Altheide (1976), is that television will "decontextualize" the event to make it explainable to the public. In this decontextualization, the complexities of chemical leaks will be explained by the displacement of families at Love Canal. The result is "media logic" (Altheide & Snow, 1979), a way of seeing and interpreting reality in a format for the media. "The doings of the world are tamed to meet the needs of a production system" (Schlesinger 1978, p. 47).

At Chernobyl, several constraints made the story difficult to report. Soviet silence, the complexity of the reactor, and inaccessibility to the story were only some of the problems the networks faced. Yet each devoted large portions of time to the story for the month following the accident. The networks achieved this largely through the process of changing the story into some of the medium's "limited repertoire of consistent predictable narratives" (Smith, 1973, p. 75).

Network Coverage: An Overview

In recent years, technology has not been without its problems. Although natural disasters have been part of the worlds news agenda for many years, in the 1970s human-caused catastrophe has begun to take on equal significance. The 1978 explosion in Mexico City in which more than 1,000 died, the Three Mile Island nuclear accident, and the gas leak in Bhopal, India, have come to highlight the phenomenon of "normal accidents" (Perrow, 1984)—predictable accidents in highly integrated and complex technical systems. Further, national self-interest dictates that most countries continue to build and to support high-risk systems.

> Catastrophes are possible where community and regional interests are not mobilized or when they are over-ridden by national policy, where the economic costs of the disaster can be displaced from the private or governmental organization in charge to the rest of society, and where superorganizational goals, such as the economic health of an industry deemed vital or the control of outer space, are served. No one wants disaster, and better design, safety measures and regulations can help redress their likelihood. But, as long as national goals are served by risky systems, we will continue to have them and their catastrophes. (Perrow, 1986, p. 356)

Scholarly studies of media coverage of various crises (Friedman, 1981; Nimmo, 1985; Wilkins, 1987) indicate that media coverage of such events seldom questions the underlying political and economic decisions that contributed to their development.

News media reports of the Chernobyl disaster relied on versions of reality that, in several cases, differed significantly from the facts. The following factors affected the coverage:

- U.S. stereotypes about the Soviet monolithic culture and political system
- Atom angst (Lifton, 1967), a psychological preoccupation with nuclear war and its by-products
- Reliance on sources who attempted to put their own "spin" on the news
- Given the almost total lack of reliable data from the accident site itself, these themes had a larger affect on the news coverage than would have been the case had Soviet reports been more timely and comprehensive.

THE INFLUENCE OF STEREOTYPE ON TELEVISION CONTENT

> Russia is a riddle wrapped in a mystery inside an enigma.
> —Tom Brokaw quoting Winston Churchill as part
> of NBC's coverage of the Chernobyl disaster

Such a view of adversaries leads to the reinforcement of stereotype, even in a profession that prides itself on reliance on facts. Television stories about the disaster were flavored by three stereotypes that not only colored the tone of the news but also made it possible for the networks to accept as fact reports that were gravely mistaken.

The "Low-Tech" Stereotype

First, the Soviets were portrayed as low-tech bumblers. Such a view was pervasive in a number of areas: the media's portrayal of the problems with the Chernobyl plant design, the refusal to grant Soviet scientists status as "experts," and the repeated discussion of Soviet inability to extricate themselves from the myriad of problems caused by the accident, including medical treatment of the victims and extinguishing the fire in the reactor core.

Almost 20% of the 61 stories broadcast raised the issue of the faulty plant design, including one story that mentioned the problem eight separate times. In addition, 11% of the stories included a reference to the Russian inability to cope with the various problems that were a part of the recovery effort.

The Chernobyl plant was referred to as a "design for disaster" in April 29 coverage, which also included misstatements of fact. The most frequent factual error was the journalistic insistence that the Chernobyl plant either had melted down or was in the process of doing so. Forty percent of the stories contained such a reference. Other common errors included assertions that the reactor itself was designed with no containment and that a second reactor might be involved in the accident. These "facts" about Chernobyl were carried on all three networks on April 30.

For example, the Soviets were alleged to have constructed a basic "off-the-rack" reactor. In an April 29 segment on ABC, the Chernobyl reactor design was referred to as "a low budget, no frills reactor" that Americans have long since abandoned. Other segments aired on CBS and NBC claimed that the reactor was plagued by "cost cutting and ineptitude." In fact, NBC as "kicker" to its May 1 report quoted extensively from an article written by a Soviet critic of the plant that had been published just 4 months before the accident.

There was, of course, an implication, in such reports: Americans and American engineers could design safer nuclear plants. Such a view was not unilateral, for all the networks quoted experts who insisted that nuclear accidents were possible in U.S. plants, although representatives from the nuclear power lobby quoted as part of the Chernobyl coverage insisted that the industry was quite safe. There was also the issue of what was omitted. Although all three networks, for example, provided coverage of the Hanford, Washington, nuclear power plant that has a graphite core, none of them mentioned WHOOPS, the huge nuclear power plant construction consortium that had gone bankrupt in the same state 2 years before Chernobyl for, among other reasons, shoddy workmanship and inferior design. Although the WHOOPS story had made the earlier national newscasts, the networks simply chose not to remind viewers that problems similar to those ascribed to the Chernobyl plant also had plagued the domestic nuclear power industry. Only 25% of all the stories broadcast even mentioned other nuclear power plants, and many of those instances did not refer to problems at those plants.

If the plant and its Soviet design got little respect in the American media, Soviet scientists fared even worse. Although 101 scientists were quoted during the initial month of the coverage, only 11 of them were Soviet. Although Soviet scientists, at least during the initial phases of the disaster, were unavailable for comment, this figure still represents a striking bias toward Western sources for scientific answers. Soviet scientists were seldom referred to as *experts* in most newscasts, although the term was liberally applied to Americans and Western Europeans. Soviet scientists were referred to as *officials* and *senior science advisers*, whereas the graphics used to provide on-screen identification seldom carried academic or other titles when referring to Soviet citizens. This tendency is illustrated by a CBS segment that aired on May 9. "Experts here (Washington, DC) agree that not only have the Soviets botched the operation of their reactor, they botched the response to the emergency, dangerously delaying the evacuation, because, as one Soviet official ruefully said, the early measurements showed there was nothing to fear."

The "Evil Empire" Stereotype

Soviets, at least according to the American television presentations, did not value human life. This second stereotype was reflected in the way television reported the "slow" evacuation from the disaster site, unwillingness to accept help from other countries, the lack of specific radiation readings made available to Soviet citizens, and, in contrast to the Soviet portrayal of those who fought the reactor fire as heroic, the portrayal of an uncaring government sending its citizens into a dangerous area with little protection and even less warning.

Perhaps the most extreme example of this Stalinesque stereotype was aired May 1 on NBC when the network noted, "Intelligence sources say the Soviets are willing to sacrifice people to fight the fire." However, the slant of an uncaring Soviet bureaucracy began on the first day of the coverage, when CBS reminded viewers that "thousands" had died or been killed in an "unreported" nuclear accident in 1957 in the Ural mountains. All three networks discussed the fact that the power station had been built near a heavily populated area—without reminding viewers that such a practice is common in Western Europe and the United States. One network pointed out that the water reservoir for Kiev was built between the power stations and the Dnieper River.

The Soviets were portrayed as both uncaring and bumbling in the media's report of the evacuation of Chernobyl and the surrounding area. CBS on May 5 noted that "the evacuation of the town of Chernobyl, population 40,000 to 50,000 was still in progress at least as late as this weekend. That is days after the biggest radiation spew from the nuclear plant." All the networks noted the contradictions between when the Soviets reported the accident and when they said evacuations from various areas actually began.

The "Pack of Lies" Stereotype

When the American networks perceived that the Soviets were lying to them, each network felt free to construct a "truth" of its own. In this myth, Soviet officials were seen as potential liars and propagandists, while their American counterparts in various agencies were accepted as the source of truth about Chernobyl. The networks never explicitly called the Russians liars. Instead they implied it 36 separate times, in 41% of all the stories broadcast.

More often than that, however, the networks accused the Russians explicitly and implicitly of withholding information about Chernobyl. In 27% of the stories broadcast, the accusation was explicit: The Russians are withholding information. This accusation was present from the first day of the story when the Russians were portrayed as deliberately withholding information about the spread of radiation from the damaged plant. In nearly half of the stories, the networks implicitly described the Russians as secretive: The Russians said one thing that was contradicted by a variety of U.S. officials. One such example was the networks's unwillingness to accept the Russian-reported death toll, opting instead to interview Western experts who placed the likely death toll much higher even though these experts had no first-hand knowledge of Chernobyl. Only after Dr. Robert Gale, a "reliable American" source, appeared on the scene did the networks' pattern change.

From the very earliest incident, American networks were willing to accept most of what was said by U.S. government sources and accepted it largely without skepticism or seeking independent confirmation. ABC's April 30th coverage began with this statement: "But because the Soviets are so stingy with their information, the real facts are hard to come by. We begin with what Washington knows." This pattern was followed throughout the crisis: What the Russians would not supply, the news media would look to the U.S. government to produce.

When the early network reports relied on the government as a primary information source, in effect, they played right into the administration's hands. On April 29 the Reagan administration ordered all scientists in the Department of Defense, the Nuclear Regulatory Commission, and the Department of Agriculture to be silent on Chernobyl. The gag order was repeated four times, according to Stewart Diamond, *New York Times*, May 22, 1986. The media resource center reported fielding a record number of calls from the press but finding virtually no scientists able to comment. So, in the absence of Soviet information, and while working within the constraints of an administration gag order, the networks were left with only one frame for what little information did exist: a cultural view that made the Soviets out to be the villains in the situation. Ironically, the networks never mentioned the gag in their newscasts, a situation vastly different than the universal condemnation of the media ban on the earlier invasion of Grenada.

The networks almost never let a Russian have the last word. An initial indication of this bias was the low number of Soviet scientists who were quoted in the reports. The few Russians who were quoted in television reports were government spokespersons or common people on the street. On the other hand, a wide variety of Americans and Europeans were quoted. During the month after the accident, Soviet reassurances were repeatedly contrasted with precautions taken by other governments, particularly the Polish government. Although the Soviets said the radiation levels were safe, the Poles were shown giving their children potassium–iodine solution. And, the Soviet's problems in Chernobyl were inappropriately generalized to other political arenas. In a CBS report on May 8, Rather commented, "The U.S. said Soviet failure to be up front about Chernobyl raises new questions about whether the Soviets can be trusted on arms control." Of the stories aired, 13% linked American reticence to come to an arms control agreement with the Russians, based on their problems at Chernobyl.

As the networks perceived the Soviets to be lying, they proceeded to give the administration the last word regarding death tolls, casualty figures, and cleanup progress, even though there is no clear evidence that the administration had access to reliable information. An example is the May 3 broadcast by NBC in which it was reported that the Soviets had released new casualty figures. Secretary of State George Schultz "expressed the administration's growing scorn" that the Soviets were hiding the number of people killed. Schultz called the casualty figure "very low" and offered the assembled journalists a $10 bet that the number of casualties exceeded the Soviet figure. However, despite administration prodding, the higher casualty figures were not universally accepted. Half the stories broadcast about the disaster included mention of the much lower Soviet death report whereas only 10% included only the higher figure.

Although American stereotypes about Soviet Russia explain much of the Chernobyl coverage, our very real fear of anything nuclear adds another dimension. This concept, known as *atom angst*, was pithily reflected by Freeman when he told Dan Rather during an interview that "anything that can meltdown, will meltdown."

THE ATOMIC CONTEXT

The concept of atom angst was first developed by psychiatrist Robert Lifton in his research on the psychological responses of the victims of Hiroshima. As described by Lifton, atom angst, among those survivors, came to represent a psychological state where all misfortune in life was ascribed to the dropping of the atomic bomb. Nuclear metaphors pervaded the literature of Hiroshima survivors, art work was cast in tones of black and white and lacked the traditional symbols of life: growing things and water. The survivors themselves linked almost all activities in daily life to the bomb—and their fears were not only for themselves but for future generations. Lifton was the first to document the lingering effects of radiation in the human psyche, and since his initial research, Lifton has broadened his concept of nuclear fear to include the political possibility of nuclear war and nuclear winter. "Nuclear fear is intensified by a quality of the unknown—by the amorphousness, mystery, and totality of impact we associate with the weapons. Nuclear fear does not occur in isolation but interacts with the rest of life's more ordinary struggles" (Lifton, 1986, pp. 91-92). Systematic survey research by other scholars supports Lifton's view. One of the most intractable problems uncovered in work on public risk perception has been the distinct way the public perceives risks of *anything* nuclear as compared to other risky systems. "We have argued that people's strong fears of nuclear power and their political opposition to it are not irrational, but can be understood as logical consequences of their concerns such as equity, catastrophic potential, and the safety of future generations" (Slovic, Fischhoff, & Lichtenstein, 1980, p. 29).

Media coverage of Chernobyl, too, made such connections—both rhetorical and pictorial—to the underlying nuclear terror.

The words of Chernobyl were telling. Only 8 of the 61 broadcasts did not contain a reference to radioactivity. In the remaining stories, the word or a synonym was used a total of 538 times. One story referred to radiation or radioactivity caused by the leak 35 separate times. The word "nuclear" occurred almost as frequently: A total of 432 times. In addition, 23% of the stories contained some verbal reference to nuclear war, atomic tests, or nuclear explosions unrelated to the accident.

But the network's version of atom angst was not limited to words. The coverage included 10 separate visual references to nuclear war, in 7 different stories. Nearly 75% of all the stories included videotape of disaster victims—people who had been forced to change their lives due to an accident that happened thousands of miles away and to a largely invisible force.

This American coverage contrasted with the Soviet television reports aired on American newscasts (Sanders, 1986). The Soviets, in the process of generating their own version of integrative propaganda, aired videotape of normal rural life, including images of cows grazing on green grass and May Day celebrations. These bucolic scenes were interpreted cynically by the American news media. For example, CBS on April 30 provided the following comment about the Russian video: "And the Soviets stuck to their story that there are but two dead, the air and water around Kiev is safe." As if for emphasis, the newscast showed a feature of happy Kiev Soviets preparing for May Day. "But, that is the official story. Tourists leaving Kiev today told of much higher casualty figures...." one network noted. The contrast of the American words with the Soviet visual imagery was startling.

References to nuclear war included in the Chernobyl coverage were both pointed and vivid. On April 29, ABC aired newsreel footage of the Hiroshima victims receiving medical treatment; NBC followed suit the same day. CBS's April 29th coverage, although not including World War II footage, used instead a segment on the Department of Energy's nuclear facility in Hanford, Washington, which, the network pointedly noted, manufactures nuclear bomb components. ABC did a similar segment on Hanford the following day, whereas CBS's April 30 coverage included film footage of Hiroshima. By May 1, NBC had resorted to using the newsreel footage of Enrico Fermi's original atomic bomb experiments at the University of Chicago, and the same network discussed the impact of radiation on Chernobyl's victims in terms of the medical findings about Hiroshima survivors the next day.

Although both visual and rhetorical cues about nuclear war were prominent in the network coverage, there were other rhetorical anomalies. Fallout was translated into a variety of contexts (i.e., political fallout, economic fallout, and propaganda fallout). The word "nuclear" dominated reports of the event—in fact, Chernobyl was almost never referred to as a power station, it was as *nuclear reactor* in network parlance. American reactors, on the other hand, were characterized as "commercial" or "industrial" reactors. Other rhetorical flourishes were more vivid, although less pervasive. CBS's early coverage characterized Chernobyl as a "reactor gone wild," and NBC referred to the accident, in both a standing graphic and in text, as a "nuclear nightmare."

This unconscious and generalized fear of the atom allowed the networks to continue to air—unchallenged—reports that a second reactor may have become involved in the accident and that a core meltdown of reactor #4 actually had occurred. Both speculations were incorrect, but the networks continued to play them as distinct possibilities for almost 2 weeks after the accident.

Lifton has argued that atom angst is a response to the very real tragedies engendered by the atomic bomb. Other scholars have documented that nuclear risks, including nuclear power plant failure, carry the same "dreaded" connotations as the bomb itself, lingering, uncontrollable, unfair, acute, fatal, and delayed (Fischhoff et al., 1981). And, the public believes nuclear accidents are far more likely to occur than statistical analysis would indicate. The tone of 98% of the television stories about Chernobyl matched this construct of "dread" risk. It was an unconscious, but not necessarily irrational construction. The public, too has its nuclear nightmares—and television journalists, as members of that public, reflected them in what they said and wrote.

THE SOURCING PROBLEM

As mentioned previously, the executive branch had ordered many of the country's knowledgeable sources not to talk about the incident, and that meant scientists at facilities such as Oak Ridge National Laboratories or Lawrence Livermore were unable to talk to the media. Losing that potential information pool had two immediate effects. First, journalists were forced to rely almost exclusively on government sources—particularly sources in the intelligence community and within the Department of Defense—for much of their daily information about what was happening at Chernobyl. Second, for scientific explanations, the media—again unable to reach those sources arguably most current on nuclear technology—were forced to line up "experts" on the polar sides of the nuclear debate and interview them, often without the sort of background information that would have placed their views in context.

The scientists quoted in early television newscasts generally represented the extremes of the nuclear debate. James MacKenzie and other members of the Union of Concerned Scientists, a group that has been outspoken in its antinuclear views, were asked to comment on the safety of nuclear power plants. Their comments were countered by those of industry, for example, the president of Toledo Edison. Viewers were left without guidance as to how they should interpret such divergent views. Due in large part due to the gag order, the U.S. government view was represented by two key figures—Lee Thomas, head of the Environmental Protection Agency, and Harold Denton, head of the Nuclear Regulatory Commission. The government's analysis of the science of the event was funneled through these two officials, neither of them a true expert in the field and both of them political appointees.

With access to more traditional scientific sources restricted, reporters turned for daily information about what was happening at the power stations to intelligence sources, the Department of Defense and "spy satellites." One 20-second segment from NBC on April 29th illustrates this pattern of reliance on government sources throughout the Chernobyl coverage.

> *Spy satellite photographs* taken this morning confirmed the worst to *administration officials*—that there is a meltdown at that Soviet nuclear reactor. *Administration sources* who have seen the first reconnaissance pictures say that the top of the reactor building was blown off, that only ragged walls remain, encircled by a fire that, as of this morning, was still out of control. The *sources* said that the *spy photographs* apparently taken by a KH11 satellite, and which will not be released, clearly show towering clouds of smoke and flame that one *source* said could endanger the second reactor nearby. *Sources* are certain from the visual evidence that a chemical explosion occurred sometime on Saturday, but, *analysts* do not know what came first, the explosion or the meltdown. *Sources* also say that reports of more than 2,000 dead seem about right.

The preceding excerpt indicates that government information was sometimes correct, sometimes faulty, but always used.

The Challenger tragedy provided an ironic counterpoint to the official view. The shuttle disaster was referred to in several contexts in the Chernobyl reports, including serving as an example of the superiority of the American technological infrastructure. Another common use, despite the federal gag order, was to show Challenger as an example of American forthrightness and contrast it to Soviet behavior at Chernobyl. "The U.S., when faced with a public catastrophe, stayed public, " said Bruce Morton in CBS's coverage on May 1. "The Soviets, faced with an inevitably public catastrophe, chose silence."

Challenger also was used to show the inevitability of technological accidents. "The Challenger showed us that anything that can go wrong, might," said David Freeman, former head of the Tennessee Valley Authority, in a CBS interview (May 1). Finally a Soviet citizen reminded ABC News (May 3) that although the Soviets grieved at America's tragedy, the attitude demonstrated in the Western media toward the Chernobyl disaster was vastly different.

Thus, in the absence of confirmable facts about Chernobyl, the networks relied on government sources, became the victims of their own atomic angst, and fell back on widely held stereotypes about the Soviet people and culture. In this context, exaggerated death figures became believable, administration officials normally viewed with skepticism were willingly accepted as sources, and rhetoric replaced reportage.

CONCLUSION

Propaganda, in its broadest sense, results from the interaction of a culture, institutions within that culture, and certain significant events. The Chernobyl disaster represents such a nexus—a convergence of a specific event with cultural and governmental need as filtered through a mediated reality that was ripe for a particular interpretation. Although some of the factors previously outlined were the results of deliberate policy decisions, others emerged unconsciously and unexamined from a cultural and psychological milieu. It is these various sets of interactions that is telling for the role of propaganda in the late 20th century.

Chernobyl occurred in a context that was set by both the U.S. and Soviet governments. The accident happened in the first 18 months of Gorbachev's ascension to power in the Soviet Union—a rise Gorbachev himself heralded with the concept of *glasnost* or openness. Furthermore, he had used the concept as a lever in both Eastern and Western Europe to move the on-again, off-again arms control talks in Vienna toward the Soviet view. Although it is difficult to document precisely, the general consensus was that Gorbachev has been partially successful, particularly in western Europe where the pressure for some tangible arms agreement was both a real and a considerable factor in government policy.

Molotch and Lester (1975) argue that accidents act as an important resources through which the public can learn about those who ordinarily possess the resources to shield themselves from view. For example, Chappaquiddick functions as a close-up glimpse into the private world of Ted Kennedy. Three Mile Island allowed the public to see some of the inner workings and even some of the backstage chaos of the Nuclear Regulatory Commission. In this sense, Chernobyl functioned as a window into the Soviet infrastructure. What the American networks saw through that window differed from the Soviet proclamations of *glasnost* and more closely resembled Soviet business as usual.

Before Chernobyl, the Reagan administration had been only partially successful in countering the Soviet leader's stated intent. Reagan's refusal to negotiate on items like the Strategic Defense Initiative, his brush-off of Gorbachev's requests for additional summit talks, and the general uneasiness of the Western allies with some of the administration's foreign policy, all left the U.S. government in search of an issue to "unveil" what the administration believed was the Soviets' real intent: world domination.

Thus, for the two governments involved, Chernobyl was a critical event. Considering what is now known about the accident, it is apparent that the Soviet bureaucracy was no quicker to react well to the crisis than local, state, and federal governments in the United States had been to react to Three Mile Island. This predictable bureaucratic bungling (Downs, 1967; Durkheim, 1933), left the Reagan administration with an ideal vehicle to counter the Soviet policy of openness. The Soviets, deep in their own disaster, had to deal with the domestic crises before they could consider world opinion.

The administration, in turn, seized the opportunity in at least two ways. First, as indicated previously, it developed a "party line" about the nature and extent of the disaster, as evidenced by the gagging of all scientists under the government's control. Second, the administration established a presidential commission on the accident—the first time such a commission has been established to examine a *foreign* catastrophe. The Reagan administration essentially hoped to scoop the Russians about their own disaster. And for about the first 10 days of the event, that is precisely what happened.

In this context, the Reagan administration attempted to produce agitative propaganda to undermine the Soviet program of openness, replacing an international conception of a changing Soviet posture with the world view espoused by the administration. The administrative view was produced primarily for export, and the message was a fairly simple one: If the Soviets cannot be trusted about a nuclear accident, how can they be trusted about something as central to world survival as arms control?

However, just as there were government imperatives, there were institutional, and underlying cultural, imperatives in the broadcast news industry. By the time the networks had completed their own evaluation of the news from Chernobyl and embedded it in a system based on competition for ratings points, the story had changed yet again.

Chernobyl was a truly significant story, one of the networks could ignore only at the peril of losing an obviously interested audience. But, the journalists charged with gathering the story also had very little real information to go on. Goaded by competition the networks were forced to scramble for a story that, in its early days, was not all that easy to report.

There were some significant results.

The networks, initially, relied heavily on the governments for information about what as going on in Chernobyl, and thanks to the institutional imperatives at work in the two governments involved, wound up with very incomplete coverage. Blocked from using more traditional sources, the journalists resourcefully turned to the less traditional. For instance, commercial satellite photographs and the data tapes from them became central sources of information. Relying on purchased material created a network vulnerabilty demonstrated by both ABC and NBC about 3 weeks after the tragedy, when they aired what they claimed was a videotape of the power plant one day after the accident. The tape turned out to be photographs of a power plant in Triest, Italy.

When the networks were not relying on the government for information, they were at the mercy of both the environmentalists and the nuclear power lobby. Although rich in information, these sources lacked objectivity, and the story of Chernobyl was lost in nuclear rhetoric.

This lack of readily accessible facts threw the networks back on their own internal resources. Those resources, imbedded as they were in the larger culture, included a stereotypical view of the Russians and the expected Russian response to events, and a worldwide psychological preoccupation with the atom and its potentially destructive results.

None of this was deliberate. Gans has noted that certain values emerge from almost all American news stories, among them ethnocentrism, altruistic democracy, responsible capitalism, individualism, an emphasis on the need for and maintenance of social order, and leadership. Filtered through this lens, the events of Chernobyl changed yet again. What had begun as administration-generated agitative propaganda toward the Soviet Union was translated into integrative propaganda by the mass mediated culture. In essence, what the networks said was the United States would have handled the accident differently, that Americans were superior in any number of ways to the Soviets, and that the Soviets could not be trusted with anything nuclear—the distinctions between power plants and missiles somehow blurring in the overall portrait. Such a view fit so neatly into the American cultural psyche and was in such harmony with the organizational imperatives of the two governments involved and the networks themselves that it became recognizable as news. Chernobyl was no longer merely news—it had become a symbol. It was, as Ellul has characterized integrative propanganda: a gigantic sales pitch on the American way of nuclear technology.

But, the symbolic message was two-edged, for the networks, while couching the story in traditional values, could not ignore its nontraditional focus: the atom. Few viewers were neutral about the atom before the disaster, and many feared it. Despite its propagandistic overtones, the network coverage of Chernobyl was not an anthem to the virtues of atomic development. Scientific and technological progress did not remain unquestioned, and in questioning the concept of progress, particularly as a fruit of technology, network reports challenged the twin myths underlying all propaganda: science and history (Ellul, 1965, p. 40). Such questioning was not overt, but rather the function of atom angst buried deep within the reports.

In some sense, the television coverage of Chernobyl began the work of substituting a new myth for the old—a myth of a technology no one can control and that produces uncertain benefits. The theme was never dominant, but its presence revealed a wariness about the technological risks of nuclear energy—translated by the networks into nuclear *anything*—which crossed both political and governmental boundaries. In this sense, this underlying theme provides a clue for a new form of the propaganda of integration: that technology is powerful, and people are powerless. Governments, in this relationship, are a placebo. They can react to normal accidents, but they cannot prevent them.

9
It's the Nuclear, Not the Power And It's in the Culture, Not Just the News

Russell E. Shain
University of Colorado-Boulder

Nuclear energy advocates have paid no small amount of attention to the disparity between public views and technical estimates of the risks of nuclear hazards. The public consistently overestimates the severity of nuclear hazards, and at least one nuclear physicist blames journalists for this disparity. He argues that the public error would be corrected if the media would report the appropriate perspective.

The physicist, Bernard L. Cohen (1983a) of the University of Pittsburgh, made such an argument in *Before It's Too Late: A Scientist's Case for Nuclear Energy*, as well as in other articles and public appearances. In *The Wall Street Journal*, Cohen (1983b) said that a

> poll found that more than 80 percent of the public believes that nuclear power is more dangerous than its principal competition, coal burning, which is typically estimated to kill 10,000 Americans each year with its air pollution—some studies estimate 50,000. Every scientific study (at least 20, including one by Union of Concerned Scientists) has reached the opposite conclusion, that coal burning is much more dangerous. Clearly, the 80 percent is badly misinformed. This is a tragic situation unnecessarily killing thousands of people and wasting billions of dollars every year. Who is to blame? Since the public gets its nuclear information from the media, electronic and print, journalism must be the culprit. (p. 34)

In making his critique, Cohen indicted journalists for these sins:

1. Overcovering of nuclear hazards,
2. Using inflammatory language,
3. Failing to help the public understand radiation dangers,
4. Consulting only a handful of nonrepresentative scientists, whom Cohen labeled renegades,
5. Failing to put risks into perspective,
6. And, treating scientific issues like political or social issues on which everyone is entitled to an opinion (Cohen, 1983b, p. 34).

As long as Cohen focused his attention on journalistic performance, he made a strong case. If the news media are not providing a comprehensive and balanced coverage of nuclear energy, then they should be criticized. They should examine their practices and change them in appropriate ways.

Whether such coverage would lead to more accurate risk assessment by the public is unclear. Indeed, Allan Mazur's 1981 study casts some doubt. Mazur concluded that as mass media coverage about safety issues increases, so does public doubt. Thus, merely increasing the amount of media support for nuclear safety would not necessarily lead to changes in public perceptions. Indeed, according to Mazur, even a small probability of risk from nuclear energy may negate the many potential benefits in the eyes of the public. "It appears that the public has an inherently conservative bias. If doubt is raised about safety issues, many in the public prefer to err of the side of safety, as if saying, 'When in doubt, reject the technology—better safe than sorry' " (Mazur, 1981, p. 114).

Understanding risk assessment, particularly that of low-probability, high-danger risk, requires more than looking for an isomorphic relationship between news content and public perceptions (see Fischoff, 1981, for a discussion of risk assessment). Understanding communication requires a broader perspective, one that acknowledges the role of communication as a cultural phenomenon and that considers media behavior in relation to other institutions and the society as a whole (Carey, 1983, p. 313).

This postulated linear relationship between news content and public perception reflects one tradition in American communication research. The perspective is, according to Carey (1979),

> grounded in a transmission or transportation view of communication. (American Researchers) see communication...as a process of transmitting messages at a distance for the purpose of control. The archetypal case of communication then is persuasion, attitude change, behavior modification, socialization through the transmission of information, influence, or conditioning. (p. 412)

From a transmission perspective, the erroneous news stories limit American public opinion to a negative attitude toward nuclear energy. In an overly simplistic view, putting the correct information into the news would lead to an appropriate attitude change. However, the cultural issue of nuclear energy, as are most issues, is much more complex. It transcends news as well as rational, logical, or scientific debate. News is a part of a cultural whole. People give meaning to news within a cultural frame. So the meaning cannot be understood unless the culture is understood.

This cultural perspective provides what Carey (1979) called a

> ritual view of communication (that) is not directed toward the extension of messages in space but the maintenance of society in time; not the act of imparting information or influence, but the creation, representation, and celebration of shared beliefs. If a transmission view of communication centers on the extension of messages across geography for purposes of control, a ritual view centers on the sacred ceremony which draws people together in fellowship and commonality. (p. 412)

Thus, although the accuracy of reporting is a major concern, the nature and roots of values, beliefs, and fears that draw people together in opposition to things nuclear should be inspected. In addition, how media depictions fit or do not fit the broader cultural picture need to be considered.

One way of studying these nuclear concerns in a cultural context is to examine media imagery. Although any medium could be used for an analysis, motion pictures are particularly useful. According to Kracauer (1947), clues to a nation's mentality lie beneath surface meanings of films. An examination of film content is one way of attaining what Raymond Williams (1966) said is "the most difficult thing to get a hold of, in studying any past period...this felt sense of the quality of life at a particular place and time; a sense of the ways in which the particular activities combined into a way of thinking and living" (p. 47).

This "way of thinking and living" nuclear is wrapped into a political, social, and economic context that began to develop in the late 1940s and continues today. After the dropping of the first atomic bombs during World War II, an ambivalance that combined awe and fear arose. The bomb had helped to end World War II, and, yet, fear of what the bomb had unleashed existed among a substantial population. In 1945, the Gallup Poll found that 69% of the American public thought it was good that the atom bomb was developed and 47% were confident that atomic energy would be developed within a decade. Only 17% reported that the bomb's development was bad, and 14% had no opinion (Gallup, 1972, p. 69). Two years later, 17% of the American public regarded the atomic bomb as the greatest invention ever; 29% thought electric light and appliances were (Gallup, 1972, p. 625).

Americans did have an ominous, ill-defined concern about the future. One reporter described the feeling in this way:

> Cold War fear is gripping people here abouts. They don't talk about it. But it's just as real and chilling as the current 11 degree weather. Fear of what? Most people don't know exactly. It's not fear of Russia alone. For most think we could run Joe's nose in the dirt. It's not fear of the atomic bomb. For most think we still possess a monopoly. But it does seem a reluctant conviction that these three relentless forces are prowling the earth and that somehow they are bound to mean trouble for us. (cited in Goldman, 1960, p. 119)

The atomic bombs dropped at Hiroshima and Nagasaki had left an indelible impression. The appearance of nuclear weapons "symbolized by the visual image of an overwhelming mushroom cloud, evoked a broader conceptual image: that of man's extermination of his species by means of his own technology" (Lifton, 1986, p. 81).

By the 1950s and 1960s, this imagery had become a mixture of issues related to peace, the military, and the Cold War. Atomic bombs were viewed as necessary evils loaded with significant danger. After the Soviet Union developed missles for delivering the bomb and radiation dangers became clearer, nuclear weapons were perceived as less desirable, yet necessary (Gallup, 1972, p. 1,741).

The Cold War and the possibility of nuclear attack were united not only in the public mind but also in films of the 1950s and 1960s. Two unlikely allies, the federal government and the American film industry, encouraged the production of such films. The two had become quite familiar with each other in the late 1940s and the early 1950s, when Hollywood was besieged by the House Un-American Activities Committee and was thrown into economic disorder by the Paramount Consent degree (for a more complete discussion of these events, see Shain, 1974). Television's inroads into movie audiences compounded these problems. As a result, the movie industry became very sensitive to pressure. Hollywood executives became

> so busy trying to prove that the picture industry is a right-living, right-thinking and right-producing community that they have gone far out of their way to offend no one—whether it be (J. Parnell) Thomas, the Catholic Church, the Jews, the Negroes, the President, the American Dental Society, or the Institute of Journeyman Plumbers of America. (Variety, 1948, p. 3)

This sentisitity spawned a blacklisting of hundreds of artists suspected of left leanings. It also led to several motion pictures about the Cold War and a profitable relationship between Hollywood and the Pentagon. Between 1948 and 1962, the Pentagon assisted with 45% of Hollywood's war films. The assistance ranged from providing access to film clips of real battles to allowing use of military technology and bases at minimal charge This assistance was not without cost. The Pentagon required submission of scripts as a prerequisite for assistance and demanded changes in those that did not meet its approval (Shain, 1972).

9. NUCLEAR ENERGY AND THE MEDIA

The government also became its own producer, or more accurately, it became three producers: the Atomic Energy Commission (AEC), the Federal Civil Defense Administration, and the military (Titus, 1983). Each sponsor had its own message, and the messages were not always consistent.

The Atomic Energy Commission promoted the use of atomic energy with such films as *A Is for Atom* (1953), *The Magic of the Atom* (1953), *Atoms for Peace* (1959), and *Atoms for the Americas* (1963). Presenting factual data to explain the atom and how it could be split, these films argued for peaceful use of atomic power. The films were directed at a general audience and used often in classrooms (Titus, 1983, pp. 5-7).

The military produced films to indoctrinate military personnel on the need for nuclear weapons. In these films, nuclear weapons were depicted as critical ingredients in a Cold War policy of deterrence. Nuclear weapons were necessary assets with some side benefits. In *The Big Picture*, a pending atomic blast was described as "one of the most beautiful sights ever seen by man" (Titus, 1983, p. 3). Originally directed only at military personnel, these proweapon films were later declassified and made available to the general public. Such films produced for the military included *Target Crossroads* (1949), *Effect of an Atomic Bomb Explosion* (1951), *Operation Sandstone* (1951), and *Target Nevada* (1953) (Titus, 1983, pp. 5-7). Many of these films engaged in what Lifton called "nuclearism"—a "spiritual aberration in which there is the exaggerated dependence upon, and even worship of, nuclear weapons. We embrace the weapons for purposes of safety and 'security' and seek in them a means of keeping the world going, a form of salvation" (Lifton, 1986, p. 93).

Many of Hollywood's films also reflected nuclearism during the 1950s. Films about the Cold War depicted the Soviet Union as a "dark and ominous force" ready to gobble up the United States. Against this force, the typical American was powerless (Shain, 1974). This image of powerlessness contrasted sharply with civilian films produced from 1942-1945. In these films, the civilian often could defeat the enemy with little or no training, and a prosperous, happy future awaited the end of the war (Shain, 1976). Instead of a bright future, Cold War films promised only containment and deterrence, with the helpless civilian protected by professional warriors and their tools.

These tools implicitly included atomic weapons and explicitly depicted the sophisticated technology needed to launch them. Films like *Strategic Air Command* (1955) and *Bombers B-52* (1957) portrayed, in wide screen and living color, the joys and sorrows of the men and machines in America's first line of defense. As Jimmy Stewart learned in *Strategic Air Command*, "This is a new kind of war. We've got to stay ready to fight." Staying ready depended on hardware and the dedication of a professional team. After all, as Stewart's commander told him, the new jet was "a ship and a crew working together to put a bomb on target" (Shain, 1972, p. 645). The Pentagon's assistance of Hollywood during the 1950s guaranteed public presentation of an argument for a stronger defense based on technology. Films about planes and ships were expensive to produce. So during the worst of the Cold War years, when Hollywood produced 53 motion pictures about military technology, the Pentagon assisted in 50 of them.

Military films, government and commercial, portrayed nuclear weapons and military technology as necessities. Nuclear power was a possession to be prized, not feared. Yet, fear lurked just beneath the surface. Sophisticated technology would not be required if nuclear confrontation with the Soviet Union were not possible. The United States would have had little need for professional warriors with their technology and nuclear tools, if the threat of nuclear attack were not perceived to be real.

Hollywood's Cold War films left the results of an unthinkable nuclear attack to the imagination. Not so those films produced by the Federal Civil Defense Administration. Their message simply was "Find the nearest hole and make like a mole" (Titus, 1983, p. 5).

Thousands of school children received this advice. In *Duck and Cover* (1951), the most widely distributed Civil Defense Administration film, an animated character named Burt the Turtle gave small children hints on surviving an initial atomic blast (Titus, 1983, p. 6). Other productions included *Atomic Survival* (1951), *Survival Under Atomic Attack* (1951), *Shelter on a Quiet Street* (1953) *House in the Middle* (1954), *Survival City* (1955), *Town of the Times* (1964), and *About Fallout* (1964). Some of these were so vivid that filmmakers in the 1980s used clips from them to produce antinuclear movies (Titus, 1983, pp. 2-4).

Commercial films of the 1950s said little about nuclear issues outside the context of U.S.-Soviet confrontation. Atomic secrets became the object of confrontation, not debate. They were the occasion for a battle of good and evil. Films like *The Iron Curtain* (1948), *Walk a Crooked Mile* (1948), and *The Atomic City* (1952) told stories of Soviet attempts to obtain atomic secrets and the efforts of U.S. agents to stall the enemy.

Set in Los Alamos, New Mexico, *The Atomic City* follows the agony of an atomic scientist weighing his son's safety against his country's security. The film opens with a shot of the first atomic bomb blast and finds the scientist (played by Gene Barry) and his family in a state of bliss until his son is kidnapped. The scientist tries to confront his dilemma but cannot resolve it without the help of FBI agents. This helplessness is a common theme of Cold War films. In this scenario, the civilian, whether nuclear physicist or movie star, turns for salvation to professional warriors, the FBI in this case. In another movie era (1940-1946), the civilian would have solved his own problem and defeated the enemy.

If *The Atomic City* told of the lengths the villainous Soviets would go to get atomic secrets, *Invasion USA* (1952) and *Hell and High Water* (1954) specified what would happen if the Soviets possessed them. In *Invasion USA*, a hypnotist weaves a story in which an enemy force takes over Alaska, uses atomic bombs to capture the state of Washington, destroys New York, and invades the District of Columbia. Playing a former submarine commander, Richard Widmark works diligently in *Hell and High Water* to prevent another world war by keeping an atomic bomb from being dropped. Widmark takes a multinational group of scientists into the Arctic to find an atomic arsenal controlled by the Chinese Communists, and their efforts are successful when his crew shoots down a captured American bomber as it takes off with its deadly load on board.

While other films such as *Rocket Attack USA* (1961) had similar themes, some tried to separate the East-West conflict from the the nuclear issue. Some like *The Next Voice You Hear* (1950) and *The Story of Mankind* (1957) addressed the potential of mankind's self destruction without explicitly addressing the atomic bomb.

Another production, *The Beginning or the End* (1947), raised questions about the consequences of the atomic bomb but at the same time celebrated the successful story of joint efforts of business, science, and government in creating and producing weapons. The film begins with the burying of a time capsule, which is to be opened in 2446 A.D. This capsule contains a film recording the events of *The Beginning or the End*, which follows the project from beginning to end, the roles of key scientists, and the resignations of some after it became a "munitions project."

Although the title apparently came from President Harry S. Truman, who is quoted as saying, "Make it a good picture. This is either the beginning or the end" (*Time*, 1947, p. 106), the film failed to live up to his recommendation. "First of all there were big problems with security. And it is obviously impossible to make a free swinging, forceful picture if every foot of it has to satisfy the official and personal tastes of numerous politicians, brass hats, and scientists" (*Time*, 1947, p. 106).

Like *The Beginning or the End*, most American films did not deal directly with the human consequence of nuclear war until the late 1950s. *Children of Hiroshima* (1952) did, but it was Japanese produced. The film depicts Hiroshima 7 years later. Leslie Halliwell (1983) called it, a "restrained yet harrowing social documentary in fiction form, with the most efficient use of flashbacks to show the horror of the bomb and its aftermath" (p. 268).

These early films of the Cold War and military technology were produced in the pre-fallout era of civil defense. Explosions killed, and the strategy of civil defense was to avoid the explosion. Shelters were an early solution; later, evacuation plans replaced them (Kerr, 1983, pp. 35-63).

Strategy began to change when the fallout threat was placed before the public in 1955. In that year, a nuclear test, called Bravo, took place in the Marshall Islands and cast radioactive fallout over a 7,000-mile area. "Because of this widespread distribution of radioactive debris, coupled with unanticipated changes in wind direction, a number of people were directly exposed to radiation. The dangers of radioactive fallout had been recognized for a number of years, but the degree and scope of the peril were yet to be fully understood" (Kerr, 1983, p. 68).

At first, the Atomic Energy Commission de-emphasized the Bravo accident. The AEC announced simply that "28 Americans and 236 Marshall Islanders (had) been 'unexpectedly' exposed to 'some radiation' during the course of 'a routine test'." In addition, "some Japanese fishermen, aboard their trawler, the *Fortunate Dragon*, had inadvertently strayed into the test area on the day of the shot and had been exposed to a two-hour rain of 'white ashes' " (Kerr, 1983, p. 69). No injuries were reported.

AEC Chairman Louis Srauss issued a statement suggesting that the burns suffered by the fishermen were due not to radioactivity but to coral being raised from the sea by the explosion. He also reported an earlier statement "that the Marshall Islanders who had been exposed appeared 'well and happy' and that neither they nor the American naval personnel had suffered any ill effects from the experience" (Kerr, 1983, p. 69).

The Bravo blast and its aftermath focused attention on the dangers of radiation. Political controversy revolved around the issue as Senator Estes Kefauver and Congressman Chet Holifield held a series of intensive hearings, separately, during the next few years. Radiation, unlike the Soviets and their potential nuclear attacks, became an enemy from which to hide. In 1961, President John F. Kennedy unveiled a civil defense plan based on providing 50 million shelter spaces, giving impetus to the notion that the consequences of nuclear attack and radiation were beyond traditional political and military control.

Until the emergence of the radiation issue, most commercial films commented about possible consequences of nuclear war only in the guise of science fiction. Although not the first, *Godzilla* (1955), a Japanese-produced film, typifies these films. Godzilla, of course, is a prehistoric monster awakened by nuclear bomb tests that moves on to attack Tokoyo.

Among U.S. films that dealt with nuclear war and radiation in a science-fiction, and almost supernatural, setting were films like: *The Beast from Twenty Thousand Fathoms* (1953), in which a rhedosaurus awakened by an atomic bomb test in the Arctic terrorizes the East Coast; *The Cyclops* (1956), where explorers in Mexico find animals turned into monsters by radiation; *World With End* (1956), with a spaceship breaking the time barrier only to find that mutants have driven intelligent humans underground in the earth of 2058; and *The Incredible Shrinking Man* (1957), in which a man shrinks to microsize after being caught in a radioactive mist. (See Halliwell, 1983, for descriptions of others of the genre, such as *Attack of the Crab Monsters* and the *Attack of the Fifty Foot Woman*.)

Between 1959 and 1964, Hollywood made three significant pictures that helped create a new pattern. Focusing less on the evil potential of the Soviet Union, the new wave (including *On the Beach*, 1959; *Dr. Strangelove*, 1964; and *Fail Safe*, 1964) concentrated on the evil consequences of nuclear weapons regardless of user.

Stanley Kramer's *On the Beach* dramatically, and directly, addresses the human agony of nuclear war. In 1963, a nuclear war has wiped out the Northern

Hemisphere and radioactivity is spreading southward. In Melbourne, Australia, with one slight exception, all that can be done is to wait. A faint radio signal fosters hope that the Northern Hemisphere survived, and the atomic submarine, the USS Sawfish, makes its way to San Francisco to check. That hope expires as San Francisco shows no sign of life; the radio signals were accidental

Back in Australia, life becomes despondent. Some quiet moments of love turn into suicide, pills are handed out, auto races turn into mad death dashes, and the Sawfish crew returns to sea to die. The end comes, and "a short time later the only sign of movement in Melbourne is the flagging banner left over from a religious meeting in the town square. The banner says—'There is still Time...Brother' " (*FilmFacts*, 1960, p. 299).

Other films also tried to depict the aftermath. In the first, *The World, the Flesh and the Devil* (1959), Harry Bellafonte emerges from 5 days in a caved-in mine to find a world devastated by atomic war. He makes his way to New York and develops a relationship with a White woman that evolves into a conflict with a White man. The gloomy conclusion casts a pall over what remains of mankind. No lessons were learned, and the conflict evolves into a war in the streets between the two men. *Panic in the Year Zero* (1962) stays on the surface (both in setting and script), following a family on a fishing trip near Los Angeles when a nuclear attack occurs. They encounter hoodlums, looters, and fear of radiation on the way to a hopeful meeting at the U.N.

Of course, *On the Beach* received the most notice of these three films. It was also the most pessimistic. Nothing was to survive, regardless of who started the war. In fact, no one could remember who started the conflict. "Somebody pushed the button," nuclear scientist Fred Astaire said in the film. No one and everyone was to blame.

Two 1960s films explored this theme with poignant depth. Departing from the stereotypical depictions in Cold War films, these pictures distributed blame to both the United States and the Soviet Union. *Dr. Strangelove; or, How I Learned to Stop Worrying and Love the Bomb* (1963) made the point in satirical fashion; *Fail Safe* (1964) did it in a more traditional dramatic style.

Strangelove features an insane U.S. Air Force general who launches a nuclear attack on the Soviet Union. Recalls fail. Retaliation is certain. All that can be done is wait—and watch the black comedy antics of Peter Sellers, who plays three parts, including the U.S. President, a Royal Air Force captain, and a mad German-American scientist. The American war room sets the scene for the after world as Pentagon strategists begin to worry about the postnuclear mine shaft gap.

Fail Safe ends with a trade: New York City for Moscow. A plane's fail-safe device sends American bombers on a mission to Moscow. President Henry Fonda tries but fails to stop them and then attempts to persuade the Russians that what is to happen is an accident. He succeeds, only by ordering New York City destroyed. Who is to blame? The president says, "We're to blame ourselves. We let our machines to get out of hand. Men are are responsible. We're responsible for what happened to us" (cited in *Variety*, 1966, p. 112).

As sobering as these films were, they did not match the reality of the Cuban missile crisis in 1962. The crisis dramatically illustrated the perils of nuclear confrontation, raising in a forceful manner the question of whether a nuclear war would have any winners. Only a few years later, a British film, *The Bedford Incident* (1965), explored the lunacy of nuclear confrontation in a game of tag between a U.S. destroyer and a Russian submarine in the Arctic.

Later, *Silent Running* (1971) depicted members of a space station crew doing space gardening for earth, which had been subjected to nuclear devastation. And the *Planet of the Apes* series hypothesized natural orders that had been turned upside down by nuclear war. In the fifth, *Battle for the Planet of the Apes* (1973), the apes in charge of society repeat human errors and begin to battle among themselves.

Silent Running and the *Planet of the Apes* series were exceptions as the use of nuclear issues in films declined from 1965 to 1980. This was natural because after all they were only "indicative of the imagination, problems and issues of the society which produced and bought them" (Dean, 1978, p. 36). Just as earlier films had reflected the crises of their time so too did the films of the 1970s. These mirrored

> a developing neo-isolationism (perhaps a result of a costly involvement in Southeast Asia); a diminishing fear of nuclear apocalypse (partially a result of the thaw in the Cold War); and a growing concern with domestic terrestrial issues—most of which are related to totalitarian government control of people's lives or to over-population, food shortages, pollution and ecology. (Dean, 1978, p. 36)

The decline in nuclear themes also coincided with a fadeout of political interest in issues related to civil defense. Kerr (1983) pointed out, "The 1964 burial in the Senate of the Shelter Incentive Bill signalled the beginning of a 12-year period during which civil defense ceased to be an issue in U.S. politics" (p. 133). Even press coverage declined. "In 1963 the *New York Times Index* listed 72 articles dealing with civil defense. In 1966, 1967, and 1968, the *Index* listed 20, 7, and 4 articles respectively. Assuming this to be a rough indicator of newsworthiness, it is quite clear that civil defense had become virtually a non-issue in U.S. politics within a very short span of time" (Kerr, 1983, p. 1345).

At the same time that media and political establishments lost interest in civil defense, public sppport for civil defense programs continued at a high level. However, support may be high but not salient. "Thus, although the American people had generally supported civil defense in the mid-1960s, their support was neither intense nor was it the product of reasoned thought.... To make matters even bleaker..., the attention of the nation turned to the war in Vietman" (Kerr, 1983, p. 141).

Thus, the political and social arena, like the movie culture of the late 1940s to early 1960s, shifted attention away from the nuclear question without answering it. Film culture abandoned the issue with *Strangelove*, *Fail Safe*, and *On the Beach*. The dangers had been presented without a secure resolution. Nuclear power was to be feared, whoever possessed it. Films of the 1950s and the 1960s and the broader culture initially placed an ambivalent value on atomic weapons and eventually evolved to a state that resembled what Lifton (1986) labeled "nuclear fear."

> What we call nuclear fear, then, includes fear of death, our own and that of our family members and others close to us; fear of bodily assaults, including severe burns and keloids; and the special terror of "invisible" contamination "—the unending danger of delayed radiation effects that haunted Hiroshima survivors. Nuclear fear is intensifited by a quality of the unknown—by the amorphousness, mystery, and totality of impact we associate with the weapons. Nuclear fear does not occur in isolation but interacts with the rest of life's more ordinary struggles." (pp. 91-92)

Not until 1979 did a nuclear theme return to prominence in motion pictures. That film, *The China Syndrome* (1979), helped raise the spectrum of a catastrophe, putting fears into living color with Jane Fonda and Jack Lemmon. Released within a month of the March 28, 1979, Three Mile Island accident, it featured efforts by a controller of a nuclear power plant and a television reporter to make public an operational flaw. The flaw could have led to the China Syndrome, an event in which the core of an out-of-control nuclear plant would eat its way deep into the earth. That the authorities in the film cared little about the dangers, and, in fact, tried to cover them up left a chilling warning.

Unlike 1950s promotional films by the Atomic Energy Commission, *The China Syndrome* did nothing to promote the peaceful use of nuclear energy. It promoted fear not energy. It depicted the nuclear power industry in a less than favorable light. Even if the message had been favorable, it perhaps would have had little impact on its audience. Previous cultural imagery in decades of films had almost universally the same message. That message was: Anything nuclear was to be feared. Only dire consequences could evolve from the use of nuclear power. After all, the consequences of the atomic bomb and been demonstrated and could not be forgotten.

Contemporary writers, Lovins and Lovins (1980) and Ramberg (1980), provide additional variations on the warning. Ramberg called nuclear power plants an unrecognized military peril that would be attractive targets for attack. Lovins and Lovins describe the possibility of nuclear plants becoming the source of nuclear weapons. They argue that for 4 decades efforts have been made unsuccessfully to separate nuclear energy from nuclear bombs. They say that the promotion of nuclear energy should be abandoned because it has not fulfilled its potential and nuclear energy plants present dangerous opportunities for proliferation of nuclear weapons (Lovins & Lovins, 1980, p. 5).

Thus, nuclear is to be feared, whether it is energy or bombs. The fear certainly was nuclear not energy for college students and members of the League of Women Voters in Eugene, Oregon, in 1979. *The Journalist's Guide to Nuclear Energy* reported that about 40% of the students and league members said they believed it possible for a nuclear plant to explode like an atomic bomb, even though such an explosion is impossible. The guide added, "A large percentage of the Oregon residents said they expected a nuclear disaster causing 10,000 to 100,000 deaths to occur in their lifetime. Conservative studies put the probability of a worst-case accident at one in 100,000" (Edelson, 1985, p. 61).

This imagery of the atomic bomb and all things nuclear has become a vivid part of our social, political, and economic context. While an examination of movies within this matrix primarily during the 1950s and 1960s provides a beginning, the analysis is not finished. It should be extended in time and to other parts of the culture. News as well as entertainment needs to be analyzed from this cultural perspective. When this analysis is complete, without doubt, it will be found that the opposition to nuclear energy is in the nuclear, not the energy, and in the culture, not just the news.

10
Tales from the Darkside:
Ethical Implications of Disaster Coverage

Deni Elliott
Dartmouth College

Disaster strikes and, today, media representatives are essential players. It took little exposure to the coverage of the 1986 Challenger explosion to agree with the observation in *Time* magazine that, "The deluge of TV and press coverage that follows a disaster has become an unavoidable feature of the media age" (*Time*, February 10, 1986, p. 42).

News coverage of disasters can have potentially positive effects. Warnings before a crisis may prevent some disasters by alerting citizens and public officials to dangers. News analysis both during and after a disaster can help people understand why the disaster happened. The coverage can help people decide whether future disasters can be prevented or made less devastating, and it can help people understand what the disaster means in a larger context.

However, if news media *should* do any of this, it is because media have a particular function in society. This is not to argue that the free press ought to be forced to do anything. The press is free to meet or not to meet societal responsibilities. This chapter is simply an attempt to flesh out what those responsibilities are in times of disaster.

It is reasonable to expect media to respond to disaster, like other powerful organizations in the community, by helping to mitigate harm. In fact, The National Research Council's Committee on Disaster and the Mass Media provides the following list of media responsibilities: (a) preparing the public to meet emergencies; (b) providing mitigation, warning, and coping information; (c) providing reassurance and a mode for grieving or assuaging guilt in the aftermath of a tragedy; and (d) providing a record of activities related to the natural hazard (Wilkins, 1985, p. 51).

Only the fourth responsibility fits with the conventional "documentarian" responsibility of the press. Disaster creates additional responsibilities for news media, including a demand for cooperation with official sources. Media and official sources form partnerships in times of crisis.

First, what of the role of government during disasters? Holton (1985) said:

> The fundamental responsibility of all government is to ensure the safety and well-being of its citizens. That mission cannot be carried out in an information vacuum. The public must know if and when there is danger, and when the danger has passed. And people also have the right to know the fate of their neighbors. (p. 16)

If there were a U.S. government owned medium that relayed messages directly to the people, the privately owned press would not be needed to be the government's information arm. But, as it is, victims, support groups, and concerned citizens depend on media representatives and officials to work together during disasters.

FUNCTIONAL OBLIGATIONS

By definition, media communication and, by function, news media communicate messages that tell people how to work effectively in society. Although this functional duty is interpreted differently in different cultures, it is the responsibility of the U.S. mass market press to tell citizens what they need to know to make intelligent decisions for self-governance.

Communication of any message to a mass audience is a powerful function, a function often expressed in a cliché about media influence: The media may not tell people what to think, but they tell them what to think about. People are vulnerable to media; even the most cynical consumers of news get most of their information about the world from media. This power that media hold over the populace implies some obligations, ethically if not logically.

One of the few areas of agreement throughout 2,000 years of moral philosophy is that people in power have at least a prima facia duty to avoid harming those who are vulnerable to them. Some philosophers, such as Plato, have gone much further, arguing that those in power must promote good. Mass communicators, in particular, have a duty to do good for the community and individuals, according to the Platonic dialogue, *Gorgias*.

Whether we want to argue that mass communicators should work actively to promote a particular view of the perfect society, they should at least provide important information for people about their world. In addition, the morality of power dictates that news organizations must refrain from causing indiscriminate harm.

U.S. news media have even more obligations, based on promises made by individual news organizations to the audiences they serve. Through promotional literature and through more subtle means, news organizations both implicitly and explicitly have promised to provide accurate, complete, balanced, and relevant information to their audiences. This promise is so universally accepted that travelers can read any mass market daily in any U.S. city and trust that the account they read represents the local journalists' attempt to approximate the truth.

Thus, three basic obligations for the news media follow:

1. News media should give readers and viewers information that tells them what they need to function effectively in society.
2. This information should be given without causing harm.
3. News media should make every attempt to provide accurate, complete, balanced, and relevant information.1

However, finding examples of media obligations in conflict is not difficult. For example, telling the public about corruption in the Nixon administration certainly caused harm to many administration officials. Yet, voters needed to know so they could make informed decisions. The *need* for the public to have the information justified the harm caused. It is often difficult to judge if news media are meeting their obligations because in meeting one, they may violate another. The question becomes even more difficult during disaster coverage with the forced interdependence between media and government and with the urgent public need for media messages.

TENSIONS OF INTERDEPENDENCE

Media representatives know they need official statements during a crisis, and officials know they need the media to get their messages out. Hazards researchers know that both media and government are crucial to the victims of disaster. Nevertheless, tension exists between government and news media during disasters.

Wilkins (1987) has pointed out that hazards researchers identify media as highly effective means of public education but that media can only be effective if reporters have access to information. However,

> analysis of actual media messages about hazards indicate that some of the information the public needs to receive is never made available to the media or

that reporters and editors lack the education and training to understand information they do receive. (p. 9)

Many "community plans for disaster preparedness seem to place contact with the media in a somewhat secondary role" (Wilkins, 1985, p. 52).

If media representatives are treated as secondary during a crisis, it should not be surprising that, as noted by Scanlon, Tuukko, and Morton (1978), media representatives exaggerate the extent of the crisis, are confused, disorganized, carry conflicting information, and interfere with disaster response. These authors conclude that most disaster literature is

> in agreement on one point: during a crisis or disaster, the media will be carriers of inaccuracies and rumors. Journalists covering such events will be, at best, a problem for those responding to the media of crisis-striken communities. (p. 68)

If media interfere with governmental response to stricken citizens, it may be through the reporter's sincere attempt to discover what is really going on. There is ample evidence that officials want to manipulate information and public sentiment about disasters.

Blyskal and Blyskal (1985) point out that disasters lead to the public relations ploy of "crisis management." Management of the 1979 Three Mile Island nuclear accident provides a good illustration. Stephens and Edison (1982) report that during that crisis, "the press briefings were tense and at times intentionally obscure, the sources often hostile and tightlipped" (p. 199). According to Friedman (1981):

> A number of newspeople placed much of the blame for poor local coverage of (TMI) on Med Ed (Metropolitan Edison Power Company). Most felt that while Met Ed did inform the media of TMI events, it did so in a way what was not useful. The city editor at the Harrisburg *Evening News* accused Met Ed of hiding the seriousness of problems encountered and propagandizing when it could. With few exceptions, the reporters and editors agreed that Med Ed had mislead them about the severity of events. (p. 122)

The Three Mile Island reactor had been far from trouble-free prior to the crisis. But reporters charged that the little information that was given to them was presented in a way that covered up the seriousness of the problems. The reporters' own lack of technical understanding allowed for official minimalization of the problem.

Similarly, reporters charged that officials misled them when the Soviets shot down Korean airliner KAL 007 in August of 1987. Boot (1983) explained:

> ...readers and viewers were overrun by a veritable stampede of reports and editorials—echoing the official Reagan administration line—which charged

> unequivocally that the Soviets had identified the craft as an airliner but had deliberately destroyed it for straying into Russian airspace.
> CBS asserted on September 1 that the attack was "a premeditated act of murder." The *New York Times* described the attack in its September 2 lead editorial as "cold-blooded mass murder."
> It was frequently a case of write first, ask questions later—questions such as: Where was the unmistakable evidence that the Soviets had known they were shooting down an airliner? President Reagan insisted he had such evidence, but the administration later backtracked. After information leaked out that a U.S. spy plane had crossed paths with the jetliner, U.N. Ambassador Jeane Kirkpatrick said that the attack might have been an accident. (p. 27)

Official sources may have withheld information and lied in these cases, but journalists share the blame for inaccurate reporting. It should come as no surprise to journalists that officials may lie, and increasingly savvy public relations tactics allow for even greater possibility of deception. So, as Blyskal and Blyskal warn, "reporters, writers and editors must learn some new additions to the traditional five Ws: Who are the PR people behind the story? What are they not telling you? Why (and how) is PR attempting to manipulate and influence the story?" (p. 55).

THE ROLE OF MEDIA IN DISASTER PREPARATION

The public, scholars, and officials alike expect that news media will help people prepare for disasters. In particular, Sorenson (1983) pointed out that scholars and officials

> are typically quick to reason that public education and the dissemination of information will result in more adaptive behavior when disaster strikes. Over time, it is concluded, losses from hazards such as hurricanes, floods, earthquakes, and other geographical events will be reduced. (p. 438)

Sorenson (1983) showed that people depend on the media for this public education. When he asked college students to decide what sources taught them adaptive behavior and preparedness for threatening natural disasters, he found that media topped the list. The students chose media over school, governmental agencies or family (p. 447).

Although this seems to affirm media credibility, news organizations do not capitalize on this consumer dependency. Journalists do not often write stories that prepare people for disasters.

News coverage of the 1982 Denver blizzard illustrates this. Wilkins (1985) found that 62% of the stories were concerned with disaster impact and emergency response. Not only were there relatively few warning stories for this predicted event, but many of the stories related to preparedness came long after they could have helped people cope. "The media told Denver residents how to survive in cars that had become mired in the show, what to put in the trunk of a car to avoid such an event...well after the blizzard and its immediate aftermath" (p. 56). While the reality of stranded people inspired such stories, the probability of these events during major snow storms is such that journalists should provide coping information along with storm predictions.

Unwilling sources can be an acute problem when media try to warn of potential disasters. Sometimes, as Kueneman and Wright (1975) noted, officials delay warnings because of the uncertainty that a disaster will strike. "Faced with the problem of crying wolf, community officials occas sionally refrain from warning of a possible flood so as not to generate panic and when the warning is finally given, too little time remains to move or protect property" (p. 674).

Officials may also minimize the threat of danger because of special interest groups, as seemed to be the case during the Mount St. Helens volcano eruption. If the media had raised questions about the officially designated zone, some of the 36 deaths might have been averted. One analyst noted, "Crucial sections of that 'red zone' (danger zone) did not follow predicted paths of devastation from a major eruption.... In areas where geologists accurately forecast that the danger could extend 20 miles or more, the boundary was less than 3 miles from the summit (Morain, 1983, p. 6).

Morain further suggested that reporters' attention on the "red zone" could have forced an expanded restricted area or, at least, "might have increased public awareness that land outside the red zone was not necessarily safe" (p. 6). Investigation after the disaster revealed that the "boundary on what proved to be the most dangerous side of the mountain simply followed the line dividing federal parkland from property owned by the Weyerhaeuser Company, the region's major employer" (p. 6).

Morain warned that reporters should resist what may be a natural tendency to doubt that the worst may happen and should examine emergency planning schemes with a eye toward the possible conflicts of interest in official decisions about safety (p. 10).

THE MEDIA MYTH OF HELPLESS VICTIMS

If people are not adequately prepared to deal with disasters, they will feel out of control when confronted with one. This feeling of helplessness leads to a weakened motivation to respond and greater emotionality (Levine, 1977, p. 100). Media emphasize helplessness.

Sometimes the nature of a disaster limits individual control, but media focus on devastation over prevention, and coping courts future crisis. According to Wilkins (1986), events like the 1984 Union Carbide chemical accident in Bhopal,

India, provide "an example of a new cultural myth in the making, a myth of mass extinction and individual helplessness which does not bode well for the policy decisions technological hazards will require of the world's citizens" (Wilkins, 1986, pp. 24-25).

Helplessness is reinforced in editorials like one that appeared in the *New York Times* after the eruption of Mount St. Helens. The writer called the eruption a tragedy with "no guilt." Statements such as, "You can't blame a volcano" (Morain, p. 6) fostered helplessness and diverted attention from culpability for poor disaster management and from planning for future disasters.

There was even helplessness in the coverage of Chernobyl. Seemingly, there was little to do but question the accuracy of Soviet body counts (because they were provided by the Soviets), track the radioactivity released into the atmosphere, and watch to see which of the world's citizens would be affected.

Are citizens and media better prepared to face nuclear disasters of the future in the wake of Three Mile Island and Chernobyl? As the Soviet accident illustrated, such a disaster potentially can touch every town in every part of the world. Virtually every news organization could prepare to empower readers and viewers in a world with nuclear accidents.

DEATHS IN LIVING COLOR

Without or without stories on preparedness, media are there either when disaster strikes or immediately after, when people and property are still in danger. In the midst of crisis, problems associated with accuracy, media self-censorship and putting the disaster into context come to the fore.

When faced with the choice between reporting uncertain information or reporting nothing, journalists often report what they have. Disasters are chaotic events. Media and governmental goals conflict. While government is responding to the physical needs of those affected, media are trying to get the big picture to meet information needs. Inaccuracies result in confused times.

In a paradoxical way, the journalist's motivation to cover the disaster in progress may lead to unintentional distortion. For example, on-site satellite transmission makes it possible for journalists to cover the blood, gore, and on-going chaos during a crisis. While such transmission is certainly "true" in the sense that the cameras are faithfully recording what is happening, the dramatic "happening" may not be the accurate, complete information that facilitates viewer understanding.

Accurate, complete, and balanced information is information selected and presented in a way that allows the best opportunity for the consumer's creation of meaning. Presentations of chaos and random dramatic events exploit victims without increasing consumer understanding of the disaster.

The journalists' lack of concern for the panic and confusion caused by such transmission is problematic, but so is the self-censorship that may result from too much journalistic concern. In an analysis of broadcast stations' policies on covering civil disturbances and disasters, Kueneman and Wright (1975) found that "the perception of public excitability was found to be strongly related to the withholding of information.... The perception of the anticipated audience response directly affects the release of information concerning such events" (p. 674).

Of the stations in Kueneman and Wright's sample, 72% treated information related to disaster in a special way.

> The following comments from interviews are characteristic of their orientation. "You must be very careful that you don't overemphasize what's taking place." "I think you can create a good deal of panic if you're not very careful on the air; you can scare people out of their wits." "We are caught in a dilemma: we try not to minimize the danger, yet try not to create panic." (pp. 671-672)

Scholars analyzing the coverage of Three Mile Island echoed these comments. Stephens and Edison (1982) said:

> At Three Mile Island reporters also faced a pressure that was new to science reporting. Residents of the area monitored news reports for hints of whether to flee. Overly alarming coverage could have spread panic; overly reassuring coverage could have risked lives. (p. 199)

During disaster coverage, then, journalists put themselves in an unusual role—that of releasing only the information that they believe will not lead to undue public reaction. Suppression of information can promote feelings of helpless by allowing people to learn too little too late, focus on chaos and trauma, and promote feelings of helplessness as well.

The way out of this too much/too little dilemma is for journalists to determine what kind of information the public *needs* during disasters. For example, the more complex the story, the more help the consumer needs in defining unusual terms. During the Three Mile Island crisis, the *New York Times* did this, literally providing the reader with a glossary of scientific terms needed to understand the developing story (Krieghbaum, 1979).

Such attention does not always occur. Wilkins (1985) noted that in reporting the 1982 Denver blizzard, "about 94 percent of the stories did not contain any definition, either paraphrased or precise, of a blizzard.... While such definitions might have been superfluous in stories written weeks after the storm, initial stories certainly would have been more precise if they defined the term" (p. 56).

Reports of the April 1986 Soviet nuclear disaster provide more illustration of media not putting the story into precise context. A May 4, 1986, UPI story described the area around the Chernobyl plant as a "desolate wasteland" in the accident's aftermath. Translating this description into specific affects on flora and fauna was left to the readers' imaginations. Readers searching for an understanding of the effects of nuclear accidents need to know details.

In addition, disasters, as reported in the media, are frequently reported without historical context. Just as comparisons between events at Three Mile Island and Chernobyl appeared long after initial coverage, the Three Mile Island story was reported initially without the reactor's own troubled history.

Wilkins (1987) echoed this lack of history in disaster reporting in her discussion of Bhopal.

> Only one story, in Reuters, mentioned the green revolution or the fact that India has been able to feed itself for most of the past ten years. Only 2.6 percent of the stories discussed, in any detail at all, the economic and political reasons the plant was built in India. (p. 20)

A lack of understanding often limits the journalists' ability to cover a disaster as something people can cope with. If journalists see disasters as events that just happen, they certainly can not empower their readers. As Holton (1985) pointed out in his discussion of Three Mile Island, the journalists "had no prior planning to turn to, no memoranda of understanding, no disaster exercises to look back to. The result was a cacophony of conflicting statements, warnings, assumptions and explanations" (p. 15).

Media shy away from dealing with the hard issues raised by disasters. Wilkins (1986) characterized the event-oriented coverage of the Bhopal disaster as "knowledge without meaning" (p. 29). Yet, when television journalists quickly began speculation about how the Challenger disaster would affect government policy regarding future launches, questions were raised about whether media were reflecting or creating public opinion. Were media forecasting (as yet unvoiced) government intention or dictating governmental response? Perhaps it is more fruitful to discuss which role is appropriate for the media.

HOW MEDIA OUGHT TO COVER DISASTERS

How should media cover disasters? One basis for formulating guidelines is the set of minimal obligations presented earlier: News media should publish accurate, complete, balanced information that tells people what they need to function effectively in society without, as much as possible, causing harm.

Given these obligations and the special audience needs for news coverage of disasters, I suggest six guidelines.

First, journalists should become well versed in the context in which disasters occur and should be skeptical of information provided by official sources.

Officials may deceive out of self-interest. Journalists have an obligation to uncover the real story because that is what citizens require to be intelligent decision makers. The real story occurs in context. Prior to disasters, journalists should become aware of potential problems and should know the relevant context before a problem occurs.

Second, news organizations ought to help the public prepare for dealing with disasters. This requires that journalists fight their own disbelief and that of officials that "the worst" might happen. They should be willing to become active information seekers rather than reactive documentarians. Preparation can prevent disasters by alerting the public to problems and can help those effected have more control.

Third, journalists should provide as much information as possible during the coverage of a disaster.

Media can cause harm by omission as well as commission. Public panic is more likely to be caused by giving too little information too late than by crying wolf. Saying nothing when something should be said causes harm. Information should be given that enables citizens to take control.

Fourth, journalists must also provide accurate information, particularly during a crisis.

Acknowledged uncertainty makes for better reporting than the reporting of erroneous facts. Media credibility is vital during disasters. The most accurate media message may be the assessment that no one is really sure of the situation at the moment. Journalists are obligated to keep their promise of accuracy; there is no competing ethical principle to justify being first with possibly inaccurate information.

Fifth, media should focus on the contextual meaning of the event rather than on victims or drama during coverage of the disaster.

The audience needs a way to put the disaster into a context that helps them make intelligent decisions of how to cope with the disaster in progress and how to deal with the disaster after the fact as part of public policy. Victims do not want or need further victimization by media focusing on their trauma, nor does this focus fulfill reader/viewer needs.

Sixth, media knowingly and responsibly ought to participate in setting the agenda for public and governmental discussions on issues involved with the disaster.

News media comprise the one U.S. institution with the obligation of getting the issues out for public discussion. Informative reports are necessarily catalytic. Fear of swaying public opinion sometimes makes journalists hesitate to grapple with the big issues or put disasters in the context of policy discussions. Rather than deny this important agenda-setting function, news media ought to raise questions about disasters. There can never be too much public attention on questions of preventing and mitigating harm.

11
Conclusion: *Accidents Will Happen*

Lee Wilkins
University of Colorado-Boulder

By the time this book reaches you—the reader—accidents *will* have happened. The Mexican and Los Angeles earthquakes, continuing hunger in Africa, and the spread of the retrovirus that has become modern humanity's worst plague—AIDS—are among the better known.

But, although events themselves become dated, the research outlined in this book does delineate some emerging trends and indicates some paths for further research. The emerging trends can be grouped into two categories: (a) media performance, and (b) the role of the mass media within the larger (usually American) culture. The paths for further research remain somewhat less clear, but certainly center on three basic questions: (a) what is the optimal role of the mass media in warning and mitigation; (b) how do the mass media convey information about risks, and how might they be employed in both natural and technological disasters; and (c) how might the mass media, at least in a democratic society, more accurately reflect the series of choices that disasters and technological accidents pose both to individuals and to social and political systems.

MEDIA PERFORMANCE

The research outlined in several chapters in this book makes a convincing case that the mass media can be expected to behave in certain predictable ways in time of disasters and crisis. These institutional tendencies may be summarized as follows:

- As indicated in the essays about the coverage of Three Mile Island, Bhopal, hurricanes Danny and Alicia, Chernobyl, and Scanlon's study of terrorism, the mass media will report disasters and crises as discrete events rather than as "normal" occurrences within certain sorts of technological and political systems. At one level, this tendency to treat disasters as events has an important social benefit: the media believe it is their ethical duty to, when possible, warn of impending events. Hurricane warnings and watches, even if not always heeded or if double-checked by the public, thus become an important media story. Further, as Friedman's study of the continuing Three Mile Island coverage notes, the media actually may be improving their ability to cover some sorts of "impending" events. Although technological crises may be impossible to predict in anything other than the most statistical terms, these studies indicate journalists are capable of learning from previous errors and, in some instances, sustaining some rather quality coverage of important events.

On another level, however, this tendency to report disasters as events leads to a serious form of decontextualization on at least three fronts.

First, in technological accidents, such as Three Mile Island, Bhopal, and Chernobyl, the accidents themselves are wrenched from underlying technologies. They become disasters rather than the predictable malfunctioning of complicated systems. Although this trend is not universal—for example the continuing coverage of Three Mile Island by some local news outlets or the occasional *New York Times* investigative piece about Bhopal—it is pervasive enough that scholars can begin to argue media portraits of such occurrences are fundamentally inaccurate on a deep level.

Second, other crises such as terrorist incidents are separated from an underlying political or social context. Some terrorists—not all, as Scanlon has pointed out—may be viewed as criminals. Others, such as some members of the IRA, are responding to 400 years of history. Other sorts of crises are erroneously imbedded in stereotypical politics: Chernobyl became a debate between the workings of communism and capitalism. Media reports either omit or fail to distinguish between these various contexts, and in the attempt to "get the very latest" often cross those ethical boundaries that Elliott outlined as fundamental to good disaster and crisis coverage.

Third, as Burd has noted, the media decontextualize crisis by searching for a quick answer rather than a more systemic cause. The "cure" for AIDS thus becomes condoms or safe sex rather than changing intimate behavior. The way to rid the world of more Bhopals is to build safer and more highly regulated chemical plants rather than to examine the role of the Green Revolution in the developing world. This lack of contextual layers compartmentalizes disasters and hazards away from the systems that produced them, making debate over genuine solutions difficult at best.

• The media can be expected to rely on predictable sourcing patterns, particularly those in government and industry. Science will, in terms of information gathering, take a back seat to elite politics, and as the Chernobyl study showed, may sometimes be replaced by politics altogether. In addition, as Friedman and Burd illustrate, when official sources are confused or in conflict, the resulting media coverage may focus on the debate between sources rather on than the disaster itself. What the media seek, as Friedman and Scanlon have noted, are authoritative and trusted spokespersons—preferably one or two prominent individuals.

Yet, as other authors have indicated, technological crises and disasters are themselves areas of scientific debate; one or two spokespersons may not be able to provide the necessary breadth and insight. Or, the media may select precisely the wrong spokesperson—the terrorist himself, or the U.S. Secretary of State, certainly not a trained scientist, to provide the latest information about radiation-related deaths at Chernobyl. As the research conducted by Ledingham and Masel Walters indicates, the audience to such reports may not be so easily led. At least when it comes to warning, no single source in considered so authoritative that audience members do not chose to "check it out" in other ways.

• Finally, scholars know little about the impact of new communications technologies on these patterns of information collection and distribution. There have been relatively few studies of international information flow, but those that have been done, for example Wilkins' work on wire service reports on Bhopal, indicate international sources behave much the same way as more provincial ones. Scanlon's work indicates that new technologies, for example direct satellite feed of the latest terrorist update, served to collapse the time journalists have to make rational and ethical choices. Simultaneously, those same messages may provide actors in a terrorist scenario with information they should not have. There has been no systematic and comparative study of international coverage of what are becoming global hazards, for example, the greenhouse effect or the recent pollution of the Rhine River. And, there has been little study of how information passes from one country to another, and how the ever-increasing rate of information transmittal may affect pre-disaster warning and preparedness.

THE CULTURE OF DISASTER

Although scholars accuse journalists of decontextualizing events, other research indicates that a variety of disaster cultures exist within which news is interpreted.

Quarantelli's early work on the culture of disaster indicates that, in some societies and some subgroups, a specific set of expectations about disasters and their impact exists. Subsequent work, this time in a variety of international settings, has substantiated this notion. Thus, media reports about hazards and technology not only must reflect specific technological, social, and political contexts, but also must be understood within a larger frame as well.

The Perry and Lindell chapter provides one example, at least as it is discussed among those whose work it is to mitigate hazards. The local disaster official, in his or her job, becomes part of a larger disaster culture which, of necessity, includes the mass media. Although such an assertion seems self-evident in this mediated age, the realization that disaster officials have media responsibilities is a relatively new one, and one that has a number of ramifications. On the one hand, officials at the disaster scene may be ill-equipped to work with a variety of media outlets, particularly as hundreds of reporters and cameras descend on the scene during the immediate impact phase of the event. Increasingly, government agencies are learning the lesson of Three Mile Island: Accurate communication with the media is an essential part of mitigating any disaster.

Neil Frank, in his role as chief hurricane forecaster for the National Weather Service, went one step further. At the onset of a hurricane, reporters become his allies in providing prediction and warning information. Frank, at a variety of national conferences, has argued that journalists need direct access to scientists in the event of disaster so that stories will more accurately reflect both the uncertainties of various technical debates and the urgency of particular situations. The disaster culture, and the intrusion of the mass media into that culture, thus has become an important new element for the hazards community to both understand and harness for certain goals.

That rather specific culture, however, is imbedded in much broader national understandings. As several of the authors in this volume have indicated, nationally funded studies of various hazards reflect not only technological events but also a variety of information sources, some of them mediated fiction, some of them the "facts" of news, and some of them deeply held cultural and political stereotypes. It is this larger cultural understanding that so frustrates the scientific community, which cannot understand why the public "just can't get the facts straight." Nesbitt and Wilson (1977) and others have pointed out that people often hold opinions or know "facts" for which they have no cognitive base. Consequently, what a person might "know" to be true about nuclear energy might instead be true about nuclear bombs; however, the individual has arranged the information cognitively to believe its veracity. Some branches of mass media scholarship indicate that most people do not distinguish between when they learn on the news and what they learn through entertainment programming and that, over time, those rather hazy distinctions blur to the point of extinction.

As other authors have noted, modern reliance on science and technology has developed over a period of hundreds of years, yet the ethical issues raised by such a reliance are only now becoming part of contemporary social and political discourse. The result, as many of the volume's authors indicate, is a mediated reliance on the technological fix of mythic structures as a way of understanding the problems raised by a variety of technological and natural hazards. However, these stereotypical views may inhibit new definitions of the problem that might lead to different qualities of insight. And, as Scanlon has pointed out, such an unwillingness to abandon traditional views has, to a large extent, become an institutionalized pattern of media behavior. Until the sort of ethical system Elliott proposes actually becomes part of media behavior patterns in times of crisis, it is likely the same mistakes, which contribute to an evolving cultural understanding, will continue to be made.

Predictable media performance within various layers of cultural understanding is one theme that emerges from this volume. A parallel theme, that the media have certain ethical imperatives that revolve around the role of debate and discussion in a democracy, also emerges. Both call for significant changes in journalistic behavior, not only for the values intrinsic within the profession itself but for those norms of dignity and representation that are the root of democratic decision making.

THE ROLE OF FURTHER RESEARCH

The Optimal Role of the Media in Warning and Mitigation

The optimal role of the mass media in conveying warning and mitigation information about certain sorts of natural hazards is clear: When there is even minimal time for advance warning, the media are an effective warning device. Further, for certain sorts of hazards, for example hurricanes, the mass media can be used to effectively educate the public about generalized activites that may mitigate disaster losses. Research indicates that, when there is some advance warning about a specific event or a fairly consistent pattern of such events, the mass media should become a hazard mitigation tool. Program implementation, not further research, is what is needed. That implementation, however, must include new information dissemination technologies.

For other sorts of disasters and hazards, particularly technological events, mediated mitigation may, in fact, be more appropriate after the event itself. In these types of disasters, the chief role of the media is to reconstruct the event at a later date, instructing the viewer or reader why the recent event happened and how to interpret future occurrences. This view is a radical departure from traditional hazards scholarship. But, it reflects the institutional constraints, as well as the cultural milieu, in which media systems function and which have been outlined by a variety of authors in this volume. The key in this mediated reconstruction, however, is a portrayal of crisis that is significantly more geared to prediction and prevention of future disasters than is currently the case. Such a reconstruction may be difficult considering the existing definitions of news, although it may be more possible in "fictional" accounts such as film.

Mediated Risk Communication

The entire field of disasters and hazard research has led, in the last decade, to the first systematic exploration of the risk analysis-risk perception-risk communication process. Only within the past 2 to 3 years, however, has the mass media's role in this linkage been explored. Although the field itself is just emerging, early research indicates the mass media—both through news and fictional portrayals—may play a significant role in the formation of cultural attitudes about risk. Preliminary content analysis of news reports about a variety of risks (Singer & Endreny, 1987) has found news tends to portray risks in terms of harm. The construct of "news" itself may lead to inaccurate portraits of risk, reports that attribute too much responsibility to the individual and not enough to underlying social and political causes (Wilkins & Patterson, 1987). Scholars need to do additional work analyzing the content—pictoral as well as verbal—of both "fact" and "fictional" mediated risk messages. An important but heretofore unexplored area is how the public interprets these mediated messages, and how those interpretations influence interpretation of similar messages about subsequent, but not necessarily similar, events.

The Costs and Benefits of Disasters

Gilbert White, in his original development of the field of hazards research, based his scholarly inquiry on the notion that greater societal information about planning for hazards could save both lives and money. Since his 1940s dissertation, White and others have expanded the field dramatically to include disaster and relief workers, the mental health effects of disasters, and the entire range of technological and "elusive" hazards. In a 1986 reprise of his work, White said he believes the next significant area of disaster and hazards research needs to focus on the values and choices underlying societal planning for and interpretation of the events.

Clearly, in a democracy, the underlying value—the costs and benefits—of various choices about hazards and risk needs to be explained to the public. The mass media is the single institution generally assumed capable of performing that role, but as the research in this book indicates, the mass media have not perceived

11. CONCLUSION: ACCIDENTS WILL HAPPEN

the reporting of costs and benefits as part of the disaster story. Although the media have focused on the tangible "costs" of disasters, they have ignored the "benefits" that society accrued from the technology before the disaster occurred. Therefore, the media will focus on the costs of cleaning up Love Canal while ignoring the culprit—the products that modern society finds itself unable to do without. Further, the mass media, perhaps best in fictionalized form, need to find a way to reflect the psychological costs of hazards and disasters—the costs to the healthy workings of a democratic government of a widely held public belief that governments continue to allow hazards that are unfair, uncontrollable, and dreaded. Perhaps the greatest research effort should be expended in outlining in some significant detail both fictionalized and factual media accounts of hazards and disasters. This understanding should then be coupled with a detailed study of public understanding of such events. Only then can enlightened public policy be formulated.

References

ABC nuclear documentary draws mixed reviews. (1985, June). *AIF Press Info, 171*, pp. 2-4.
Adams, D. (1974). *A description and analysis of a radio station operation during a forest fire* (Preliminary Paper #14). Newark, DE: University of Delaware, Disaster Research Center.
AIDS: What is to be done? [Report of forum of experts at Princeton Club]. (1985, October). *Harper's*, pp. 44.
AIF, GPU protest ABC documentary. (1985, July). *AIF Press Info, 172*, pp. 5-6.
Alexander, D. (1980). Florence floods—what the papers said. *Environmental Management, 4*, 27-34.
Alexander, Y. (1978, June). Terrorism, the media and the police. *Police Studies*, 45-52.
Alter, J. (1985, September 23). Sins of omission. *Newsweek*, p. 25.
Altheide, D.L., (1976). *Creating reality: How tv news distorts events*. Beverly Hills, CA: Sage.
Altheide, D.L. & Snow, R.P. (1979). *Media logic*. Beverly Hills, CA: Sage.
Anderson, W. (1970). Tsunami warning in Crescent City, California and Hilo, Hawaii in the great Alaskan earthquake of 1964. In National Academy of Sciences (Ed.), *Human ecology volume* (pp. 116-124). Washington, DC: National Academy of Sciences.
Bagdikian, B.J. (1980, February). Patriotic television. *The Quill*, p. 19.
Barnes, K., Brosius, J., & Mitchell, J.K. (1979). *Response of impacted populations to the Three Mile Island nuclear reactor accident*. New Brunswick, NJ: Rutgers University, Department of Geography.
Barton, A. (1970). *Communities in disasters*. New York: Anchor Doubleday.
Bassiouni, M.C. (1981, Spring). Terrorism, law enforcement, and the mass media: Perspectives, problems, proposals. *The Journal of Criminal Law & Communication*, pp. 1-51.
Beady, C., & Bolin, R. (1986). *The role of the black media in disaster reporting to the black community*. Boulder, CO: Institute for Behavioral Sciences.
Bedell, D.H. (1983, February 28). [Letter from Douglas H. Bedell, Manager, Communications Services, GPU Nuclear, to Robert Giles, Editor, Rochester *Times Union*].
Blyskal, J., & Blyskal, R. (1985, December). Making the best of bad news: How corporations in crisis use the press. *Washington Journalism Review, 5,* 4-5.

Boot, W. (1983, November/December). Beating the tribal drums. *Columbia Journalism Review*, pp. 27–28.

Brooks, J. (1970). *A sociological study of commercial broadcast organizations*. Unpublished doctoral dissertation, Ohio State University, Columbus, OH.

Brouillette, J.A. (1966). *A tornado warning system: Its functioning on Palm Sunday in India* (Research Rep. #15). Newark, DE: University of Delaware, Disaster Research Center.

Budd, R.W., Thorp, R.K., & Donohew, L. (1967). *Content analysis of communications*. New York: The MacMillan Company.

Bucher, R. (1957). Blame and hostility in disaster. *American Journal of Sociology, 62*, 467–475.

Burd, G. (1978, October). *Social science methods as precision journalism and urban functions in preventive journalism*. Paper Presented at the Community College Social Science Association, St. Louis, MO.

Burd, G. (1980, April). *Preventive journalism: A perspective derived from the health sciences and applied to a newspaper*. Paper presented at Western Social Science Association, Albuquerque, NM.

Burd, G. (1981, August). *Press responsibility for health news: Beyond precision and toward prevention*. Paper presented at Association for Education in Journalism, East Lansing, MI.

Burd, G. (1983, October). *Editorial positions and government policies on decline of the Northeast and expansion of the urban Southwest (Sunbelt)*. Paper presented at Southwest Symposium Journalism and Mass Communication, Austin, TX.

Burton, I., Kates, R.W., & White, G.F. (1978). *The environment as hazard*. New York: Oxford University Press.

Cale, D. (1987). *Victory the ultimate goal of the terrorist*. Unpublished manuscript, Carleton University, Ottawa, Canada.

Campbell, A., Converse, P., Miller, W., & Stokes, D. (1960). *The American voter*. New York: Wiley.

Carey, J.W. (1969). The communication revolution and the professional communicator. In P. Halmos (Ed.), *The sociology of mass media communicaton* (pp. 23–38). Keele, Staffordshire, England. University of Keele.

Carey, J.W. (1975). A cultural approach to communication. *Communication, 2*, 1–21.

Carey, J.W. (1979). Mass communcation research and cultural studies: An American view. In J. Curran, M. Gurevitch, J. Woollacott, J. Marriott, & C. Roberts, (Eds.), *Mass communication and society* (pp. 409–425). Beverly Hills, CA: Sage.

Carey, J.W. (1983). The origins of the radical discourse on cultural studies in the United States. *Journal of Communication, 33*(3), 311–313.

Casey victory top Pa. Story. (1986, December 31). *The* (Allentown) *Morning Call*, p. A4.

Cawley, D.F. (1974, January). The Williamsburg incident. Anatomy of a seige. *The Police Chief*, pp. 30–34.

Chaffee, S. (1981). Mass media in political campaigns: An expanding role. In R.E. Rice & W.J. Paisley (Eds.), *Public communication campaigns*. Beverly Hills, CA: Sage.

Chase, M. (1987, May 18). AIDS costs—In lives and dollars, the epidemic's toll is growing inexorably. *Wall Street Journal*, pp. 1, 20.

Christians, C. & Carey, J. (1981). The qualitative approach to mass communication research. In G.H. Stempel & B.H. Westley (Eds.), *Research methods in mass communication*. New York: Prentice-Hall.

Clutterbuck, R. (1978). *Kidnap and Ransom: The response*. London, England: Faber & Faber.

Cohen, B.L. (1983). *Before it's too late: A scientist's case for nuclear energy*. New York: Plenum Press.

Cohen, B.L. (1983b, November 30). Most scientists don't join in radiation phobia. *Wall Street Journal*, p. 34.

Collier, P., & Horowitz, D. (1983, July). Whitewash. *California Magazine*, p. 54.

Committee on Disasters and the Mass Media. (1980). *Disasters and the mass media*. Washington, DC: National Academy of Sciences.

Connelly, J. (1985, May 12). Life amid the ruins. *Seattle Post-Intelligencer*, p. E1.

Cooper, H.A. (1979). Terroristic fads and fashions: The year of the assassin. *Chitty's Law Journal, 27*(3), 94–100.

REFERENCES

Crandall, W., & Mullineaux, D. (1978). *Potential hazards from future eruptions of Mt. St. Helens volcano*, Washington (Geological Survey Bulletin 1382-C). Washington, DC: U.S. Geological Survey.

Crisis cop raps media. (1977, June). *More*, pp. 18–21.

Cunningham, A.M. (1986). Not just another day in the newsroom. In S.M. Friedman, S. Dunwoody, & C.L. Rogers (Eds.), *Scientists and journalists: Reporting sciences as news* (pp. 202–211). New York: The Free Press.

Davies, J.C. (1971). *When men revolt and why*. New York: The Free Press.

Dean, J.F. (1978). Between *2001* and *Star Wars*. *Journal of Popular Film and Television, 7*(1), 32–41.

Detjen, J., & Fitzgerald, S. (1985a, February 10). Three Mile Island: Accident without an end. *Philadelphia Inquirer*, pp. 1A, 18–21A.

Detjen, J., & Fitzgerald, S. (1985b, February 11). Three Mile Island: Accident without an end. *Philadelphia Inquirer*, pp. 1A, 6–7A.

Detjen, J., & Fitzgerald, S. (1985c, February 12). Three Mile Island: Accident without an end. *Philadelphia Inquirer*, pp. 1A, 8–9A.

Diamond, E. (1983, October 22). TV news and AIDS: How bad reporting scared America. *TV Guide*, p. 8.

Dombrowski, W. (1981). *Another step toward a social theory of disaster* (Preliminary Paper #70). Newark, DE: University of Delaware, Disaster Research Center.

Douglas, D., Westley, B., & Chaffee, S. (1970). An information campaign that changed community attitudes. *Journalism Quarterly, 47*(4), 479–487.

Downs, A. (1967). *Inside bureaucracy*. Boston, MA: Little Brown.

Drabek, T. (1986). *Human system responses to disaster: An inventory of sociological findings*. New York: Springer-Verlag.

Durkheim, E. (1933). *The division of labor in society*. New York: Macmillan.

Dye, T.R. & Ziegler, L.H. (1971). *The irony of democracy*. Belmont, CA. Duxbury Press.

Dynes, R. (1974). *Organizational behavior in disaster*. Newark, DE: University of Delaware, Disaster Research Center.

Dynes, R., & Quarantelli, E.L. (Eds.). (1973). Urban civil disturbances. [Special issue]. *American Behavioral Scientist, 16*, 305–440.

Dynes, R., Quarantelli, E.L., & Kreps, G. (1972). *A perspective on disaster planning*. Newark, DE: University of Delaware Disaster Research Center.

Dynes, R., Quarantelli, E.L., & Kreps, G. (1981). *A perspective on disaster planning*. Newark, DE: University of Delaware, Disaster Research Center.

Eckholm, E. (1986, June 17). Broad alert over AIDS: Social battle is shifting. *New York Times*, pp. 19–20.

Edelson, E. (1985). *The journalist's guide to nuclear energy*. Bethesda, MD: Atomic Industrial Forum, Inc.

Edelstein, A. (1956). Evaluation of editorials through model technique. *Journalism Quarterly, 33*, 324–334.

Editorials on File. (1984, April 16–30). *Progress on AIDS?, 15*(8), 470–475. New York: Facts on File.

Editorials on File. (1985, September 16–30). *Should AIDS kids be in School, 16*(18), 1106–1114. New York: Facts on File.

Editorials on File. (1985, November 16–30). *Special survey: U.S. AIDS Epidemic Spreads, 16*(22), 1374–1385. New York: Facts on File.

Editorials on File. (1986, July 1–15). *Pornography Report Released, 17*(13), 798–803. New York: Facts on File.

Editorials on File. (1986, July 1–15). *Supreme Court: Georgia Sodomy Ruling, 17*(13). New York: Facts on File.

Editorials on File. (1987, February 1–15). *Liberace dies amid controversy, 18*(3), 168–169. New York: Facts on File.

Editorials on File. (1987, February 15–28). *Special survey: Condom ad debate, 18*(4), 222–231. New York: Facts on File.

Editor's notes. (1980, January). *The Quill*, p. 2.

Elliott, D. (1986). *Responsible journalism*. Beverly Hills, CA: Sage.
Ellul, J. (1965). *Propaganda*. New York: Alfred A. Knopf.
Esslin, M. (1982, Fall). Violence as entertainment. *The Stanford Magazine*, pp. 35–37.
Fenyvesi, C. (1977, July-August). Looking into the muzzle of terrorists. *The Quill*, pp. 16–18.
FilmFacts. (1960, January 6).
Findley, R. (1981, December). Mt. St. Helens aftermath. *National Geographic, 160*, 713–733.
Fischoff, B., Lichtenstein, S., Slovic, P., Derby, S.L. & Keeney, R.L. (1981). *Acceptable risk*. Cambridge, England: Cambridge University Press.
Fisher, W.R. (1970). A motive view of communication. *Quarterly Journal of Speech, 56*, 132–139.
Ford, D.E. (1982). *TMI: Thirty minutes to meltdown*. New York: Penguin.
Frank, R.S. (1973). *Message dimensions of television news*. Lexington, MA: Lexington Books.
Friedman, B., Lockwood, D., Snowden, L., & Zeidler, E. (1986). *Mass media and disaster: Annotated bibliography* (Miscellaneous Report #36). Newark, DE: University of Delaware, Disaster Research Center.
Friedman, S. M. (1981). Blueprint for breakdown: Three Mile Island and the media before the accident. *Journal of Communication, 31*,(2) 116–120.
Friedman, S.M. (1984a, August 5–8). *Local coverage of Three Mile Island during 1981–82*. Paper presented at Association for Education in Journalism and Mass Communication, Gainesville, FL.
Friedman, S.M. (1984b, December). Environmental reporting: Before and after TMI. *Environment, 26*(10), 4–5, 34.
Friedman, S.M. (1985, Winter). Lessons from TMI. *The Journalist*, pp. 24–25.
Friedman, S.M. (1986). A case of benign neglect: Coverage of Three Mile Island before the accident. In S.M. Friedman, S. Dunwoody, & C.L. Rogers (Eds.), *Scientists and journalists: Reporting science as news* (pp. 182–201). New York: The Free Press.
Friedman, S.M., Gorney, C.M. & Egolf, B.P. (1987). Reporting on radiation: A content analysis of Chernobyl coverage. *Journal of Communication, 37*(2), 58–79.
Fritz, C. (1961). Disaster. In R. Merton & R. Nisbet (Eds.), *Contemporary social problems* (pp. 651–694). New York: Harcourt Brace World.
Fritz, C., & Marks, E. (1954). The NORC studies of human behavior in disaster. *Journal of Social Issues, 10*, 26–41.
Fritz, C.E., & Williams, H. (1957, January). The human being in disaster. *The Annals of the American Academy of Social Sciences, 309*, 42–51.
Gallup. G. H. (1972). *The Gallup poll, Public opinion, 1935–1971*. New York: Random House.
Gans, H. (1979). *Deciding what's news. A study of* CBS Evening News, NBC Nightly News, Newsweek, *and* Time. New York: Vintage.
Gelb, L. (1986, April). Was the tragedy overplayed? *Washington Journalism Review*, p. 52.
General Accounting Office. (1982). *Federal involvement in the Mt. St. Helens disaster* (Document GAD/RCED-83-16). Washington, DC: Comptroller General of the United States.
Genovese, M. (1986, August). Terrorism. *Presstime*, pp. 26–32.
Gifford, W.L. (1983, January 17). [Letter from William L. Gifford, Vice President, Communication, GPU Nuclear, to Van Gordon Sauter, President, CBS News].
Giles, R. (1982, January 29). How reporters see same story different ways. *Rochester Times-Union*, p. 21.
Gillins, P. (1985, May 12). Effects of Mt. St. Helens' 1980 eruption still felt. *The Arizona Republic*, p. 12.
Goldman, E.F. (1960). *The crucial decade—and after*. New York: Vintage Books.
Goldschen, S.A. (1965). *United States editorial reaction to the 1962 Cuban crisis*. Unpublished master's thesis, University of California, Berkeley, CA.
Goltz, J. (1984). Are the news media responsible for the disaster myths? A content analysis of emergency response imagery. *International Journal of Mass Emergencies and Disasters, 2*, 345–368.
GPU Nuclear. (1985, March 4). *GPU Nuclear replies to misleading Inquirer series on TMI-2*

cleanup (GPU Nuclear New Release #19-85N).
Graber, D. (1980). *Mass media and American politics*. Washington, DC. Congressional Quarterly Press.
Graham, K. (1986, March 6). *Terrorism and the media*. ANPA Government affairs dinner, p. 6.
Gray, M., & Rose, I. (1982). *The warning: Accident at TMI*. New York: W.W. Norton.
Green, K. (1983). *A case study analysis of the relationship of local newspapers and disaster related citizen groups* (Preliminary Paper #27). Newark, DE: University of Delaware, Disaster Research Center.
Greenberg, B. (1964). Diffusion of news of the Kennedy assassination. *Public Opinion Quarterly, 28*, 225-232.
Greene, M., Perry, R.W., & Lindell, M. (1981). The March, 1980 eruptions of Mt. St. Helens: Citizen perceptions of volcano hazard. *Disasters, 5*(1), 49-66.
Halliwell, L. (1983). *Halliwell's film guide*. New York: Charles Scriber's Sons.
Hannigan, J. (1976). *Newspaper conflict and cooperation content after disaster: An exploratory analysis* (Preliminary Paper #27). Newark, DE: University of Delaware, Disaster Research Center.
Hannigan, J., & Wigert, S. (1973). *The newspaper as a functional entity and as an indicator after disaster*. Unpublished manuscript available from Disaster Research Center, University of Delaware, Disaster Research Center, Newark, DE.
Harless, J., & Rarick, G. (1974). *The radio station and the natural disaster*. Unpublished manuscript available from Disaster Research Center, University of Delaware, Disaster Research Center, Newark, DE.
Harolde, E., & Harvey, K. (1979). The diffusion of 'shocking' good news. *Journalism Quarterly, 56*(4), 771-775.
Hartsough, D., & Mileti, D. (1985). The media in disaster. In J. Laube & S. Murphy (Eds.), *Perspectives on disaster recovery* (pp. 282-294). Norwalk, CT: Appleton Century Crofts.
Hassel, C.V. (1975, September). The hostage situation. Exploring the motive and the cause. *The Police Chief*, pp. 55-58.
Herron, M. (1985, Fall). Living with AIDS. *Whole Earth Review, 48*, pp. 34-53.
Hickey, H. (1976, July 31-August 7). Terrorism and television. *TV Guide*, pp. 10-13.
Hiroi, O., Mikami, S., & Miyata, H. (1985). A study of mass media reporting in emergencies. *International Journal of Mass Emergencies and Disasters, 3*, 21-49.
Hirose, H. (1986). The psychological impact of the Tokai earthquake prediction: Individual's responses and mass media coverage. *Japanese Psychological Research, 28*, 64-76.
Holton, J.L. (1985, November). Planning out chaos: The time to prepare for disaster coverage is now. *The Quill*, pp. 15-22.
Holsti, D. (1969). *Content analysis for the social sciences and humanities*. Reading, MA:Addison-Wesley.
Jackson, G. (1977, November 11-19). We've got enough problems—Give us some answers. *TV Guide*, pp. A4-5.
Jaehnig. W.B. (1978). Journalists and terrorism: Captives of the Libertarian tradition. *Indiana Law Journal, 53*, 718-744.
Janis, I., & Feshback, S. (1953). Effects of fear-arousing communication. *Journal of Abnormal and Social Psychology, 48*, 78-92.
Jenkins, B., Johnson, J., & Ronfeldt, D. (1977). *Numbered lives: Some statistical observations from 77 hostage episodes*. San Francisco, CA: The Rand Corporation.
Jenkins, B. (1976). *Hostage survival: Some preliminary observations*. San Francisco, CA: The Rand Corporation.
Jensen, C. (1972). *The use and abuse of media in the aftermath of a disaster: An analysis of the 1970 Southern California fires*. Unpublished master's thesis, University of California at Santa Barbara.
Joslyn-Scherer, M.S. (1980). *Communication in the human sciences—A guide to therapeutic journalism*. Beverly Hills, CA: Sage.
Kaplan, A. (1983, July 14). Viewpoint. *ABC Nightline*.

Katz, E., Blumler, J., & Gurevitch, M. (1974). Uses of mass communication by the individual. In W. Davidson & F.T. Yu (Eds.), *Mass communication research* (pp. 11–35). New York: Praeger.

Keir, G., McCombs, M., & Shaw, D.L. (1986). *Advanced reporting—Beyond news events*. New York: Longman.

Kellett, A. (1981). *International terrorism: A retrospective and prospective examination*. Ottawa, Canada: Department of National Defense.

Kerr, T.J. (1983). *Civil defense in the U.S.: Bandaid for a holocost?* Boulder, CO: Westview Press.

Killian, L.M. (1953). *Evacuation of Panama City for Hurricane Florence*. Unpublished manuscript, National Academy of Sciences, Washington, DC.

Knott, J., & Wildavsky, A. (1979, June). If dissemination is the solution, what is the problem? *Knowledge, 1*, 537–578.

Korosec, M., & Rigby, J.G., & Stoffel, K. (1980). *The 1980 eruption of Mt. St. Helens, Washington, Part I: March 20-May 19, 1980* (Information Circular Number 71). Olympia, WA: Washington State Department of Natural Resources, Division of Geology and Earth Resources.

Kracauer, S. (1947). *From Caligari to Hitler: A psychological history of the German film*. Princeton, NJ: Princeton University Press.

Kraus, S., Davis, D., Lang, G.E., & Lang, K. (1975). Critical events analysis. In S.H. Chaffee (Ed.), *Political communication* (pp. 195–216). Beverly Hills, CA: Sage.

Kreps, G. (1980). Research needs and policy issues on mass media disaster reporting. In National Research Council (Ed.), *Disasters and the mass media* (pp. 35–74). Washington, DC: National Academy of Sciences.

Krieghbaum, H. (1956). What's the matter with editorial writing? In H. Krieghbaum, *Facts in perspective* (pp. 68–102). Englewood Cliffs, NJ: Prentice-Hall.

Krieghbaum, H. (1979, Spring). Three Mile Island: A crash course for readers. *Mass Comm Review, 6*(2), 2–10.

Kueneman, R.M., & Wright, J.E. (1976). News policies of broadcast stations for civil disturbances and disasters. *Journalism Quarterly, 52*(4), 670–677.

Lagadec, P. (1985). *Communication strategies in crisis situations*. Unpublished manuscript available from Disaster Research Center, University of Delaware, Disaster Research Center, Newark, DE.

Laquer, W. (1976, March). The futility of terrorism. *Harper's*, pp. 101–105.

Larson, J. A.(1980). A review of the state of the art in mass media disaster reporting. In National Research Council (Ed.), *Disasters and the mass media* (pp. 75–127). Washington, DC: National Academy of Sciences.

Lasswell, H.D. (1948). The structure and function of communication. In L. Bryson (Ed.), *The communication of ideas* (pp. 37–52). New York: Harper & Row.

Lasswell, H.D. (1965). *World politics and personal insecurity*. New York: The Free Press.

Ledingham, J., & Masel-Walters, L. (1985). Written on the wind: The mass media and Hurricane Alicia. *Newspaper Research Journal, 6*(2), 50–58.

Lerner, D. (1980). The revolutionary elites and world symbolism. In D. Lerner, H. Lasswell, & H. Spier (Ed.), *Propaganda and communication world history, emergence of public opinion in the West* (pp. 371–394). Honolulu, HI: University of Hawaii.

Levin, G.F. (1977). Learned helplessness and the evening news. *Journal of Communication, 27*(4), 100–105.

Lifton, R.J. (1967). *Death in life*. New York: The Free Press.

Lifton, R.J. (1986). Imagining the real: Beyond the nuclear 'end.' In L. Grinspoon (Ed.), *The long darkness* (pp. 76–99). Binghamton, NY: Vail-Ballou Press.

Lindy, J., & Lindy, J. (1985). Observations on the media and disaster recovery period. In J. Laube & S. Murphy (Eds.), *Perspective on disaster recovery* (pp. 295–303). Norwalk, CT: Appleton Century Crofts.

Lindell, M.K. & Perry, R.W. (1983, January). Nuclear power plant emergency warning: How would the public respond. *Nuclear News, 26*, 49–53.

Lippmann, W. (1949). *Public opinion*. New York: The Free Press.
Love, R. (1969). *Television and the death of a president: Network decisions in covering collective events*. Unpublished doctoral dissertation, Columbia University, New York.
Lovins, A. B., & Lovins, L.H. (1980). *Energy/war breaking the nuclear link*. San Francisco, CA: Friends of the Earth.
MacDougall, C. (1973). *Editorial writing*. Dubuque, IA: William Brown.
Machalaba, D. (1983, August 24). High-technology age causes news problems in coverage by media. *Wall Street Journal*, pp. 1, 15.
Mark, R. (1976, Spring). Kidnapping, terrorism and the media. *Nieman Reports*, pp. 15-18.
Marks, E. (1954). *Human reactions in disaster situations*. Chicago, IL: University of Chicago, National Opinion Research Center.
Martin, T.L., & Latham, D.C. (1963). *Strategy for survival*. Tuscon, AR: The University of Arizona Press.
Maury, R., & Pfeiffer, K.G. (1960). How not to write an editorial. In R. Maury & K.G. Pfeiffer (Eds.), *Effective editorial writing* (pp. 87-91). Dubuque, IA: William Brown.
Mazur, A. (1981). Media coverage and public opinion on scientific controversies. *Journal of Communication, 31*(2), 106-115.
Mazur, A. (1984). The journalists and technology: Reporting about Love Canal and Three Mile Island. *Minerva, 22*, 45-66.
McCombs, M., & Shaw, D.L. (1972). The agenda-setting function of mass media. *Public Opinion Quarterly, 36*, 176-187.
McKay, J. (1984). Newspaper reporting of bushfire disasters in Southeastern Australia—Ash Wednesday, 1983. *Disasters, 7*, 1-8.
McQuail, D. (1969). *Towards a sociology of mass communications*. London, England: Collier-Macmillian.
McQuail, D. (1983). *Mass communication theory*. London, England: Sage.
Meltzner, A. (1979). The communication of scientific information to the wider public. *Minerva, 17*(3), 331-354.
Metropolitan Edison Press Releases. (1978, May 5). Releases no. 66-78c. LER output on events at Three Mile Island 1 and 2 from 1969 to the present, Nuclear Regulatory Commission (Docket No. 05000320, LER no. 78-021/-3L-0, Event Date 3/29/78, Report Date 5/1/78). Washington, DC: Nuclear Regulatory Commission, p. 70.
Mills, C. W. (1956). *The power elite*. New York: Oxford University Press.
Molotch, H., & Lester, M. (1974). Accidental news: The great oil spill. *American Journal of Sociology, 81*, 45-66.
Molotch, H., & Lester, M. (1975). News as purposive behavior: On the strategic uses of routine events, accidents, and scandals. *American Sociological Review, 39*, 101-112.
Moore, H. (1958). *Tornadoes over Texas: A Study of Waco and San Angelo in disaster*. Austin, TX: University of Texas Press.
Moore, H., Bates, F., Layman, M., & Parneton, V. (1963). *Before the wind: A study of response to Hurricane Carla* (Disaster Study No. 19). Washington, DC: National Academy of Sciences.
Morain, C. (1983, September/October). Aftershocks at Mount St. Helens. *Columbia Journalism Review*, pp. 6-10.
Morentz, J. (1980). Communications in the Sahel drought: Comparing the mass media with other channels of international communication. In National Research Council (Ed.), *Disasters and the mass media* (pp. 158-186). Washington, DC: National Academy of Sciences.
Nesbitt, R., & Wilson, T. (1977). Telling more than we can know: Verbal reports on mental processes. *Psychological Review, 84*, 231-259.
Nigg, J. (1982). Communication under conditions of uncertainty: Understanding earthquake forecasting. *Journal of Communication, 32*, 27-36.
Nimmo, D. (1985). TV network news coverage of Three Mile Island. Reporting disasters as technological fables. *International Journal of Mass Emergencies and Disasters, 2*, 115-145.
Nimmo, D., & Combs, J. (1985). *Nightly horrors: Crisis coverage in televison network news*. Knoxville, TN: University of Tennessee Press.

Northorp, B. (1978, September). *Press handling of terrorism and violence*. Address to Commonwealth Press Union. Toronto, Canada.

Notes on the press—By the press. (1984, March). *AIF Press Info, 168*, p. 5.

Notes on the press—By the press. (1985a, July). *AIF Press Info, 172*, pp. 5-6.

Notes on the press—By the press. (1985b, October). *AIF Press Info, 175*, pp. 4-5.

Ostland, L. (1973). Interpersonal communication following McGovern's Eagleton decision. *Public Opinion Quarterly, 37*, 601-611.

Paths of Glory. (1980, September). *National Geographic, 158*, p. 360.

Perrow, C. (1984). *Normal accidents: Living with high-risk technologies*. New York: Basic Books.

Perrow, C. (1986, October 11). The habit of courting disaster. *The Nation*, pp. 329,347.

Perry, R.W. (1985). *Comprehensive emergency management*. Greenwich, CT. JAI press.

Perry, R., & Greene, M.R. (1982, Fall) Ethnicity in the emergency decision-making process. *Social Inquiry, 52*, 309-334.

Perry, R.W., & Lindell, M. (1985). *Twentieth century volcanicity at Mt. St. Helens*. Tempe, AR: Arizona State University, School of Public Affairs.

Perry, R.W., & Mushkatel, A.H. (1986). *Minority citizens in disasters*. Athens, GA: University of Georgia Press.

Perry, R.W., & Nigg, J. (1985, January). Emergency management strategies for communicating hazard information. *Public Administration Review, 45*, 72-77.

Perry, R.W., Greene, M.R., & Lindell, M. (1980). *Human response to volcanic eruptions: Mt. St. Helens, May 18, 1980*. Seattle, WA: Battelle Human Affairs Research Center.

Perry, R.W., Greene, M.R., & Mushkatel, A.H. (1983). *American minority citizens in disasters*. Columbus, OH: Battelle Memorial Institute.

Perry, R.W., Lindell, M., & Greene, M.R. (1979). *Evacuation decision-making and emergency planning in four communities*. Seattle, WA: Battelle Human Affairs Research Center.

Prince, S. (1920). *Catastrophe and social change*. New York: Columbia University.

Psyching out terrorists. (1977, November 15). *Medical World*, pp. 5-17

Quarantelli, E.L. (1954). Nature and conditions of panic. *American Journal of Sociology, 60*, 267-275.

Quarantelli, E.L. (1970). Emergent accommodation groups. Beyond current collective behavior typologies. In T. Shibuteni (Ed.), *Human nature and collective behavior* (pp. 111-123). Englewood Cliffs, NJ: Prentice-Hall.

Quarantelli, E.L. (1971). Changes in Ohio radio station policies and operations in reporting local civil disturbances. *Journal of Broadcasting, 15*, 287-292.

Quarantelli, E.L. (1977). Social aspects of disasters. *Disasters, 1*(1), 98-107.

Quarantelli, E.L. (1980). Some research emphases for studies on mass communication systems and disasters. In National Research Council (Ed.), *Disasters and the mass media* (pp. 293-299). Washington, DC: National Academy of Sciences.

Quarantelli, E.L. (1981). The command post point of view in local mass communication systems. Communication. *International Journal of Communication Research, 7*, 57-73.

Quarantelli, E.L. (1983). *Emergent citizen groups in disaster preparedness and recovery activities: An interim report* (Miscellaneous Rep. #33). Newark, DE: University of Delaware, Disaster Research Center.

Quarantelli, E.L. (1984). *Inventory of disaster field studies in the social and behavioral sciences, 1919-1979* (Book & Monograph Series #20). Newark, DE: University of Delaware, Disaster Research Center.

Quarantelli, E.L. (1985a). An assessment of conflicting views on mental health. In C. Figley (Ed.), *Trauma and its wake* (pp. 173-215). New York: Brunner Mazel.

Quarantelli, E.L. (1985b). *Organizational behavior in disasters and implications for disaster planning* (DRC Report Series #18). Newark, DE: University of Delaware, Disaster Research Center.

Quarantelli, E.L. (1985c). Realities and mythologies in disaster films. *Communications, 11*, 31-44.

Quarantelli, E.L. (1986). *Disaster studies: An historical analysis of the influences of basic* sociology and applied use on the research done in the last 35 years (Preliminary Paper #111). Newark, DE: University of Delaware, Disaster Research Center.

Quarantelli, E.L., & Dynes, R.R. (1972, February). When disaster strikes. *Psychology Today, 5*, pp. 66-70.

Rabe, R. (1977, November 17). Terrorism and the media. Remarks made at City University, New York City, New York.

Ramberg, B. (1980). *Nuclear power plants as weapons for the enemy.* Berkeley, CA: The University of California Press.

Rice, R., Blair, J.H., Chen, M., Dimmick, J., Dozier, D.M., Jacob, M.E., Johnson, B.M., Penniman, W.D., Svenning, L.L., Rogers, E.M., Rothenbuhler, E.W., Ruchinskas, J.E., & Williams, F. (1984). *The new media.* Beverly Hills, CA: Sage.

Robinson, M.J. (1976). Public affairs television and the growth of political malaise: The case of The Selling of the Pentagon. *American Political Science Review, 70,* 409-432.

Rogers E., & Sood, R. (1980). Mass media communication and disasters: A content analyses of media coverage of the Andrha Pradesh cyclone and the Sahel drought. In National Research Council (Ed.), *Disasters and the mass media* (pp. 139-157). Washington, DC: National Academy of Sciences.

Rogers, E. (1980). *Proceedings of the Committee on Disasters and the Mass Media Workshop.* Washington, DC: National Academy of Sciences.

Rogers, E., & Sood, R. (1981). *Mass media operations in a quick onset natural disaster: Hurricane David in Dominica.* Boulder, CO: Institute for Behavioral Sciences.

Rosengren, K., Arvidson, R., & Sturesson, D. (1975). The Barseback panic: A radio programme as a negative summary event. *Acta Sociologica, 18,* 303-321.

Roscho, B. (1975). *Newsmaking.* Chicago, IL: University of Chicago Press.

Rothman, S. & Lichter, S.R. (1982, August/September). The nuclear energy debate: Scientists, the media and the public. *Public Opinion,* p. 51.

Sanders, J. (1986). The Soviets first living room war: Soviet national television's coverage of the Chernobyl disaster. Unpublished manuscript.

Sandman, P.M., & Paden, M. (1979, July/August). At Three Mile Island. *Columbia Journalism Review,* pp. 48-49.

Sanford, D. (1985, August 29). Need we guess why young men are dying? *Wall Street Journal,* p. 18.

Santoianni, F. (1983). *Mass-media ed emergenza.* Gorizia, Italy.

Scanlon, J. (1976). The not so mass media: The role of individuals in mass communication. In G. S. Adams (Ed.), *Journalism, communication and the law* (pp. 104-119). Scarborough, Ontario: Prentice Hall of Canada.

Scanlon, J. (1978). Day one in Darwin: Once again the vital role of communications. In J.I. Reid (Ed.), *Planning for people in natural disasters* (pp. 134-155). Townsville, Australia: James Cook University of North Queensland.

Scanlon, J. (1980a). The media and the 1978 Terrace floods: An initial test of a hypothesis. In National Research Council (Ed.), *Disasters and the mass media* (pp. 254-263). Washington, DC: National Academy of Sciences.

Scanlon, J. (1980b, Spring). Hostage taking and media ethics. *Carleton Journalism Review,* pp. 6-7.

Scanlon, J. (1981). Coping with the media: Police-Media problems and tactics in hostage takings and terrorist incidents. *Canadian Police College Journal, 5*(3), 135.

Scanlon, J. (1984). Terrorism and the media: Live coverage of crime. *Canadian Police College Journal, 8*(2), 144-178.

Scanlon, J., & Alldred, S. (1982). Media coverage of disasters. The same old story. *Emergency Planning Digest, 9,* 13-19.

Scanlon, J. (1986). *The media in hostage situations: The way it is.* Unpublished paper, Carleton University, Ottawa, Canada.

Scanlon, J., & Frizzell, A. (1979). Old theories don't apply: Implication of communcations in crises. *Disasters, 3,* 315-319.

Scanlon, J., Dixon, K., & McClennan, S. (1982). *The Miramichi earthquakes. The mediaresponse to an invisible emergency.* Ottawa, Canada: Carleton University, Emergency Communication Research Unit.

Scanlon, J., Tuukko, R., & Morton, G. (1978) Media coverage of a crises. Better than reported, worse than necessary. *Journalism Quarterly, 55,* 66–72.

Schmid, A. & de Graaf, J. (1982). *Violence as communication.* London, England: Sage.

Schlesinger, P. (1978). *Putting reality together.* London: Constable.

Schuman, H., Ludwig, J., & Krosnick, J.A. (1986, Winter). The perceived threat of nuclear war, salience, and open questions. *Public Opinion Quarterly, 50*(4), 519–536.

Shabad, T. (1986). The Soviet press and Chernobyl. Unpublished paper.

Shain, R.E. (1972). Effects of Pentagon influence on war movies, 1948–70. *Journalism Quarterly, 49*(4), 641–647.

Shain, R.E. (1974). Hollywood's cold war. *Journal of Popular Film, 3*(4), 334–350.

Shain, R.E. (1976). *An analysis of motion pictures about war released by the American film industry, 1939–1970.* New York: Arno Press.

Singer, E., & Endreny, P. (1987, Summer). Reporting hazards: Their benefits and costs. *Journal of Communication, 37*(3), 10–26.

Slovic, P., Fischhoff, B., & Lichtenstein, S. (1980). Facts and fears: Understanding perceived risk. In R. Schwing & W. Albers (Eds.), *Societal risk assessment* (pp. 67–93). New York: Plenum.

Smith, J. (1979). Look away, look away, look away, movie land. *Journal of Popular Film and Television, 2*(1), 29–46.

Sobran, J. (1986, May 23). The politics of AIDS. *National Review,* pp. 22–26+.

Sood, R. (1981). *News media operations in natural disasters.* Unpublished doctoral dissertation, Stanford University, Palo Alto, CA.

Sorenson, J.J. (1983). Knowing how to behave under the threat of disaster. *Environment and Behavior, 15*(4), 438–457.

Staff. (1947, February 14). *Time,* p. 16.

Staff. (1985, August 23). Editorial. *Houston Post,* Section B, pg. 1.

Staff. (1985, June 28). Editorial. *Chicago Tribune,* Section 1, p. 22.

Staff. (1986, February 10). *Time,* p. 42.

Stallings, R. (1967). *A description and analysis of the warning systems in the Topeka, Kansas tornado of June 8, 1966* (Research Rep. # 20). Newark, DE: University of Delaware, Disaster Research Center.

Stein, M.L. (1985, November). AIDS: Getting the facts. *Editor and Publisher,* pp. 16–17.

Stephens, M. (1980). *Three Mile Island.* New York: Random House.

Stephens, M., & Edison, N. (1980). Coverage of events at Three Mile Island. *Mass Communication Review, 7,* 3–9.

Stephens, M., & Edison, N. (1982). News media coverage of issues during the accident at Three Mile Island. *Journalism Quarterly, 59,* 199–204.

Stokes, G. (1985, October 25). Press clippings. *Village Voice.*

Streitmatter, R. (1984, May). AIDS—It's just a matter of time. *The Quill,* pp. 22–26.

Swift, C., & Kresch, D. (1983). *Mudflow hazards along the Toutle and Cowlitz rivers from a hypothetical failure of Spirit Lake blockage.* Tacoma, WA: Office of the District Chief, U.S. Geological Survey.

Taylor, V. (1978). Future directions for study. In E.L. Quarantelli (Ed.), *Disasters: Theory and research* (pp. 251–280). Beverly Hills, CA: Sage.

Terry, H. A. (1978). Television and terrorism: Professionalism not quite the answer. *Indiana Law Journal, 53.* 748–777.

The Getty Affair. (1975, June–July). *International Criminal Police Review,* pp. 166–170.

The Inquirer gave you its view of TMI in 30,000 words—Here's some of what was left out. (1985, March 3). Advertisement by GPU Nuclear in *Philadelphia Inquirer,* pp. 10–11A.

The Right Words: The Edward J. Meeman Award. (1986). [Flyer from Scripps Howard Foundation National Journalism Awards].

Titus, C. (1983). Back to ground zero: Old footage through new lenses. *Journal of Popular Film and Television, 11*(1), 2–11.

Travis, R., & W. Riebsame. (1979). Communicating environmental uncertainty. *Journal of Geography, 78*(5), 168–172.

Trounstine, P.J. (1977, June). We interrupt this program. *More,* p. 15.

Tuchman, G. (1978). *Making news: A study in the construction of reality.* New York: The Free Press.

Turner, B.A. (1976, November). The development of disasters: A sequence for the origins of disaster. *The Sociological Review, 24,* 753–774.

Turner, R. (1980). The mass media and preparation for natural disaster. In National Research Council (Ed.), *Disasters and the mass media* (pp. 281–292). Washington, DC: National Academy of Sciences.

U.S. Government Printing Office. (1979a). Met Ed public relations; What the public knew about TMI before the accident. In S.M. Friedman (Ed.), *Report of public's right to information task force, staff report to the President's Commission on the Accident at Three Mile Island* (pp. 29–49). Washington, DC: Author.

U.S. Government Printing Office. (1979b). *Report of the public's right to information task force, staff report of the President's Commission on the Accident at Three Mile Island.* Washington, DC: Author.

U.S. Government Printing Office. (1979c). *Report of the President's Commission on the Accident at Three Mile Island, the need for change: The legacy of TMI.* Washington, DC: Author.

Variety. (1948, July 7), p. 3.

Variety. (1966, September 6), p. 112.

Vaughan, L. (1986, May 16). Efforts to stop spread of AIDS faulted. *Austin American Statesman,* p. A5.

Waxman, J. (1973). Local broadcast gatekeeping during natural disaster. *Journalism Quarterly, 50,* 751–758.

Weiman, G. (1981). Terrorists or freedom fighters: Labeling terrorism in the Israeli press. *Political Communication and Persuasion, 2*(4), 443–445.

Weller, J. (1979). *What is news after a disaster.* Unpublished manuscript available from Disaster Research Center, University of Delaware, Disaster Research Center, Newark, DE.

Wenger, D. (1985). *Mass media and disaster* (Preliminary Paper #98). Newark, DE: University of Delaware, Disaster Research Center.

Wenger, D., & Friedman, B. (1985). *Local and national media coverage of disaster: A content analysis of the print media's treatment of disaster myths* (Preliminary Paper #99). Newark, DE: University of Delaware, Disaster Research Center.

Wenger, D., Dykes, D., Sebok, T., & Neff, J. (1975). It's a matter of myths: An empirical examination of individual insight into disaster response. *Mass Emergencies, 1,* 33–46.

Wilkins, L., (1985, Summer). Television and newspaper coverage of a blizzard: Is the message helplessness? *Newspaper Research Journal, 6*(4), 51–65.

Wilkins, L. (1986). Media coverage of the Bhopal disaster: A cultural myth in the making. *International Journal of Mass Emergencies and Disasters, 4,* 7–33.

Wilkins, L. (1987). *Shared vulnerability: The mass media and American perception of the Bhopal disaster.* Westport, CT: Greenwood Press.

Wilkins, L. & Patterson, P. (1987). Risk analysis and the construction of news. *Journal of Communication, 37*(3), 80–92.

Williams, E. (1956). *A study of letters to the editor of the* Waco Times-Herald *and* New Tribune *following the tornado of May, 1953.* Unpublished master's thesis, University of Texas, Austin, TX.

Williams, H. (1956). *Communications in community disaster.* Unpublished doctoral disseration, University of North Carolina, Chapel Hill, NC.

Williams, R. (1966). *The long revolution.* New York: Harper & Row.

Yamamoto, Y., & Quarantelli, E.L. (1984). *Inventory of the Japanese disaster research literature in the social and behavioral sciences* (Book and Monograph #19). Newark, DE: University of Delaware, Disaster Research Center.

Author Index

A

Alexander, D. 9
Alexander, Y. 125, 127, 129
Alter, J. 87
Altheide, D. 14, 23, 135
Altheide, D. & Snow, R. 135
Anderson, W. 3

B

Bagdikian, B. 123, 128
Barnes, K., Brosius, J., & Mitchell, J. 59
Barton, A. 2, 6, 10, 15
Bassiouni, M. 125
Beady, C., & Bolin, R. 10
Bedell, P. 79
Blyskal & Blyskal 164, 165
Boot, W. 165-165
Brooks, J. 9
Brouillette, J. 3
Budd, R., Thorp, R., & Donohew, L. 134
Burd, Gene
  about xiii, 85, 86
  by 85-113
Burton, L., Kates, R., & White, G. 29

C

Cale, D. 125
Campbell, A., Converse, P., Miller, W., & Stokes, D. 29
Carey, J. (Bhopal), 134, 150, 151
Cawley, D. 122
Chaffee, S. 37
Chase, M. 109
Christians, C., & Carey, J. 134
Clutterbuck, R. 119-120, 127
Cohen, B. 149-150
Collier, P. & Horowitz, D. 87
Cooper, J. 123
Crandall, W., & Mullineaux, D. 51

D

Davies, J. 29
Dean, J. 158
Detjen, J., & Fitzgerald, S. 75-79
Diamond, E. 87
Dombrowski, W. 5
Douglas, D., Westley, B., & Chaffee, S. 52
Downs, A. 145
Drabek, T. 6, 7, 10, 12
Durkheim, E. 145

Dye, T., & Ziegler, H. 29
Dynes, R. 10
Dynes R., & Quarantelli, E. L. 11
Dynes, R. Quarantelli, E. L., & Kreps, G. 6, 53

E

Eckholm, E. 86
Edelson, E. 160
Edelstein, A. 88
Elliot, D.
  about xiv, 175
  by 161–170
Ellul, J. 133, 147
Esslin, M. 115

F

Fenyvesi, C. 121
Findley, R. 49
Fischhoff, B. et al. 142, 150
Fisher, W. 22, 132
Ford, D. 67
Fritz, C. 6, 10, 11
Fritz, C., & Marks, E. 5
Fritz, C., & Williams, H. 36
Frank, R. 134
Friedman, S.
  about xiii, 9, 64, 71, 81, 132, 136, 164, 172, 173
  by 63–83
Friedman, S., Gorney, C., & Egolf, B. 82
Friedman, B., Lockwood, D., Snowden, L., & Zeidler, E. 8

G

Gallup, G. 151, 152
Gans, H. 16, 133, 146
Genovese, J. 128, 130
Gifford, 77
Gillins, R. 49
Goldman, E. 152
Goldschen, S. 88
Goltz, J. 9, 11
Graber, D. 21
Gray, M., & Rose, I. 67
Green, K. 9
Greenberg, B. 36
Greene, M., Perry, R., & Lindell, M. 54

H

Halliwell, L. 155, 156
Hannigan, J. 9

Hannigan, J. & Wigert, S. 16
Harless, J., & Rarick, G. 9
Harolde, E., & Harvey, K. 36
Hartsough, D., & Mileti, D. 15
Hassel, C. 129
Herron, M. 87
Hickey, H. 118, 125
Hiroi, O., Mikami, S., & Miyata, H. 10
Hirose, H. 8, 10
Holsti, D. 134
Holton, J. 162, 169

J

Jackson, G. 86
Jaehnig, W. 117, 121
Janis, I., & Feshback, S. 36
Jenkins, B. 124
Jenkins, B., Johnson, J., & Ronfeldt, D. 123
Jensen, C. 9
Joslyn-Scherer, MM. 85, 86

K

Kaplan, A. 87
Katz, E., Blumler, J., & Gurevitch, M. 37
Keir, G., McCombs, M., & Shaw, D. 85
Kellett, A. 126
Kerr, T. 155, 156, 158
Killian, L. 5, 36
Knott, J., & Wildvasky, A. 52
Korosec, M., Rigby, K., & Stoffel, K. 48
Kracauer, S. 151
Kraus, S., Davis, D., Lang, K., & Lang, G. 30
Kreps, G. 61, 16
Kreighbaum, H. 10, 88, 168
Kueneman, R., & Wright, J. 2, 9, 11, 18, 166, 168

L

Lagadec, P. 8, 17
Laquer, W. 129
Larson, J. 16, 36
Lasswell, H. xii, 21, 22, 23, 30
Ledingham, John
  about xii, 173
  by 35–45
Ledingham, J., & Masel-Walters, L. 36, 38
Lerner, D. 85
Levine, G. (Bhopal) 166
Lifton, R. 28, 140, 142, 152, 153, 159
Lindell, M.
  about xiii, 174
  by 47–62

AUTHOR INDEX

Lindell, M., & Perry, R. 59
Lindy, J., & Lindy, J. 18
Lippmann, W. 134
Lovins, A., & Lovins, L. 159–160

M

MacDougall, C. 88
Machalaba, D. 76
Mark, R. 119, 127
Marks, E. 5
Maury, R., & Pfeiffer, K. G. 88
Mazur, A. 9, 150
McCombs, M., & Shaw, D. 36
McKay, J. 10
McQuail, D. 22
Meltzner, A. 52
Mills, C. 29
Molotoch, J., & Lester, M. 17, 145
Moore, H. 9
Moore, H., Bates, F., Layman, M., & Parneton, V. 36
Morain, C. 166, 167
Morentz, J. 8, 9
Mulder, D. 120

N

Nesbitt, R., & Wilson, T. 174
Nigg, J. 10
Nimmo, D. 8, 9, 21, 126
Nimmo, D., & Combs, J. 134
Northrop, B. 118, 126

O

Ostland, L. 36

P

Patterson, P.
  about xiv
  by 131–147
Perrow, C. 21, 31, 136
Perry, R.
  about xiii, 53, 59, 61, 174
  by 47–62
Perry, R., & Greene, M. 36
Perry, R., Greene, M., & Lindell, M. 54, 56
Perry, R., Greene, M., & Mushkatel, A. 36, 56
Perry, R., Lindell, M., & Greene, M. 59
Perry, R., & Mushkatel, A. 36
Perry, R., & Nigg, J. 53
Prince, S. 3

Q

Quarantelli, E. L.
  about xi, xii, 2, 5, 6, 8, 11, 12, 18, 23, 53, 174
  by 1–19
Quarantelli, E. L., & Dynes, R. 6, 36, 60

R

Rabe, R. 123
Ramberg, B. 159
Rice, R. et al. 2, 18
Robinson, M. 29
Rogers, E. 36
Rogers, E., & Sood, R. 9
Roscho, B. 135
Rosengren, K., Arvidson, R., & Sturesson, D. 8

S

Sanders, J. 10, 141
Sanford, D. 87
Santoianni, F. 8
Scanlon, J.
  about xi, xiv, 8, 9, 16, 121, 125, 173, 175
  by 115–130
Scanlon, J., & Alldred, S. 8
Scanlon, J., Dixon, K., & McClennan, S. 8
Scanlon, J., Tukko, R., & Morton, G. 11
Schlesinger, P. 135
Schmid, A., & de Graaf, J. 119, 123, 124, 128
Shabad, T. 10
Shain, R.
  about xiv, 2, 152, 153
  by 149–160
Singer, E., & Endreny, P. 176
Slovic, P., Fischhoff, B. Lichtenstein, S. 61, 141
Smith, J. 135
Sobran, J. 87
Sood, R. 9
Sorenson, J. 165
Stein, M. 87
Stephens, M. 67
Stephens, M., & Edison, N. 10, 164, 168
Stokes, G. 87
Streitmatter, R. 87
Swift, C., & Kresch, D. 49, 50

T

Terry, H., 123
Titus, C. 153, 154
Travis, R., & Riebsame, W. 52
Trounstine, P. 117, 126
Tuchman, G. 14, 15, 22
Turner, B. A. 36
Turner, R. 10

V

Vaughan, L. 86

W

Walters, L.
 about xii, 173
 by 35–45

Waxman, J. 10
Weiman, G. 130
Weller, J. 10
Wenger, D. 12, 18
Wenger, D., Dykes, D., Sebok, T., & Neff, J. 6
Wenger, D., & Friedman, B. 9, 10
Wilkins, L.
 about xii, 8, 10, 22, 136, 162, 163–164, 165–166, 167, 168, 169, 173
 by 21–34, 171–177
Wilkins, L., & Patterson, P. 176
Williams, E. 9
Williams, R. 150

T

Yamamoto, Y., & Quarantelli, E. L. 8

Subject Index

A

ABC 75, 79, 80, 81, 116, 123, 128, 137, 139, 142, 144, 146
Accuracy xiv, 5, 6, 11, 14, 40, 69, 77, 78-79, 117, 137, 139, 140, 143, 146, 163, 164, 167, 169, 170, 172, 174
Agenda setting 36, 43, 162, 170
AIDS xiii, 85-87, 92-112, 171
Arms control 140, 144, 145
Atomic Industrial Forum 77, 80, 81
Atom angst (nuclear fear) xiv, 26, 28, 136, 140-144, 146-147, 151-153, 159
Associated Press 24, 77, 78, 80, 81
Audience recall 28-29
Audience response xi, xii-xiii, 13-14, 15, 28, 36, 42, 52, 57, 61, 176

B

Barrons 77
Bioengineering 17
Bhopal xii, 10, 13, 21-27, 32-33, 135, 136, 166, 169, 172
Blizzards 9, 10
Brochures 56

C

Cable television 17
Cancer 26, 28
CBS 77, 116, 117, 123, 137, 138, 140, 141, 142, 144
Challenger disaster 135, 144, 161, 169
Carter, H. 76
Chemical spills (see also Bhopal) 13, 21
Chernobyl xiv, 9, 10, 13, 17, 63, 76, 131-133, 167, 168-169, 172, 173
Civil defense 154, 156, 158
Civil disturbances 18
Civil rights xiii, 107-108
Collective behavior 11
Competition 127-128, 146
Computers 17, 18, 33
Command post view, 7, 11, 18, 23
Committee on Disasters and the Mass Media 11-12
Community 33
Condoms xiv, 110-112
Content analysis xiii, 4, 9, 10, 13, 134-135
Convergence 15
Credibility 41, 53, 57-59, 68, 71
Criminals 117, 118
Critical events 30

Cuban missile crisis 158
Cultural studies xiv, 150-151
Cultural values 133, 146, 147
Cyclones 8, 9

D

Dam failure 49-50
Decontextualization 24-25, 26, 70, 135, 167, 168, 172
Democracy 32, 176-177
Denton, H. 69
Disaster culture 174
Disaster planning (see also preparedness and warning) 9
Disaster Research Center 3, 4, 10, 11
Disaster Research Group 3, 4
Drought 8, 12

E

Earthquakes 3, 9, 10, 13, 17
Economic impact of disasters 50-51
Editorials xiii, 88-112
Efficacy 29
Elites 29-30, 33
Emergency management officials xiii, 6, 14, 18, 48, 52, 53, 54-55, 57-58, 59-60, 61-62
Emergency plans 64, 66, 67, 71
Emergency response 57
Engineers 65-66, 67, 68, 70
Environmental pollution 26
Ethics xiv, 126, 128, 130, 161-170, 173, 175
Eugene, Oregon 27
Evacuation xiii, 41, 42, 43-44, 50, 70, 137, 138, 155
Event orientation xiii, 22-25, 31, 33, 72-73, 107, 124, 172

F

Film xiv, 151-160, 176
Fires 10, 17
Floods 9, 10

G

Gag orders 139, 143
Gas 27
Gatekeeping, 14, 16
Glasnost 144
Government restrictions 130
Green revolution 24, 33

H

Helplessness 31
Hijackings 124-125
History of disaster research xii, 1, 3-7
Hostages 119, 125-126
Human response to disasters 6
Hurricanes xii, 9, 10, 37-38, 174

I

Information co-ordination 53
International disaster studies 8, 11, 14, 15, 16
Interpersonal communication 40, 52
Investigative journalism 25, 73

J

Jackson, Jesse 75

K

Koop, C. E. 110, 111
Kreim, M. 86-87

L

Learning xiii, 27-29, 53, 60, 165, 175
Lexington, Washington 48,m 51, 55
Le Monde 9
Liberace 109-110
Local media 13-14, 16
Los Angeles Times 78
Love Canal 9, 26, 177

M

Mass media 69, 81-82
  influence on evacuation behavior 31
  use of 62
Magazines (see also *Time, Newsweek,* and *U. S. News)* 9, 31
Media performance xiv, 174-176
  effects of 124
  organizational problems 7
  in terrorist incidents 116, 119, 125, 128
Media organizations—behavior 4, 5, 10, 11, 12, 14, 16
Melodrama 22
Meltdown 69, 70
Mental health 6
Metropolitan Edison 64-69, 71-76, 80
Military 152-154
Minority groups 10, 15, 36, 56

SUBJECT INDEX

Mt. St. Helens xiii, 48–51, 169
Mudslides 10, 49
Myth xi, 1, 5, 6, 11, 14, 31–32, 33, 133, 139, 147

N

Narrative 135
National Opinion Research Center 3
Natural disasters 2
NBC 9, 116, 123, 127, 136, 137, 138, 140, 142, 143, 146
New technology 16, 17–18, 174
News 14, 122, 134, 135, 150, 160, 174, 176
Newspapers (see also specific newspapers) 4, 9, 10, 41, 55–56, 61, 62, 65, 71–74, 75–76, 88–112, 129
Newsweek 25–26
New York Daily News 70
New York Post 70
New York Times 9, 25, 30, 66, 72, 74, 77, 81, 87, 165, 167, 172
NOVA 74
Nuclear—general 153
Nuclear power (see also Three Mile Island and Chernobyl) a66, 77, 80, 149–150, 154, 159
Nuclear war (see also atom angst) 140, 141, 142, 151–152, 154–155, 156–158
Nuclear waste 26
Nuclear Regulatory Commission 64, 65, 66–68, 71–75, 79, 144, 145

O

Obituaries 87
Organizational behavior 6

P

Panic xiii, 5, 6, 168, 170
Philadelphia Inquirer 72, 74, 75, 79–80
Photographs (see also visual imagery) 126
Powerful actor 30–31
Politics of disaster coverage xii, 21, 25, 29–30, 32–33, 170, 171, 172, 175, 176–177
Powerlessness 29, 31, 166–167
Preparedness (see also warning) 2, 41, 43, 48, 165
President's Commission on Three Mile Island 64, 66, 67, 70, 73
Preventive journalism (see also surveillance function) 85–86
Propaganda xiv, 133, 141, 144–147

Public broadcasting 128
Public meetings 56
Public officials 41, 43, 166, 170
Public relations 64, 164–165

R

Radiation, 68, 69, 77, 79, 138, 139, 140, 121, 142, 150, 155–157, 173
Radio, 3, 4, 9, 10, 15, 40, 55–56, 58, 61, 66, 120, 126, 129
Rand Corporation 123
Reporters 67, 68, 69, 70, 72–73, 76, 121, 125, 128, 159
Research goals 16–18
Reuters 24
Rhine River spill 13, 17
Right-to-know laws 30
Risk xii, 31, 33, 61, 171, 176
Risk perception 47, 77, 149
Role of experience 40–41

S

Salience 52
Scientists 30, 76, 137, 138, 143, 154–155, 174
Sex (see also AIDS) 86–87, 110
Sources 30–32, 72, 136, 139, 143–144, 146, 162, 164–165, 166, 169, 173
Stereotype xiv, 136–140, 144, 146, 157, 172, 174, 175
Surveillance function xii-xiii, 22–23, 27, 28, 33, 36–37, 42–43, 44, 60–61

T

Technical language 65, 68, 69, 71, 74, 75, 164
Technological disasters (see also Bhopal, Chernobyl, and Three Mile Island) 2, 17, 23, 25, 28, 135–136, 144, 167, 172
Technological "fix" xiv, 107, 112, 172, 175
Television xiii, xiv, 8, 13, 14, 26–27, 28, 30, 40, 41, 58, 66, 76, 77, 78, 110–111, 115, 118, 122, 123, 129, 132–147
Terrorism xiv, 115–122, 122–124, 172
Three Mile Island xiii, 9, 10, 17, 30, 59, 63–70, 74–76, 135, 145, 159, 164, 167, 168, 172
Time 9, 26, 161
Tone 26
Tornados 4, 5
Toutle, Washington 48, 51, 55
Tsunamies 3

U

UPI 24, 78, 168
U.S. News and World Report 25–26
Uses and gratifications 36–37, 44

V

Victims 14, 27, 122, 166–167, 170
Video malaise 29
Visual imagery 14, 27, 28, 32, 141–142, 167, 176

Volcanoes 13, 47–51

W

Wall Street Journal 77, 81
Warnings (see also preparedness) xiii, 3, 15, 23, 36, 38, 40, 43, 48, 50, 51–52, 60, 161, 171, 172, 175–176
Washington Post 25, 30, 74, 77, 78, 79
West Virginia, Institute 26, 27–29
White, G. 176
Wire service reports 8, 9, 12, 24, 30

PN 4888 .D57 B3 1985

DATE DUE			
NOV 3 '89			
APR 1 2005			